ISLAM

ISLAM

The Religious and Political Life
of a World Community

Edited by
Marjorie Kelly

Published for the
Foreign Policy Association

PRAEGER

New York
Westport, Connecticut
London

Library of Congress Cataloging in Publication Data

Main entry under title:

Islam the religious and political life of a world
 community.

 "Published for the Foreign Policy Association."
 Includes index.
 1. Islam 2. Islamic countries – History. 3. Islam
and politics. I. Kelly, Marjorie. II. Foreign Policy
Association. III. Title.
BP161.2.I882   1984   909′.097671   84-13307
ISBN 0-275-91204-3
ISBN 0-275-91615-4 (pbk.)
ISBN 0-275-91614-6 (study guide)

Library of Congress Catalog Card Number: 84-13307
ISBN: 0-275-91615-4

First published in 1984

Praeger Publishers, One Madison Avenue, New York, NY 10010
An imprint of Greenwood Publishing Group, Inc.

Printed in the United States of America

The paper used in this book complies with the Permanent
Paper Standard issued by the National Information Standards
Organization (Z39.48-1984).

10 9 8 7 6

For all that they taught me, personally and professionally,
this book is dedicated to the memories of
Malcolm H. Kerr (1931-84)
and
Elizabeth Parker (1927-82)

Preface

This volume represents the print component of an Introduction to Islamic Civilization course produced by the Foreign Policy Association in cooperation with National Public Radio and the University of Texas at Austin, funded by the Exxon Education Foundation and the Corporation for Public Broadcasting. It is written for the adult reader who has no academic background in either Islam or the Muslim world, and it therefore appears without the scholarly diversions of footnotes or diacritical marks on transliterated words. However, a glossary has been provided for easy reference, as has a bibliography, in the hope that further interest in the field has been stimulated. Islam is a world religion and, particularly in an introductory volume of this size, a great deal that could be said has been left out. It is hoped that the reader will pursue topics of interest for a fuller understanding of events and a richer appreciation of the issues.

The selection of contributors to the book was a painstaking process. The two chief criteria were scholarship and an ability to write for the nonexpert. Those with a background in Islamic studies will be familiar with the names of most of our contributors; readers new to the field need only be aware that care was taken to include material written by Muslim scholars, so that their "inside" perspective is present along with that of "outside," non-Muslim observers.

The reader may also note that while a number of authors use examples drawn from Muslim societies outside the Middle East, many of the case studies are Middle Eastern and, particularly, Arab. The explanation is simple: the linguistic and historical links between Islam and Arabic speakers are unique. The Qur'an was revealed in Arabic to an Arab in Arabia, and its message was spread by Arabs throughout an area whose heartland became not only Muslim but also Arabic-speaking. Though certainly not regarded as being limited to Arabs (who, in fact, were long ago outnumbered

by Muslims of other ethnic and linguistic backgrounds), Islam
holds a special place in Arab identity—so much so that even Christian Arabs make mention of Islam in their formulations of Arab
nationalism.

In trying to anticipate readers' needs and subsequent response
to this volume, I imagine an initial reaction of surprise that Islam is
as diverse and widespread as it is. An appreciation of this diversity
and dynamism is the key to undersanding Islam. Neither characteristic makes Islam easy to write about, because one always needs
to specify who, where, and when in discussing Islamic beliefs and
society. While Muslims regard the message of Islam as eternal and
universal, individual Muslims have, over time and around the
world, lived vastly different lives in a wide variety of circumstances.
In short, the message may be eternal but the expressions of it have
been varied.

So one talks about aspects of Islam: Islam as theology and
ritual, faith and practice, an ideology and a way of life—as well as
official Islam, popular Islam, traditional Islam, modernizing Islam,
and revivalist Islam. From the social perspective one speaks of Islamic civilization and institutions: Islamic law, banking, education,
history, sciences, art and architecture—even urban planning. Islam
has been seen as both a barrier to development and a blueprint for
the perfect society. In the end, one faces very subtle questions
about what is inherently Islamic and what has assumed an Islamic
identity by being addressed by Muslims in terminology associated
with Islam.

In trying to come to terms with the diversity of Islam, particularly if one is secular and Western, one must take care to avoid
equating Islam with tradition and, therefore, with something likely
to fade away as societies modernize. Muslims have come to realize
that modernization need no longer mean imitating the West, nor
need it necessarily imply secularization. They are endeavoring to
establish a modern Muslim society in a world that is currently dominated, if no longer controlled, by the West. This effort is made in
the belief that the superiority of Islam and the societies that em-
body it will be affirmed in the future as they have been in the past.
Hence the dynamism and diversity of Islam in today's world.

Unfortunately, on the human scale, diversity and dynamism
can also be interpreted as a lack of social cohesion and of governmental stability—which, of course, only adds impetus to the
search for authenticity and legitimacy. Given the Qur'an's silence

on many issues—but most particularly on those arising in the modern age—it is not surprising that more than one solution is proffered. As is its custom, the Muslim community (*umma*) has not foreclosed its options, and is relying on history to determine which solution is correct. But history may have caught up with the umma, for the lessons of the last century or so have indicated what does not work rather than providing a positive direction for change.

Change is never easy, and the ferment within the Islamic world and its repercussions on outside observers and societies reflect that difficulty. But perhaps "growth" is a better, more accurate description of what is occurring than is the word "change," for Islam continues to be a living tradition and remains a vital part of the religious and political life of the community that professes it.

My thanks go to the contributors to this book for helping to make it an integrated volume rather than a collection of articles; to the more than two dozen scholars who advised, critiqued, and responded to requests for help; to Lawrence Potter, for research and bibliographic assistance; and to those on both sides of several Middle Eastern borders whose friendship and hospitality have provided me with learning experiences that could have been achieved in no other way.

Marjorie Kelly

Contents

1

Faith and Practice

One of the most basic, yet misleading, distinctions made between the world's religions is that between the Western and Eastern traditions. To what does the East-West division refer? Geography alone? Clearly not. For Christianity, a Western religion, has taken root in almost every part of the world, while Hinduism and Buddhism, Eastern traditions, have a significant impact on the religious life of Europeans and Americans.

The distinction often reflects our cultural perceptions rather than geography or the intellectual structures of these traditions. Eastern religions are those we find mysterious, whose belief systems and ritual practices appear foreign, if not bizarre, and with whose cultural roots we have almost no firsthand contact. Western religions, on the other hand, represent the familiar, those world views that have been shaped by Judaism and Christianity and that form the underpinnings of European and American culture. Hence the temptation to number Islam among the Eastern religious traditions, a temptation to which educators, writers, and journalists have frequently succumbed.

When one reflects, however, on the conceptual and symbolic bases of the religion of the Muslims, Islam reveals itself to be a full member, alongside Judaism and Christianity, of the family of traditions commonly labeled Western. Islam did not spring from the soil of present-day Saudi Arabia in the seventh century C.E.* as a movement isolated from the religious currents of the age. On the contrary, the revelations transmitted to the Prophet Muhammad emphasize Islam's continuity with earlier Semitic traditions. Ac-

---

*C.E. stands for Common Era and is used in this volume rather than A.D., which has, of course, a specifically Christian referent.

1

cording to Muslim tradition, God chose Abraham to be the father of monotheism and created through his two sons, Isaac and Ishmael, the Israelite and Arab nations, respectively. In the same way He chose Moses to receive the Torah on Mount Sinai, elected Jesus to preach the good news of salvation in the Gospels, and appointed Muhammad as the seal of the prophets through whom He communicated His final revelation in Arabic, the *Qur'an.*

REVELATION IN ISLAM

Muslims affirm the Qur'an to be God's actual words; Muhammad is neither author nor editor, for no human agency influenced the formation of the text. Muhammad does not, therefore, function in the way, for example, the Evangelists do in Christianity. The majority of Christians acknowledge significant human contributions to the creation of their Scriptures. Equally critical for Christians is their belief that God's power was ever present to guide His human instruments and protect them from errors of faith. The Islamic tradition, on the contrary, is reluctant to allow even this modicum of human involvement in the production of the Qur'an. Muhammad is not a partner but a go-between, chosen from among men to transmit verbatim God's Word communicated to him through the angel Gabriel.

The Qur'an, as God's final revelation, does not, however, abrogate the Jewish and Christian Scriptures that preceded it. More precisely, the Qur'an serves as a corrective of the previous revelations, for the Jewish and Christian communities, Muslims insist, have distorted their books. Consequently the Torah and Gospels must be read through the eyes of the Qur'an and revised wherever conflict arises.

The Qur'an is neither a wholesale rejection nor a stale repetition of themes central to the Scriptures of the Christians and Jews. For the Islamic revelation blends a reaffirmation of aspects of the tradition with unique reinterpretations of fundamental theological principles. Eschatological concerns with death, judgment, heaven, and hell are familiar echoes from previous encounters with prophecy. The vision of a universe populated with numberless spiritual beings is also in tune with the Semitic world view. Gabriel, Michael, and other angels, together with lesser spirits and demons, are active participants in the spiritual life of Islam.

The role of the prophet, however, undergoes a significant transformation, for in Islam he is superseded by the *rasul* (messenger), who, according to tradition, comes to a community with a revealed message in book form. In addition, whereas the prophet might fail and be killed, a rasul is guaranteed success by God. Moreover, tradition affirms the sinlessness of both prophets and rasuls, thus guarding God's Word from any possible corruption or taint at the hands of men.

The title "prophet" is accorded to a far greater number of individuals in Islam than in either Judaism or Christianity. In fact, many figures of the Hebrew Bible and Christian Gospels are named as prophets by Muslims even though they are not so honored by Christians and Jews: for instance, Abraham, Noah, and Joseph; Zachariah, John the Baptist, and Jesus.

The title "rasul," in contrast, is far more restricted. The majority view among Muslims is that every rasul is a prophet, whereas not every prophet is a rasul. Joseph was a prophet but not a rasul; Moses, Jesus, and Muhammad are both prophets and rasuls. It is for this reason, therefore, that the Muslim confession of faith affirms the fact that Muhammad is the messenger (rasul) of God, not simply his prophet.

PHILOSOPHICAL THEOLOGY AND THE FIRST PILLAR OF ISLAM

While Islam's emphasis on continuity highlights the basic interdependence among the great Semitic religious traditions, a more thorough exploration of the Islamic belief system and Muslim religious institutions confirms Islam's right to a secure position among the traditions of the West rather than those of the East. The heart of Islam is an experience of revelation, God's active participation in history to communicate His will to mankind through His spokesman and apostle, the Prophet Muhammad. Man could not have discovered God's will unaided, for man is but a servant who, because of his finite nature, is precluded from attaining insight into the divine mind. The role of men and women is to listen and obey, to live the life outlined for them in the revelation and the traditions (*hadith*), and made specific in the law (*shari'a*).

Man is both finite and touched by evil, as the myth of Adam and Eve vividly illustrates. Not only does Satan seduce Adam and Eve but he involves himself in the life of every man and woman. The reason a child cries out at birth, the hadith explain, is because he or she is being pricked by Satan's goad. The only two humans spared this satanic involvement are Jesus and his mother, Mary. Even Muhammad was touched by evil at birth, but, tradition reveals, his heart was later claimed by the angel Gabriel. In addition, the hadith affirm that every human being possesses companion spirits, one evil and one good. Even Muhammad was thus afflicted, although his evil spirit eventually converted to Islam and became a force only for good.

The first of the five pillars of Islam, which are the foundation of the faith and the social, political, and religious structures of the Islamic community (*umma*), encapsulates the Muslim understanding of man's right relationship with God. The profession of faith (*shahada*) is a commitment to radical monotheism and to Muhammad as the instrument of God's Word and work: "La ilaha ill' Allah wa Muhammad rasul Allah" ("There is no god but God, and Muhammad is the messenger of God"). To embrace this single truth is to enter fully into the life of the community of truth, Islam, for whose members paradise has been prepared. Consciously to reject it is to be numbered among the unbelievers and hypocrites, the denizens of hell.

A commitment to monotheism is nothing new in the history of Western religious traditions. The radical monotheism of Islam, however, offers distinctive solutions to the thorny problems of the nature of God and the relationship of freedom to predestination, of good to evil, and of reason to revelation.

Islam insists on God's absolute transcendence and perfect unity, yet the Qur'an makes anthropomorphic references to God (for instance, to His face or His hands) and refers to such attributes of the divine essence as knowledge and mercy. This apparent contradiction poses a theological dilemma. Is God totally other than, or somehow like, human beings? Is His essence perfectly simple, or do the attributes have an independent existence of their own? No one answer is universally accepted; the classical synthesis, however, attempts to tread a middle path by affirming both sides of the paradox. Yes, God is transcendent, but the anthropomorphic verses have validity because they are the Word of God. God, therefore, possesses a face, hands, and the like in a way that we do not understand. As for the attributes, they must not be interpreted as simple metaphors because they, too, have Qur'anic validation. Although they are actual realities, they do not impinge on the unity of God's essence.

In similar fashion the early Muslim philosopher-theologians struggled to integrate the Islamic vision of an all-powerful creator God who continues to sustain every aspect of the universe with men's and women's seeming ability to determine their own fate. But how could human freedom be affirmed without contravening the basic Qur'anic principle that no being, earthly or otherwise, is equal to, or capable of challenging in the slightest way, the all-pervasive power of God? The granting of such independence to men and women is condemned as the cardinal sin of *shirk* (associationism—that is, associating someone or something else with God).

Throughout the formative period of Islamic intellectual life, from the eighth to the tenth centuries C.E., the issue was hotly debated: Was man's fate his own or totally predetermined? An influential group of Muslims, known as Mu'tazilites, insisted vehemently on man's absolute moral accountability for his actions. The Mu'tazilite stance in favor of human responsibility was a corollary to their defense of God's justice, for justice requires that men and women be punished or rewarded for deeds performed as a result of free moral choice. At the same time that they highlighted God's justice, the Mu'tazilites affirmed that God is not involved in the evil He condemns. Evil is understood to be the unfortunate product of the human power to choose. In the minds of the Mu'tazilites, to attribute absolute omnipotence to God would make God responsible for all actions—good or evil.

Yet this insistence on men's and women's ability to determine their moral life through free choice raised the specter of shirk, because it created the impression that human beings, solely through their own powers, earn eternal reward or punishment. The classical solution, exemplified in the work of al-Ash'ari (d. 935 C.E.) and his school, does not favor either radical freedom or predestination, although it leans toward the latter. Al-Ash'ari was a staunch defender of God's absolute omnipotence and limitless freedom, and he rejected radical freedom of the human will, teaching that all human actions are creations of God alone. He even denied secondary causality a place in the universe, lest the assertion that creation possesses an independent order of its own somehow diminish God's pervasive power. The sun rises and sets, therefore, not because of some internal law of the cosmos, but because God creates the event anew every day.

In defending God's omnipotence, al-Ash'ari needed somehow to address the question of God's involvement in man's sinful deeds. He did so by denying that human actions are intrinsically good or evil. Something is good because God commands it, evil because He forbids it. Lying, for example, is evil only because God decided it is so. If He someday decided that lying is good and ordered his faithful to lie, men and women would be expected to comply.

One learns what is good and evil first and foremost by careful attention to God's command, made explicit in the Qur'an and Muslim legal tradition, not by using reason to determine the intrinsic moral worth of a particular action. In fact, human reason can easily become a snare of self-delusion, for it appears both gloriously independent and irrefutable in its logic. Reason that has been molded in an Islamic environment will admit its fallibility and cede primacy of place to revelation whenever conflict arises. This stance should not stifle inquiry but, rather, be a reminder of human reason's fundamental limitations. Men and women may reach the stars, but in the process they cannot attain equality with the divine power from whom the universe has its life and upon whom they depend for their continued existence.

ISLAMIC PRAXIS AND THE FOUR REMAINING PILLARS OF ISLAM

Prayer

While these philosophical and theological controversies contributed to the vibrancy of Islamic intellectual life in the classical period (eighth–thirteenth centuries), such inquiries were not a preoccupation of the majority of Muslims. On the contrary, the central concern of the faithful man or woman, then as now, is to lead the life of a Muslim, not to debate theological issues. The emphasis is on praxis, the molding of every aspect of one's daily life to conform to the prescriptions laid down in the Qur'an, the hadith, and the shari'a.

The fulfillment of God's Word, therefore, demands continuing efforts to create a society that is imbued with Islamic ideals and that reflects as perfectly as possible the presence of God in His creation. Not surprisingly, the four remaining pillars of Islam are fundamental elements of this holistic vision of the Islamic umma.

The second pillar, *salat* (prayer) five times a day, envelops every period of the daily human cycle in the mantle of Islam: daybreak, noon, midafternoon, sunset, and evening. Salat may be performed anywhere, but it must not be initiated unless one is in a state of ritual purity. The ablutions preceding prayer cleanse the worshipper's body and spirit, and enable him or her to pass from profane existence to a state consecrated solely to divine worship. Although the ablutions entail the washing of the hands, mouth, teeth, nostrils, arms, head, ears, and feet, they should not be confused with personal hygiene. Not that cleanliness is ignored; the primary consideration, however, is to pass from a state of impurity, caused by bodily evacuations, sleep, and sexual contact, to a state of ritual purity. While these normal human processes are not necessarily unhygienic, they nevertheless impose a state of ritual impurity on the believer and must be counteracted.

The prayers themselves involve two, three, or four *rak'as,* depending on the time of day the prayer is performed. The rak'a is a multistage movement that combines bows, prostrations, and the recitation of prayer formulas. The time for prayer is heralded by the call of the *muezzin:*

> God is great! God is great! God is great! God is great!
> I bear witness that there is no god but God.
> I bear witness that there is no god but God.
> I bear witness that Muhammad is the messenger of God.
> I bear witness that Muhammad is the messenger of God.
> Come to prayer! Come to prayer!
> Come to prosperity. Come to prosperity.
> God is great! God is great!
> There is no god but God.

A minor change in the call to prayer occurs in the morning, when, before proclaiming the final "God is great!," the muezzin reminds the faithful, "Prayer is better than sleep. Prayer is better than sleep."

While some Muslims perform some or all of their daily prayers in the local *masjid* (mosque), this is not obligatory. The only prayer service of the week that all are encouraged to attend is the Friday noon prayer. Congregational prayer is led by an *imam,* who stands at the head of the assembled faithful. (The imam who leads prayer should not be confused with the Imam of Shi'ism, who functions as the head of the theocratic state and whose role will be discussed more fully below.) The Friday congregational prayer is solemnized further by the addition of a sermon, a tool for the revitalization of religious ideals and, on occasion, a telling barometer of the religiopolitical tensions in a particular region of the Islamic world.

The Muslim place of worship, the mosque, is traditionally an open space capable of accommodating large numbers for congregational prayer. While the architectural styles vary according to period and cultural milieu, the vast majority share common features. The *mihrab,* for example, is a niche in the mosque wall indicating the direction of Mecca. All must face toward Mecca during prayer because the *Ka'ba,* the Sacred Cube or Holy House of God, is located there. The pulpit provides the Friday preacher with a vantage point from which to deliver his sermon to the assembled believers. At the entrance to the mosque, running water is provided for ablutions. The apparatus may consist of a simple spigot and basin or an elaborate courtyard with fountains. The *minaret,* perhaps the most widely recognized feature of a mosque among non-Muslims, was traditionally the tower from which the muezzin would chant the call to prayer five times daily. Rarely these days, however, do muezzins climb to the tops of minarets to perform their duties; they use public address systems with loudspeakers.

The mosque building is primarily a place of assembly for the community; consequently it has more in common with the Jewish synagogue than with the Christian church. God does not reside in the mosque; the only edifice that is universally acknowledged to be God's house and a locus of divine power is the Ka'ba at Mecca. The mosque should be seen as a multipurpose structure intended to offer the Muslim an environment conducive both to prayer and to more mundane activities. The mosque is a place to meditate on the text of the Qur'an, to study with a learned religious teacher, to relax quietly from the turmoil of a bustling metropolis, to do one's homework, to doze in the midday heat. The expansive area of the interior of many mosques is covered with carpets, providing a comfortable, shaded space of peace and tranquility. Mosques serve as both the social and the religious centers of villages and urban neighborhoods.

Almsgiving

A third pillar of Islam, *zakat* (almsgiving), develops further the link between religious practice and social concerns. Each Muslim is acknowledged to be the equal of every other Muslim when he or she stands shoulder to shoulder with other community members to perform identical ritual movements and prayers in the mosque during congregational worship. Economic inequality between the affluent and the needy members of the community is mitigated through zakat. Islamic law requires that one tender a percentage of one's wealth and yearly production to the umma for the care of the indigent, orphans, and the needy, and for the support of clerics, the *ulama*. The amount ranges from 10 percent to much lower percentages, depending on the commodity taxed. The method of collection and the agency of distribution vary from country to country, but the basic obligation is incumbent on all. The extent of compliance, however, depends a great deal on the piety of the individual.

Ramadan

Of the five pillars of Islam, the two most visible to the observer are the month-long fast of *Ramadan* and the *hajj*, the pilgrimage to Mecca. During Ramadan, Muslims are obliged to fast from dawn to sunset, abstaining completely from both solids and liquids. For the exceptionally scrupulous even smoking and the swallowing of one's saliva are considered infractions of the fast. Because the Islamic calendar is lunar rather than solar, the Islamic months do not fall at exactly the same time each year. In fact, it takes 33 years for an Islamic lunar month to make the complete round of the seasons. Consequently, the month of Ramadan periodically falls during the summer, adding even more strain to the already arduous fast. The summer heat in a number of Muslim countries is severe, and to work for a full day without eating or drinking fluids is exhausting if not dangerously debilitating. No doubt the level of productivity and efficiency is severely affected in industrialized Muslim societies during Ramadan; but that is a small price to pay, the faithful are convinced, for the spiritual benefits to be reaped.

Fasting is characterized by some observers as anachronistic if not overtly masochistic. Yet it may be more "modern" than it appears at first glance. Fasting confronts the believer squarely with his or her physical dependencies. The individual becomes aware of the extent to which various needs (food, sex, emotional fulfillment) actually control his or her life. Has one become a slave to one's instincts? With this stark realization of physical dependency comes a renewed awareness of one's need for God, whose merciful hand provides His faithful with the strength to reestablish balance within themselves and with their surroundings.

The month of Ramadan is a period of contrasts. Whereas the days are spent in austere fasting, the nights are set aside for family feasting, visiting with friends and relatives, and for exercises of piety (such as the recitation of the whole Qur'an, one-thirtieth each night). At sunset, when the breaking of the fast occurs, all pause for a light meal and the first fluids of the day. Much later that evening a large meal is shared. After several hours of sleep, men and women rise before dawn to take nourishment before the start of the coming day's fast.

The conclusion of the month of Ramadan is the occasion for perhaps the most widely celebrated festival in the Islamic world, the *Id al-Fitr,* the Festival of Breaking the Fast, known also as the *Id as-Saghir* (Little Festival) to distinguish it from the less joyous, more religiously solemn *Id al-Adha,* the Festival of Sacrifice, or *Id al-Kabir* (Great Festival), celebrated during the pilgrimage. The twenty-seventh day of Ramadan is an especially sacred day, the *Laylat al-Qadr* (Night of Power), on which Muslim tradition commemorates the beginning of God's revelations to Muhammad.

Hajj, the Pilgrimage to Mecca

The religious pilgrimage is familiar to people of all traditions, Western and Eastern. The Muslim hajj, however, is unique among sacred journeys because it is obligatory and not simply an act of special piety or devotion. Thus it functions as an essential element of Islamic life. Every Muslim man or woman is duty bound to perform the rites of the hajj once in a lifetime, provided the journey is both physically possible for the individual and not an undue financial strain on the family.

A Muslim man or woman does not pick a random time to travel to Saudi Arabia to perform the pilgrimage. There is only one period a year (the first ten days of the month Dhu 'l-Hijja, the eighth, ninth, and tenth being the most critical days) during which the religious obligation of the hajj may be fulfilled. Of course Muslims are not prevented from visiting the holy places at other times of the year. For such visits of devotion the rites of *umrah,* the lesser pilgrimage, are prescribed. Although these rites are identical with the early rites of the Hajj (entering a state of ritual purity, the circumambulation of the Ka'ba, the running between the hills of Safa and Marwa, and so on), they do not in any way fulfill the obligation to perform hajj. Because hajj is a religious obligation while umrah is an act of devotional piety, each has a different significance in the life of Islam. Nevertheless, it is often the custom for pilgrims to perform both umrah and hajj during the pilgrimage days, umrah being performed before, at the same time as, or after the hajj proper.

Arrival at Mecca may occur anytime before the eighth of Dhu 'l-Hijja, when all pilgrims (upwards of 2 million in recent years) must be assembled to perform together the required rites and rituals. Early arrivals often take the opportunity to visit Medina and the mosque and grave of the Prophet Muhammad. Although the visit to Medina is an integral part of most Muslims' hajj, it is not, properly speaking, one of the prescribed rites.

The major ritual of the pilgrimage begins and ends with the circumambulation of the Ka'ba, the Holy House of God, in whose wall is embedded the sacred Black Stone. The initial rite of seven circumambulations is performed soon after one's arrival in the holy city. The Ka'ba was an object of pilgrimage in pre-Islamic times, before the revelations to Muhammad. According to Muslim tradition, Muhammad purified the Ka'ba of idols and restored it to its rightful place as the house of the one God, a position it held when it was built by the prophet Abraham and his son Ishmael. The Black Stone, the final building block of the Ka'ba, was brought to Abraham, it is said, by the angel Gabriel.

The circumambulation of the Ka'ba is followed by a visit to the shrine of Abraham, the father of Western monotheism, and by running seven times between Safa and Marwa to commemorate Hagar's search for water when she and her son Ishmael were abandoned in the desert. (Their search resulted in the appearance of the sacred well of Zemzem, whose waters are believed to possess special powers.) The pilgrims then travel several miles from Mecca the the village of Mina, where many pass the night as Muhammad had done on his last pilgrimage. The next day, the ninth, the pilgrims proceed to the mount of Arafat, where the rite of standing before God takes place, beginning at high noon. The hours until sunset are dedicated to prayerful repentance during which the mass of pilgrims, as representatives of all Muslims throughout the world, seek and receive from God His merciful forgiveness. This is *the* central rite of the pilgrimage; its omission nullifies the validity of the hajj.

From Arafat the pilgrims begin a return journey to Mina by way of Muzdalifah, where each pilgrim collects 49 pebbles to be used in the stoning of the three "devils," really stone pillars symbolic of the power of evil in the world. Arriving at Mina from Muzdalifah on the tenth of Dhu 'l-Hijja, the pilgrims prepare for the most solemn of Islamic festivals, the Id al-Adha. Before the sacrifice, however, seven pebbles must be cast at one of the stone devils. (Those remaining will be cast during the following two days, seven pebbles a day at each of the three devils.) Subsequent to the stoning a blood sacrifice is offered of sheep, goats, cattle, or camels. The flesh of the sacrifice was originally intended for distribution to the poor. But the vast number of pilgrims in recent years has required that many of the sacrifices be disposed of by burial in large pits or, most recently, by being processed at new food-packing plants for later distribution. On the return to Mecca from Mina, no later than the thirteenth of Dhu 'l-Hijja, a farewell circumambulation of the Ka'ba is made before the pilgrim returns to the world of everyday existence.

Just as daily prayers in Islam are preceded by preparatory rites (ablutions) that move one from a profane to a sacred plane of existence represented by the sacred state of purity (*ihram*), so the pilgrims must take upon themselves ihram for hajj, which involves physical ablutions, purification rites, and the removal of the external signs of social differentiation. No jewelry or finery may be worn, nor is one allowed to use perfume. Women are instructed to dress simply and modestly, while all men wear the same simple pilgrim's garb, two pieces of seamless white cloth; one is worn around the waist, the other covers the torso and is slung over the shoulder. Men should wear no head covering, nor should women veil their faces. All are to abstain from sex. Violence is forbidden; even anger or the harming of animal or vegetable life within the precincts of the sacred territories is outlawed.

All of these preparatory rites aim at the common goal of leveling all of the everyday differences that separate Muslims one from the other: sexual, social, economic, ethnic, cultural. During the hajj all Muslims are equal before God and are meant to experience the ideal unity hoped for in the Islamic umma. Despite the fact that Islam is composed of an astonishing cultural diversity of nation-states that at times are in political agreement, at times not; despite the economic disparity between the oil-rich nations and the Third and Fourth World Muslim countries; despite the sexual inequality that exists, the hajj provides a unique opportunity to experience for a time what the ideal Islamic umma is envisioned to be: multiethnic, egalitarian, and dedicated to the human and religious values embodied in the divine revelation. The hajj is truly without parallel in other religious traditions and has the potential to serve as a positive force for the renewal of the Islamic vision throughout the world.

As significant as the five pillars in shaping the Islamic community are the legal system (shari'a) and *jihad,* the principle of holy war. Both will be discussed in later chapters. One makes explicit the structure of life and community practice embodied in the Qur'an and hadith; the other functions as an ideal of personal reform—the war between one's God-derived impulses and the seductions of the devil—and as the means to ensure the survival of the community when it is confronted by forces hostile to Islam.

DIVERSITY IN THE UMMA: SHI'ISM

Personal human history, the social process, and the material world all play pivotal roles in the process of salvation as described within Islam and the other Western traditions. In Judaism God speaks His creative Word and history is born. He elects a concrete, historical community to be His chosen people, entrusts them with the Torah, and provides them with a particular land in which to flourish. The Christian community takes this valuation of the material a dramatic step further: God's creative Word becomes actual flesh and blood in the person of Jesus Christ. Finally, in Islam, the creative Word of God becomes book in the Qur'an.

Thus, to recognize clearly Islam's place within the continuum of Western religious history is to begin to dissipate the cloud of mystification that has for so long enveloped the Muslim world. Once again, however, we must beware lest we succumb to a different naive assumption: that there is a concrete, monolithic reality called Islam. In point of fact one "Islam" does not exist any more than one "Christianity" or one "Judaism" exists. Islams exist—or, more precisely, the Islamic world view has taken root in a variety of cultural settings: from Indonesia and Malaysia to Africa, from Iran and Central Asia to China and the Indian subcontinent, and from the Arab world to Europe and the United States. While there may be a common vision that can be abstracted from these cultural settings and labeled "Islamic," the multifaceted and evolving historical forms of Islamic civilization are the realities we encounter. Moreover, the unity of the Islamic umma is based primarily on the ideals embedded in this abstract vision, not on any serious hope to impose cultural uniformity.

The diversity of cultures in the umma has fostered pluralism in religious practice, primarily in the realm of popular piety. Doubtless each Islamic culture believes itself to be the repository of "true" Islam, as well as the manifestation of its full flowering in history. As a result, other forms of Islam are seen not simply as different but, rather, as imperfect copies of one's own reality. Consequently, negative critiques by one Muslim group of the devotional practices of another group are sparked by inherent conflict between cultural pluralism and the uniformity of an idealized religious vision.

Not only does cultural diversity produce tensions within the umma, but there also exist differing religious visions of what constitutes "true" Islam. They are the product of fundamentally different theological interpretations of Muhammad's relationship both to God and to the early community. In the same way that Christianity and Judaism comprise various sectarian groups that have come into existence because of theological disagreement on fundamental issues, so Islam has numerous divisions and subdivisions, the most important being that between the Sunni and Shi'i communities.

It has been traditional in the study of theology to designate certain sectarian communities as orthodox while condemning others as heterodox, as if they were somehow distortions of an original, authentic vision. This judgmental approach was carried over into the academic study of Islam: scholars often describe *Sunni* Islam as orthodox while they brand Shi'ism as heterodox. There is no doubt that Sunnis far outnumber Shi'is in the Islamic world; but this should not necessarily lead to the conclusion that Sunni Islam is more authentic. Nonetheless, the majority view is clearly the most influential and, for historical and social as well as dogmatic reasons, the one that has had far wider appeal in the Islamic world. We should not be dismayed, however, that insiders (those committed in faith to a tradition) continue to judge as unorthodox or "less right" those members of the same tradition who choose to align themselves with a different sect. That is the insider's prerogative. On the other hand, outsiders should couch their evaluations in terms more in tune with their role as observers, not as theologians.

Sunni and Shi'i Islam diverge primarily in their views of religious authority. After the death of the Prophet Muhammad in 632 C.E., the majority adopted a congregational solution to the problem of succession. One of the companions of the Prophet was chosen by Muhammad's inner circle to be caretaker of the political and material needs of the nascent community. True religious and legal authority was localized in the Qur'anic revelations and the remembered words and actions of the Prophet, which were eventually collected in the hadith. The power of interpretation that resided in the community came to be exercised by those members trained in the religious sciences. A tradition, attributed to the Prophet Muhammad, that corroborates this basic stance confirms that his community will never err when it agrees on an issue of religious import. This segment of the umma became known as Sunnis, followers of the well-trodden path of tradition.

A minority position, however, affirmed that succession to the prophetic office should be hereditary and that political and religious authority should remain unified in one individual who would guide the theocratic state. As God bestowed on Muhammad the unique gift of prophecy and molded him into the prophet-statesman who governed the Islamic community, so too, it was believed, would He instill in Muhammad's heirs a unique power of religious insight into the Qur'an and the charisma of political leadership. Thus one man would exercise both religious and political leadership, as God had originally intended.

None of Muhammad's male children survived him. The aspirations of those favoring a hereditary solution to the succession were focused on Ali, Muhammad's first cousin and son-in-law, the husband of Fatima, the Prophet's daughter. The hereditary faction became known, therefore, as Shi'is or partisans (of Ali). Ali was eventually named to the caliphate in 656 C.E., but he fell victim to an assassin in 661 C.E. The political hopes of the early Shi'is were dealt an even more crushing blow with the martyrdom of Ali's son Husayn in 680 C.E., at the hands of the representatives of the recently established Umayyad dynasty. The martyrdom of Husayn is the paradigm of suffering for Shi'is, who see their destiny in terms of a minority's struggle against continual persecution. The tenth day of the month of Muharram, the anniversary of Husayn's martyrdom, is the most important religious commemoration in Shi'ism. This memorial is accompanied by mourning rites, penitential processions, and the performance of ritual dramas depicting the tragic events that led to the slaughter of Husayn and his followers at Kerbela in present-day Iraq.

The heir to authority in Shi'ism is known as the Imam. (This Shi'i title should not be confused with the Sunni use of the same term to describe the one who leads congregational prayer in the mosque.) The usual transmission of the office of Imam is from father to son. Problems arose, however, in the eighth century C.E. over which son was actually designated by the sixth Imam, Ja'far al-Sadiq (d. 765 C.E.). Some followed his older son, Isma'il, while others followed the younger, Musa al-Kazim. This resulted in the most significant sectarian division among the Shi'is, one community becoming known as the Seveners or Isma'ilis, the other as the Twelvers.

The numerical appellation of each group refers to perhaps the most critical theological and political dilemma faced by the developing Shi'i community, the death of an Imam with no apparent male successor surviving. This crisis occurred in both lines descending from Ja'far al-Sadiq. For the Isma'ilis the shock was immediate, since the line was broken with the family of Isma'il himself, who died in 760 C.E. The line of Imams descending from Musa al-Kazim continued until the disappearance of the twelfth Imam, the child Muhammad al-Muntazar (al-Mahdi), around 874 C.E.

The resolution of the problem is reminiscent in some ways of the Christian interpretation of Christ's death and the doctrine of the Holy Spirit. Both Shi'i groups share the conviction that neither line was irrevocably broken. On the contrary, the last Imam did not die, but was transmuted from a physical presence in the community to a spiritual one. Neither did Isma'il's son die, say the Seveners; nor did the child Muhammad al-Muntazar die, affirm the Twelvers. On the contrary, the Imam has gone into hiding (the more technical term being occultation). He will eventually return to restore the Islamic community to its rightful place as the embodiment of the final revelation and the beacon of religious, social, and political righteousness. One subdivision of the Isma'ilis is unique in that it possesses a living Imam, His Highness Shah Karim al-Husayni, Aga Khan IV.

The Shi'i Imam is a figure of extraordinary religious power; he is the perfect mediator between God and man. Later Shi'i theology describes him as sinless, possessed of exceptional virtue and unparalleled insight into the hidden meanings of the Qur'an. Moreover, he is infallible, incapable of erring in his guidance of the Shi'i community. For some Shi'is the Imam takes on semidivine status, a physical shell in which resides the power of God Himself. His word, therefore, is not to be contested; it is to be revered as a further expression of God's will for the umma.

SUFISM

It is not only in Shi'i Islam that one discovers a fascination with the esoteric or hidden dimensions of the Qur'an and of religious experience. Beginning in the eighth century C.E., there are clear signs of a burgeoning mystical tradition in Islam, a conscious effort on the part of individuals to establish an intimate, loving relationship with God. Islamic mysticism is known as Sufism, a term usually thought to be derived from the Arab word *suf* (wool). The early ascetics of Islam, called Sufis, wore coarse woolen garments to signify their rejection of the material world.

Several scholars in the past have expressed the opinion that mysticism is not compatible with Islam, and that its presence in an Islamic environment is due to outside influences, perhaps Christian and Buddhist. One need not, however, look beyond Islam for the origins of Sufism. While it is true that the predominant vision of God in the Qur'an is that of an omnipotent creator, lawgiver, and judge who wields terrifying power, yet is eternally compassionate, a careful study of the Qur'anic text reveals a far more complex God-man relationship.

One of the most crucial Qur'anic verses for Sufis describes the establishment of the primordial covenant between God and the souls of men and women in a time before the creation of the universe (Qur'an 7:172). The goal of every Islamic mystic is to reestablish the loving intimacy between the Lord of the worlds [*sic*] and the human soul proclaimed at that moment of the covenant. Sufi tradition refers to this event as the "day of *alast,*" the day when, the Qur'anic text relates, God proclaimed His Lordship and the souls of mankind acquiesced in an act of perfect *islam* (self-surrender).

The text of the Qur'an was not the only stimulus for the burgeoning Sufi tradition; social and political forces were at work as well. The transfer of the capital of the nascent Islamic empire from Medina to Damascus, with the establishment of the Umayyad dynasty in the mid-seventh century C.E., created a dramatically new ambience: the comparatively spartan tribal life in the Arabian peninsula gave way to the sophisticated, cosmopolitan world of an urban metropolis. The relative opulence of the early Umayyad period may have influenced the ascetics who preached detachment from worldly goods and power—in fact, from all earthly attainments—as a prerequisite for creating a suitable environment in which to cultivate the experience of God's immanence.

One of the major centers for this eighth- and ninth-century phenomenon was the province of Khurasan, especially the formerly Buddhist city of Balkh. Other centers of early Sufism were in

Iraq, especially the cities of Baghdad, Basra, and Kufa, and in Egypt, which produced significant figures whose imprint on Islamic mysticism endures to this day.

Renunciation and detachment, which are so characteristic of asceticism, are often understood as ideals relating principally to regulating one's involvement with the material realm: food, clothing, money, sex, and so on. The goal of this process is, however, more than a rejection of materiality and physicality; it is often a struggle to attain a new level of freedom where one is in harmony with one's physical life, not its slave. Freedom results in the power to focus one's attention fully on mystical union.

More sophisticated understandings of the role of detachment emphasized man's emotional and psychological life, thus providing the impetus for highly sophisticated analysis of human psychology by masters like al-Muhasibi (d. 857 C.E.), who introduced the examination of conscience into Sufism. The effort to provide the Sufi initiate with organized treatments of the theoretical foundations of the Sufi life was not restricted to the realm of psychology but touched on every dimension on the spiritual life. The late tenth and eleventh centuries saw the production of important manuals that attempted to systematize the Sufi path. These works categorize and elucidate the spiritual and psychological experiences encountered at every stage of the Path. In addition, a great deal of helpful, practical advice is imparted by the well-tested master to the newly embarked novice.

A didactic literary genre of a different sort, hagiography, attained prominence during the same period. Early Qur'an commentators and street preachers often focused on the lives of the prophets for inspiration. This interest spawned works known as *Qisas al-Anbiya* (Tales of the Prophets), compilations of lively, pedagogic prophetic fables. The Sufi community also cherished the lives of its prominent members as role models. Collections of the lives of Sufis offered the reader a wealth of practical guidance in the form of the preserved sayings and teachings of particular masters as well as details about their lives.

By far the most provocative expressions of Islamic mysticism were not its ascetic literature, manuals, or hagiographies, but its ecstatic and poetic works. It is here that one encounters the most problematic and yet the most intriguing attempts by the mystics to convey in words the ultimately ineffable experience of union with the Beloved. Ecstasy in Sufism is manifest at the earliest stages of the movement. Abu Yazid al-Bistami's (d. 874 C.E.) cries of "Glory to me!" "How great is my majesty!" and similar seemingly self-divinizing expressions of ecstasy dramatically raised for the Muslim community the question of the exact nature of mystical union: Was it union with God or actual identity with Him?

While al-Bistami is the first recorded ecstatic of significant influence, his utterances are overshadowed by those of the most famous of the Baghdad mystics, Husayn ibn Mansur al-Hallaj, who was put to death by order of the Abbasid caliph al-Muqtadir in 922 C.E. Al-Hallaj's "Ana al-Haqq!" (I am the Divine Truth!) rings throughout the history of Sufism as the outstanding example of ecstatic utterance.

Al-Hallaj's mystical paradoxes ranged far beyond the subject of union with the divine. One of his most creative uses of paradox was his treatment of the Islamic devil, whose name is Iblis (derived from the Greek *diabolos*). In the Qur'an the angel Iblis fell from divine favor because he refused to obey God's command to bow down before the newly created Adam. Iblis was an angel of fiery might, and saw no purpose in bowing to a creature made of humble clay.

Al-Hallaj, however, reinterpreted this Qur'anic myth and proclaimed Iblis as the perfect monotheist who refused to turn away from his single-minded dedication to God. Iblis would not bow to another, even if his refusal resulted in his condemnation. For al-Hallaj, Iblis was the epitome of paradox: a satanic yet tragic victim, condemned for his disobedience yet perfect in loving devotion to God, tempter but also model of mystical piety.

The use of paradox to cut through to the core of the Sufi experience in dramatic fashion was a technique that many renowned Sufis used to express the essentially ineffable quality of the mystical experience. Logic, philosophy, theology—all the religious sciences, especially those that rely on rational discourse—were inadequate to encompass in verbal expressions the essence of Sufi ecstasy. More evocative modes of discourse were needed.

The mystical impulse was the catalyst for the creation of highly sophisticated poetry. Perhaps the greatest poets of the medieval period in Islam were trained in the Persian style of letters and mysticism. Attar (d. 1220 C.E.), Rumi (d. 1273 C.E.), and Hafiz (d. 1389 C.E.) are but a few of the masters whose poetry shaped a literary tradition.

The language of the traditional religious sciences in Islam has always been Arabic, even in non-Arabic-speaking environments. Persian attained a significant though not so universal ascendancy in the Muslim world, especially in the realms of poetry and mystical literature. But in the fourteenth century important works of Sufi poetry began to appear in the local languages that were much more accessible to people not trained in the Arabic and Persian intellectual traditions. Yunus Emre (d. 1321 C.E.) helped to create a vibrant poetic tradition in Turkish; writers in Central Asia and the Indian subcontinent molded the local dialects into compelling literary idioms.

The fact that mysticism occurs in the majority of Eastern and Western religious traditions is not the sole reason why Sufism is of special interest to scholars of religion. Islamic mysticism is unique in that it functions as a bridge between the Eastern and Western religious traditions. How so? Up to the late twelfth and early thirteenth centuries, the goal of Sufism was described in terms very much in tune with the predominant metaphysical and mystical ideals of Western religion. The ultimate experience was a loving relationship between the soul and God in which both remained independent realities. Moreover, the soul of the perfected mystic was to enjoy the most intimate of loving unions with God for all eternity. Yet in the twelfth and thirteenth centuries, Sufism began to take on a genuinely different character. The goal was described not as union between lover and Beloved, both eternally independent, but as the total obliteration of lover into the Beloved: unity or identity, not union.

This was not the first time that language of this sort had been used, but now the vision of mystical identity was solidly grounded intellectually in a metaphysical system by one of the greatest minds of Islam, the philosopher, theologian, and mystic Ibn 'Arabi (d. 1240 C.E.). His affirmation of a metaphysical identity between God and His creation, a type of monism, is far more reminiscent of the Hindu religious tradition than of those of the West.

Born at Murcia in Spain in 1165, Ibn Arabi traveled widely from Muslim Spain through North Africa to Mecca, finally settling at Damascus in 1230. His literary output was prodigious, its intellectual density a continuing challenge to modern scholarship. In Ibn 'Arabi's concept of *wahdat al-wujud* (the unity of being), one finds the essence of his metaphysics. Rather than affirming the traditional Islamic (and Western religious) view that a personal God created the cosmos from nothing, and that the soul is eternal and distinct from God, Ibn Arabi insisted that only an unknowable One exists who is God. The creative process was but the manifestation of the One in the plurality of created beings; creation was the process of God manifesting Himself to Himself. Plurality was ultimately an illusion, because only the One truly existed. Eventually all creation will return to the source from which it sprung, the One.

Ibn 'Arabi's mystical theories had a tremendous formative influence on later Sufism and provided Islam with a sophisticated intellectual bridge to the traditions of the East. If at first glance wahdat al-wujud appears to be a radical departure from early theological and mystical theories, on closer scrutiny it reveals itself as a logical extension of the Ash'arite synthesis that emphasized the pervasive involvement of God's determinative power in every human action. The move from perceiving God as the only true Agent to affirming Him as the only true Existent should not appear startling.

While Ibn 'Arabi was enormously influential among those trained in the subtleties of Sufism, the rise of Sufi fraternities from the eleventh through the thirteenth centuries eventualy had a far more significant impact on the religious life of the wider Muslim population. Up through the eleventh century the structure of Sufi groups remained somewhat fluid, often relying on the charismatic personality of the individual Sufi master (*shaykh* or *pir*) who attracted disciples and acted as the binding force in the group. With the shaykh's death the group often disbanded. By the thirteenth century, however, the structure of the fraternities became more stable; self-perpetuating *tariqahs,* as they were known, became the norm. These institutionalized groups preserved the spirit and teachings of the charismatic founder through a line of shaykhs who traced their initiation and training back to him.

DEVOTIONAL PIETY

Possibly the major reason for the pervasive and continued influence of Sufism on Islamic life has been the ability of Sufi fraternities to fulfill important religious needs of the general Muslim population. Involvement with a particular Sufi fraternity did not necessitate the abandonment of one's secular life and family. For some that abandonment was definitely the case. For others—in fact, for the vast majority of Muslims involved with Sufism today— affiliation consists in periodic attendance at particular ritual exercises known as *dhikr* and *sama'*.

Dhikr (remembrance) most often involves the rhythmic repetition in a group setting of one or more formulas containing the name of God. It developed complex forms in the different fraternities, often involving body movements, breathing techniques, chants, and such—all leading to some form of religious experience, be it self-induced or granted by God. The sama' (audition) is a musical recital of religious poetry, usually accompanied by Qur'an recitations and involving ritual dance. The type of poetry, music, and dance varies dramatically from group to group, ranging from the meticulously choreographed and aesthetically refined dance of the Mevlevis of Turkey (known also as the Whirling Dervishes), to the frenetic, almost hysterical sama' still found in urban and rural centers, from North Africa to Indonesia, where the music and poetry are inspired by local mystic-saints.

In addition to dhikr and sama', the veneration of renowned holy men and women took on special significance in the popular piety of Islam. The founders and most notable shaykhs of the different Sufi fraternities became the objects of the devotion of their immediate followers and the wider community. These spiritual giants were known to possess *baraka,* unique spiritual power capable of being transmitted from holy man or woman to disciple and/ or devotee. Baraka does not disappear with the death of the saint; visits to the tombs of holy men and women provide the faithful with opportunities to experience their power. A saint's baraka produces spiritual favors as well as visible miracles of all sorts.

The charismatic personality takes on a particularly critical role in the developed theology of saintship. The most spiritually proficient, and therefore most powerful, among the living saints of the age serves as the *Qutb* (Pole), the axis of spiritual power and authority on earth. The Qutb is the Perfect Man who mediates between God and creation and who heads a spiritual hierarchy that sustains the universe.

The rise of the superhuman religious figure in Islam should not, however, be attributed solely to Sufism. A similar process had been under way in the shaping of the Islamic umma's approach to the Prophet Muhammad. Although the Qur'anic and early bio-graphical evidence affirms unequivocally that Muhammad under-stood himself to be nothing more than a man like other men, the community gradually transformed him into a wonder-worker and intercessor with God. Much has been made by European and American scholars of this inconsistency between Muhammad's self-understanding and the rise of popular devotion to him. The later "cult" of Muhammad was often depicted as a degeneration of the original Islamic vision, the vulgarization of an ideal by the popular religious mind.

There has been, and continues to be, a segment of the Islamic community that has decried the popular devotionalism surround-ing the Prophet, branding it innovation and, consequently, unac-ceptable. But these voices have never won out. If the student of reli-gion were to dismiss the veneration of the Prophet as an illogical aberration, he or she would be missing the point entirely. This, like other religious devotional practices, responds immediately and creatively to the felt needs of the faithful. It is this personal experi-ence of power that sustains an important part of their religious lives. True, the textual logic may be wanting, but religion is often at its most dynamic when it moves beyond human logic, to a realm it perceives as suprarational, above reason but equally authentic.

The major feast celebrated in honor of the Prophet is his birth-day, which falls on the twelfth of the month of Rabi al-Awwal. It is marked by the recitation of particularly popular poems that depict in detail the wondrous events surrounding the Prophet's birth and the miracles of his later life. These mythic infancy narratives and hagiographic tales envelop Muhammad with cosmic signs and por-tents of his future dignity and vocation as prophet and intercessor: his birth is attended by Moses' and Jesus' mothers, who welcome him as the successor to their sons; he speaks the confession of faith immediately after leaving the womb. In later life he heals the sick, provides miraculous assistance to the needy, and performs other wonders.

Possibly the greatest miracle of Muhammad's life, other than the revelations of the Qur'an, is the Night Journey and Ascension. He is said to have been carried one night on his fabled steed, Buraq, from the precincts of the Ka'ba at Mecca to Jerusalem, from which he ascended through the seven heavens to an actual encounter with God. The rock in Jerusalem on which he stood and from which he ascended into heaven is now a preeminent shrine of Islam: the Dome of the Rock. This story has been preserved in numerous versions, with wonderfully imaginative embellishments. It is perhaps the most popular religious myth in Islam.

Among the Shi'is, devotion to Muhammad is equaled, if not superseded, by a deeply felt commitment to the power of the Imams and the members of their families. The most important shrine and pilgrimage site in Shi'i Iran is the tomb complex of the eighth Imam, Ali al-Rida, located in the city of Mashhad. Of almost equal importance is the shrine dedicated to Fatima, the sister of the eighth Imam, at Qum, which is also an important center for theological education. The two most prominent Shi'i shrines in Iraq are located at Najaf, where Ali, the first Imam, is said to have been buried, and at Kerbela, where Ali's son Husayn was martyred.

It is to such holy places that faithful Shi'is travel in search of cures, favors, and a sense of nearness to divine power. The prominence of the major shrines in Iran and Iraq should not overshadow the importance of the local sanctuaries dedicated to other holy members of the Alid line. These shrines, large and small, provide accessible and immediate contact with baraka for all men and women in every corner of the Shi'i world.

The Shi'i Imam is unique not only because he is a focal point of divine power, but also because he combines within himself both religious and secular authority. No equivalent concept exists in Sunni Islam except, perhaps, for the messianic belief held by many that the *Mahdi* (Guided One) will eventually appear to restore Islam to its pristine glory. He also will reforge the link in Sunnism between religious and secular authority. In addition to Mahdism, however, there exists in North Africa a phenomenon somewhat similar to that of the Imam, the warrior-saints known as *marabouts.* At first an individual attained the rank of marabout either by demonstrating baraka or through charismatic leadership based on sherifian lineage (descent from the Prophet Muhammad). As time progressed, however, these two qualities seemed, more often than not, to be linked in the same individual.

A fine example of the shrine of a sherifian marabout is in the village of Moulay Idris, the holiest sanctuary in Morocco, where the tomb of Idris I (d. 791 C.E.), the founder of the first Arab dynasty to rule in Morocco, is located. His son, Idris II, established the city of Fez. By combining prophetic lineage, religious dedication, and military perspicacity, he was an extremely effective leader. The modern period has seen an equally successful sherifian ruler and holy man in the person of Muhammad V, father of the present King Hassan II of Morocco. He earned the veneration of his people through his management of the colonial powers in the mid-1950s.

SOCIAL DUALISM

This brief overview of the classical belief system and the evolution of religious practice and popular piety in Islam should establish beyond a doubt the basic family relationship among the great traditions of the West: Judaism, Christianity, and Islam. Doubtless there is much about Islam that is unfamiliar. Its predominant thrust, however, is clearly in accord with the monotheisms of the revelational traditions that affirm God's active involvement in the historical process.

Islam's common heritage with Judaism and Christianity should not, however, imply cohesiveness among these communities. For the very nature of this heritage militates against such a unity. Essential to the Western religious tradition, we have seen, is the notion of divinely revealed Word. However, a value judgment is implicit in each community's conviction that it possesses the fullness of truth embodied in the Word. Moreover, the religious, social, and political institutions derived from the revealed Word are believed to mirror this same perfection. Problems arise when one community of exclusive truth confronts another, since each is convinced that its own truth is ultimate.

In Islam this opposition is described in terms of social dualism, a conflict between the *Dar al-Islam,* that portion of the world that has been permeated by the Qur'anic revelation and has begun to shape its institutions accordingly, and the *Dar al-Harb,* the realm of chaos and evil. The goal, of course, is eventually to integrate the whole world into the Dar al-Islam.

The claim by the Western traditions that each somehow possesses ultimate truth entails at the same time the implied or explicit judgment that the stances of other communities are wrong, not just different. Outsiders have freely rejected the truth and, in their hardheartedness, remain firmly attached to their distorted vision. Hence Muslims must be vigilant to prevent these imperfect, if not evil, communities from injecting their corruption into the Dar al-Islam. The textual logic seems to indicate an unresolvable conflict among the great traditions. Once again, however, we need not be victims of textual logic but, rather, can look beyond these limitations to a new avenue of entente.

Basic understanding is possibly the key. Appreciating as fully as possible how members of a community different from one's own find meaning in their lives cannot help but dissipate pent-up tensions. Not that one is expected to change allegiance because of this interaction; nor, in fact, must one learn to like or agree with others' perceptions of truth and reality. The essential requirement is respect, a respect that precludes irrational responses and that wards off the insidious temptation to reduce others to inferior or less-than-valuable human beings. This may be the true avenue of creative interaction and one that will, in time, lead to a freer movement between, and greater appreciation of, one another's worlds.

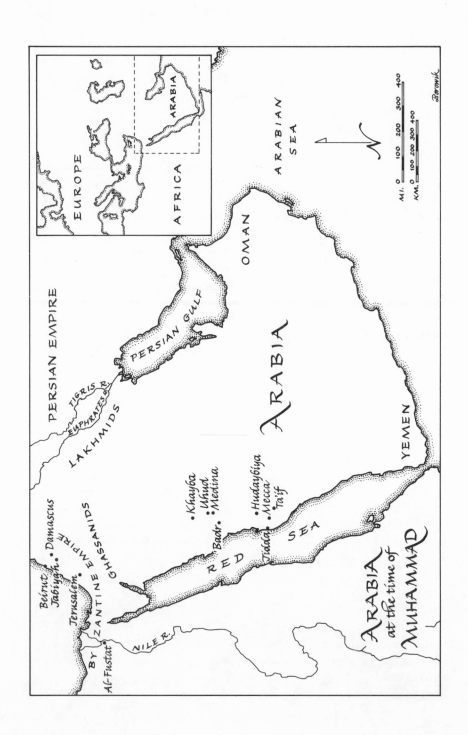

ARABIA
at the time of
MUHAMMAD

28

2

The Message and
the Messenger

Fazlur Rahman

Seventh-century Arabia lay between the Byzantine and Persian empires, which were constantly at war with each other. In present-day Iraq, to the east, and Syria, to the north, were the Christian Arab principalities of the Lakhmids and the Ghassanids, under Persian and Byzantine suzerainty, respectively. In South Arabia (present-day Yemen), where a high civilization had existed until shortly before the coming of Islam, there was a mixed population of Jews and Christians; the Persians supported the former and the Byzantines the latter through their Ethiopian vassal.

In 523 C.E., Dhu Nuwas, the Jewish ruler in South Arabia, reacted to an Ethiopian threat to his kingdom by massacring the Christians of Najran when they refused to convert to Judaism. The event had a traumatic effect on the whole of Arabia and is referred to in the Qur'an (85:4-8). Sometime before Muhammad's birth, Abraha, the Christian ruler of South Arabia, invaded Mecca, but failed to capture it because a smallpox epidemic broke out among his soldiers. The Qur'an refers to this event in *sura* (chapter) 105.

Besides the Jewish community in South Arabia, there were prosperous Jewish settlements in Yathrib (later Medina) and Khaybar. The Jews, though orthodox in religion, had become completely Arabized culturally; some wrote excellent Arabic poetry. Christianity was also present in Arabia beyond the South, having spread among several desert tribes, such as the powerful Banu Taghlib. Because of the presence of these Jewish and Christian communities, there was a general penetration of Judeo-Christian ideas in the Arabian peninsula. Mecca was a region of particular religious ferment. Individuals called *hanifs* had arrived at a vague idea of monotheism.

Astride the caravan route between India and Byzantium, Mecca was a prosperous commercial town. The large and powerful Quraysh tribe dominated the city and exercised considerable influence over desert tribes as well. Besides the income derived from trade, the Quraysh received income from the Ka'ba, the sanctuary that was the object of annual pilgrimage from all parts of Arabia, and from the special trade fairs held at the time of the pilgrimage. Along with this prosperity, however, there existed in Mecca acute problems common to any commercial community: a large number of disenfranchised persons and an underworld of slaves and hirelings, including a large number of Ethiopian slave laborers. There was thus a good deal of social disequilibrium and unrest.

Strictly speaking, the "religious" problem was polytheism. Although many had accepted the idea of one God called Allah, actual cultic worship was dedicated to other gods and not to Allah, as the Qur'an mentions repeatedly. These gods and goddesses were worshipped as mediators between man and Allah, who was supposed to be too high to be approached directly. The Qur'an also makes clear in several passages that Jews and Christians had made attempts to proselytize the Meccans but had been unsuccessful. While the mercantile aristocracy of Mecca in general felt little need to give up its ancestral religion of idol worship, the more sensitive but proud Arabs wanted a new religious dispensation of their own whereby "they would be better guided than these earlier communities," as the Qur'an puts it.

Although there was some practice of star cult in Arabia, which the Qur'an repudiates, the main features of the religion of the Arab bedouin consisted of fetishism and a belief in a blind fate, called The Time, that controlled certain critical stages of human existence: birth, sustenance, and death. For this blind fate the Qur'an substituted a powerful, merciful, and purposeful God. The Arabs also had an all-important code of honor, which consisted of bravery in defense of individual and tribal honor, especially with regard to the honor of women; generosity; and the keeping of promises and pacts. This last was especially necessary, given the precariousness of desert life, and was manifested in intertribal pacts and the institution of the four "sacred months" in the year when all feuding and fighting ceased in order to allow free travel and trade.

The last important constituent of the bedouin code of honor was vengeance, for it was believed that until a slain person's blood was avenged, his soul—transformed into a bird—cried from his grave from thirst. According to the principle of vengeance, it need not necessarily be the killer who was executed in revenge; anyone from the killer's tribe or clan equal in status to the slain man would do. This was later prohibited by the Qur'an, though retribution was deemed desirable.

In many cases women in pre-Islamic Arabia chose their husbands and exercised a certain freedom that was not regulated by any standard code. Free love existed and prostitution was common; both were prohibited by the Qur'an, which sought to regulate sex and family life. However, generally speaking, women's status in pre-Islamic Arabia was not high. The infanticide of females was fairly common and regarded as having religious sanction. The Qur'an has some sharp criticism of the socioeconomic disvalue attached to female children by Arab pagans:

> When one of them is given the good news of [the birth of] a girl, his face darkens while he tries to suppress his chagrin. He hides from people [out of shame] and [wonders] whether to keep her in disgrace or shove her under the earth. Behold how evil is their judgment. (16:59)

Female children were barred from inheritance, while a son inherited his stepmother. These practices, too, were abolished by the Qur'an.

On the whole, Arabs were, in their world view and practice, a secular people, and such religion as they had was ritualistic and cultic. Their code of honor was, in practice, their religion, emanating from the fountains of deepest human emotion. In this code of honor, called "manly virtues," the crowning place was held by tribal honor, for it was to the tribe that the Arab owed foremost loyalty. This is effectively illustrated in a poem by Durayd ibn al-Simma, who recalls how, while returning home with a party of his tribesmen from some errand, he advised his men to change their course for fear of being waylaid. His men, however, refused to listen to his advice, were attacked by their enemies, and lost some of their most precious heroes in the battle. The poet justifies his decision to follow his men by citing the ideology of tribal solidarity:

> When they rejected my advice, I also joined them while fully knowing
> That I was in manifest error in abandoning the correct path.

Am I but a member of the [tribe of] Ghaziya. Should they go
wrong,
I must do likewise as I must follow them should they choose the
right!

Yet, as was hinted at the outset, at the time of the advent of
Islam, a religious consciousness had arisen in many circles and
among sensitive individuals. Judeo-Christian ideas, notably
monotheism, had materially contributed to this consciousness, but
the temper and content of religious expression were probably
purely Arab. For example, an older contemporary of Muhammad,
Umayya ibn Abi'l-Salt of Ta'if, near Mecca, described his religion in
a collection of poems as "hanifism" and "monotheism." He was not,
however, active in founding any religion and was content to live
quietly, even praising rich men and receiving material rewards. But
some religious seekers developed into claimants of prophethood,
the most serious being Maslama (contemptuously nicknamed by
Muslims "Musailima" [the diminutive], who was a younger contemporary of Muhammad in the Najd. All of these men appear to have
represented tribal leadership. They were defeated by the Muslims
soon after the Prophet Muhammad's death, when their claims
threatened both Islam and the central Islamic political authority at
Medina.

MUHAMMAD, THE PROPHET OF GOD

Muhammad, son of Abd Allah, born at Mecca in 570 C.E., was
distinguished from false prophets not only by an extraordinary religious and ethical sensitivity and the universalist import of his message, but also by a single-minded devotion that was a central trait of
his character. Prophetic mission was not just his hobby or profession, but his entire life:

Say, [O, Muhammad!] my prayers and my devotions, my life
and my death are all for God, the Lord of the world. (Qur'an
6:163)

Muhammad's father, a trader, died before he was born, and his
mother, Amina, died when he was about six. His respected but rela-

tively poor uncle, Abu Talib, the elder statesman of the clan of Banu Hashim of the tribe of Quraysh, brought him up, gave him protection, and unflinchingly defended him against the enemies of his mission, although Abu Talib himself seems never to have accepted his nephew's faith.

Little is known about Muhammad's life before his call at about the age of 40, in 610. There is little doubt, judging from the Qur'an and contemporary accounts, that he was by temperament pensive, introverted, shy, rather aloof, and brooding. In his youth, he was called al-Amin (the trusted one), an indication of his honesty and moral sensitivity. In his early twenties, he undertook trade missions to Syria on behalf of a rich lady, Khadija, whose business he managed. She was so impressed by his honesty and ability that she offered herself in marriage to him, which he accepted. He was 25 and she was 40 years old. She bore him three sons, all of whom died in infancy, and four daughters. The youngest, Fatima, married Ali, Muhammad's cousin and the son of Abu Talib. Muhammad did not remarry until well after Khadija's death, when he was 50 years old. No male offspring resulted from his later marriages, although the Coptic Christian concubine, Mary, bore him a son who died.

Some time after his marriage to Khadija, Muhammad began to visit the Cave of Hira, a little north of Mecca, where he spent days and sometimes weeks in solitude, prayer, and contemplation. No doubt he contemplated problems of God, the Absolute Creator and Sustainer of the universe, and His creation—particularly the human problems of society: the socioeconomic disparity, the ill-gotten gains of the rich through fraudulent trade practices, and their irresponsible ways of spending their wealth in the face of the sorry plight of the poor, the orphans, and the oppressed.

One night at the age of 40 (later celebrated as the Night of Power, "when all important matters of wisdom are decided" by God), while in a deep contemplative mood in the Cave of Hira, Muhammad was called by a messenger of revelation, Gabriel, to God's message. He saw the divine messenger in a vision "on the highest horizon." While experiencing this sudden spiritual outburst, he felt totally passive. He came home trembling and perspiring. His wife reassured him by telling him that because he was a good man, he could not have been possessed by an evil spirit and must have truly experienced divine revelation. Muhammad never returned to the cave again, but embarked on his historic mission. This was the beginning of Islam as religion; Islam as a community or polity began in a latter phase of the Qur'anic revelation.

Muhammad's early preaching was private: to his family, clan, and close friends. His wife, Khadija, and his cousin, Ali, were the first converts. For the most part, his other followers were from disenfranchised and deprived classes, although some were well-to-do merchants, like Abu Bakr, and others were individuals who had experienced religious ferment for some time, like Uthman ibn Maz'un. But the mercantile aristocracy, whose members sat on the High City Council of Mecca, and those under their influence squarely rejected the new teaching. They regarded it as a threat to their two fundamental vested interests: idol worship and socioeconomic privilege. The Qur'an demanded (1) abolition of idol worship (or what the Qur'an calls "associating others with God" [shirk], in which the Meccan oligarchy had a patent religious and economic interest, and (2) social and economic justice for the have-nots, which the Meccan oligarchy perceived as an unfair levy on the wealth they had earned and felt entitled to dispose of as they liked.

Approximately two years later, when Muhammad's mission was launched publicly, there was active opposition to the religion and his less powerful followers were persecuted. Meccan leaders tried to persuade Abu Talib either to influence his nephew to relent in his mission or to withdraw his protection, but these attempts failed. They spread propaganda against the Prophet among Arab tribal chiefs at the time of the annual pilgrimage, but that action only succeeded in making Muhammad's name and his mission more widely known to Arabia.

It seems abundantly clear from numerous passages in the Qur'an that there were some Jews and Christians with messianic expectations who accepted the new dispensation. In fact, they encouraged the Prophet in his mission, even when he hesitated because of fierce opposition and religious division within families—something that was disastrous for a tribal society in which solidarity rested on blood ties.

In the face of the systematic persecution of his more vulnerable followers, Muhammad advised them to emigrate temporarily to Ethiopia, and in 615 some followers did so. At the same time, however, Islam won some influential and powerful converts, the most prominent being Umar ibn al-Khattab, who subsequently ruled as the second caliph of Islam. Panicked by these events, important members of the High City Council decided to institute a boycott of the Prophet's clan, the Banu Hashim. This excommunication, although it caused a great deal of suffering to the clan, was never fully successful; members of other clans related to the Banu Hashim covertly supplied them with food and other help. The boycott collapsed after three years.

When the Meccans saw that they could not silence Muhammad or destroy his movement, they offered to compromise. They would join his faith if he would get rid of his ragtag lower-class followers, for it would be unseemly for them to sit by his side in the presence of such people, particularly when the leaders of other Arab tribes visited him. The Qur'an warned him:

> Do not abandon those who pray to their Lord in the morning and in the evening—coveting only His pleasure; in no way are you accountable for them nor are they accountable for you. Should you cast them aside, you will be among the unjust ones. (6:53; 18:28)

Before offering their compromise, they had tried to negotiate with Muhammad on certain doctrinal issues: if he would modify his teaching to accommodate their gods as intermediaries between man and God, and possibly eliminate the idea of resurrection, they would become Muslims. Regarding resurrection, there could be no compromise. On the question of intermediary gods, Islamic tradition says that during the emigration to Ethiopia, when the nascent Muslim community was in dire straits, the Prophet did once speak favorably of them, reciting some compromising verses in sura 53. However, these were soon abrogated, castigated as satanic verses, and replaced with verses that now stand in the Qur'an.

Most modern Muslims reject the story that Muhammad ever spoke the words, but in light of the Qur'an, it seems quite plausible. For the Qur'an's standard doctrine is that no human—including a prophet—is immune from Satan's temptations and assaults; but in the case of God's good servants, truth eventually prevails and Satan's insinuations are obliterated. Thereafter, in response to demands that the Prophet make changes in the Qur'an, the Qur'anic reply was:

> Say [O, Muhammad!], it is not for me to change it by myself; I only follow what is revealed to me. I fear, if I disobey my Lord, the punishment of a mighty day. Say, if God so willed I would not be reciting it to you. . . . Do you not reflect that I have lived among you all my life before this? (10:15-16)

When, in 619, both Khadija and Abu Talib died, the Prophet lost the worldly help essential for his physical survival. He visited the neighboring town of Ta'if (now the summer capital of Saudi Arabia) in search of support for his cause. He was not only maltreated there but stoned. While returning from Ta'if, the Prophet had the following moving prayer on his lips:

> O, Lord! to You I complain of my helplessness, my paucity of resources, and my insignificance vis-à-vis other men. O most Merciful of the merciful, You are the Master of the helpless and You are my Lord. To whom will You abandon me?

Upon his return to Mecca, Muhammad visited the camps of Arab tribesmen who came to the city for their annual pilgrimage, and he met with their chiefs to offer them Islam. Some agreed to join his community on condition that after his death they would succeed him as leader, which Muhammad refused. During these encounters, he met with a group of pilgrims from Yathrib (renamed Medina when Muhammad moved there), an oasis 250 miles north of Mecca. Tired of their internecine feuding and looking for someone to whom they could entrust their affairs, the people of Medina invited Muhammad to live among them. After careful discussion of the conditions and terms during two consecutive pilgrimage seasons, the Pact of Aqaba was concluded; the emigration from Mecca to Medina took place in the summer of 622. The Prophet himself arrived there on September 24. This historic emigration, known as the *hijra,* marks the beginning of the Islamic calendar and the founding of the Islamic community.*

The first task was to build a mosque, the area of prayer that is the center of Islamic life. Within a short time after his arrival in Medina, the Prophet created a brotherhood between the new arrivals and the native population. The groups were known as *muhajirun* (emigrants) and *ansar* (helpers). While emigrants continued to trickle into Medina for years, either individually or in small parties, and occasionally a Muslim went back to Mecca as an apostate, Medina became a Muslim town, the town of the Prophet.

---

*Because the Islamic calendar is based on a lunar cycle of 354 days, the calculation of dates between the Muslim (A.H.) calendar and the Gregorian (A.D. or C.E.) calendar is not just a simple difference of 622 years.

But now a grave political problem arose, for according to the tribal law of the Quraysh, the Prophet and his Meccan followers were fugitives and traitors, and therefore had to be destroyed, even though residing in Medina. Medina itself was divided. Besides the two large feuding tribes of Aus and Khazraj, there were three Jewish tribes: the Banu Qainuqa (the smallest), the Banu Qurayza, and the Banu Nadir. Ethnically pure and religiously orthodox, the Jewish tribes had come to Arabia after the Diaspora and become completely Arabized culturally. Most of them lived in fortresses around Medina and were traders, while the Arab population was agriculturists. Although the Jews were divided and took sides in the disputes between the two feuding Arab tribes, they nevertheless constituted a distinct group by themselves.

As for the Arab population, the large majority became Muslim upon Muhammad's arrival or soon thereafter. There was, however, a group whom the Qur'an calls Hypocrites. These were followers of Abd Allah ibn Ubayy, a highly skillful and intelligent man from the Banu Khazraj who had nearly succeeded in becoming the ruler of Medina. When Muhammad arrived, ibn Ubayy outwardly embraced Islam while inwardly harboring designs to undermine it. Thus, the Hypocrites were a sort of fifth column, secretly in league with the Meccan pagans and the Jews, and constantly intriguing against the Muslims. It is a tribute to the skill of ibn Ubayy that although the Prophet was fully aware of his dangerous machinations, he could never actually lay hands on him.

Within a few months after his arrival in Medina, the Prophet drew up and promulgated a document called the Charter of Medina (or, as Western scholars term it, the Constitution of Medina). The charter spelled out the rights and obligations of all the groups residing in the city. The Prophet was recognized as the chief arbitrator of Medina in settling intercommunal disputes. The Jews were granted religious and cultural autonomy, and were recognized as "a community along with Muslims." Most important, all groups were to defend Medina in case of an attack from the outside. Despite this, however, a party of Meccans arrived by night in Medina not long after the hijra to scheme against the Muslims, and the Hypocrites gave them hospitality and a sympathetic ear.

Bear in mind that ever since Muhammad had left Mecca, the central aim of his policy had been to take the city for Islam because, aside from its commercial and political ascendancy, it was the religious capital of the Arabs. Within one year of the hijra, the Ka'ba at

Mecca was declared by the Qur'an to be the object of Islamic pilgrimage, and about six months later it was also fixed as the direction for prayer—replacing Jerusalem. Muhammad harassed and attacked Meccan trade caravans en route to Syria (Medina lay astride the route), not just to capture booty but, above all, to isolate Mecca economically and bring it to its knees before Islam.

From the very beginning of the Muslim settlement in Medina, the Meccans and Muslims were actively hostile to each other: Meccans seethed with revenge and wanted to bring Islam down, and the Muslims tried to strangle Mecca economically. This point has to be emphasized because historians, particularly some modern Western historians, have implied that with the hijra the struggle between the Meccans and the Muslims came to an end, and that it was the Prophet who offended by attacking the Meccan caravans. On the contrary, the earliest historical sources (including the Qur'an) show that the Meccans were in active pursuit of the Muslims even after they settled in Medina.

The first pitched battle took place in the year 2 A.H. (March 624 C.E.) at the plain of Badr, a few miles southwest of Medina, where Muslims planned to intercept an exceptionally large and rich Meccan caravan returning from Syria under the leadership of the Umayyad Abu Sufyan (whose son Mu'awiya later founded the Umayyad dynasty). The Quraysh reinforced their caravan with an additional 900 fighters from Mecca. The Muslims numbered only 312 and were ill-equipped compared with the Quraysh, but they won a decisive victory, killing 70 Quraysh, including some of their most important men, and taking many prisoners. Some of the prisoners were released for ransom, while others who were literate were freed on the condition that they teach Muslims how to read and write. This unusual victory was interpreted as a clear sign of God's favor and of the truth of Islam.

The following year, the Quraysh, even better equipped than they had been at the first battle, returned to avenge themselves. (A Medinese Jewish poet, Ka'b ibn al-Ashraf, who had become rich by trading in arms, wrote a poem to instigate Meccans to take revenge. He went to Mecca and recited the poem in the tradition of the Arab war bards, and was later assassinated on the Prophet's orders.) Under pressure from his companions and against his own better judgment to battle the Meccans inside the city, the Prophet decided to fight near the Uhud Hills outside Medina. When the Muslim archers stationed on the hills saw the Meccans were headed for defeat, they left their positions in order to share in the booty. With their flanks thus exposed, the Muslims were attacked by the Meccans and fell into confusion and disarray: A false rumor spread that the Prophet had fallen in battle. He did in fact lose two front teeth. The Meccans did not pursue their victory, however, and returned home. The Qur'an reprimanded the Muslims for their haste but also consoled them by saying:

> Muhammad is but a Messenger; before him have gone many other Messengers. Should he die or be slain [in battle], will you turn back upon your heels? (3:144)

Two years later (5 A.H./627 C.E.) Abu Sufyan, once again and for the last time, marched on Medina with 10,000 troops, including 600 cavalry, consisting of Meccans, bedouin tribesmen, and Jews from the Khaybar oasis in the north. On the advice of a Persian companion, Salman, the Prophet had trenches dug outside Medina, which prevented the attacking cavalry from advancing. The invaders laid siege to the city but, partly due to the Prophet's effective intelligence and partly due to bad weather, the siege had to be lifted when the bedouins became impatient at the lack of booty and pay. This was the last armed conflict between Meccans and Muslims.

The conduct of bedouin tribes, Hypocrites, and Jews throughout these wars calls for some comment. Whenever the Muslims won a battle, the bedouin were eager to conclude pacts of peace and mutual help with the Prophet; but whenever the fortunes of war turned against him, they abandoned their pacts. The Qur'an has passed some of the harshest strictures on their behavior:

> The bedouin are the most entrenched in infidelity and hypocrisy and the most apt not to observe the limits of God. (9:97)

> The bedouin say, We believe; say to them [O, Muhammad!], you have not believed but say, we have [only] surrendered [outwardly]. (49:14)

The Hypocrites vanished with the death of ibn Ubayy in 9 A.H./631 C.E. As for the Jews, it has already been pointed out that they had links with the Meccans, and their relationship with the

Hypocrites was particularly strong. The Qur'an repeatedly accuses them of breaking pacts:

> How is it that whenever they make pacts, a group among them casts it aside unilaterally? (2:100)

In fact, this is the standard charge against the Jews. It is important to note that after each of the three battles described above, the Prophet turned against one of the Jewish tribes and accused it of infidelity. After Badr, the Banu Qainuqa were accused and expelled along with their mobile possessions. They would probably have received harsher treatment but for the intervention of ibn Ubayy. After Uhud, the Banu Nadir met with the same treatment. After the Battle of the Trench, where Jews of Khaybar and of Medina had actually participated on the side of the Meccans, Muslim opinion differed sharply about the treatment of the last tribe, the Banu Qurayza. Most of the able-bodied adult males who did not repent were massacred, according to the decision of Sa'd ibn Mu'adh, whom both parties had agreed upon as the arbitrator.

The following year (628) the Prophet declared his intention to make the pilgrimage to the Ka'ba. The majority of the Meccans opposed this, and armed themselves to stop the Muslims at a place called Hudaybiya. Instead of doing battle, the Muslims signed a pact in which they agreed to postpone the pilgrimage for a year. There were other important clauses in the pact, including provision for the extradition of renegades from Mecca. It was a fundamental victory for Islam in that the haughty Meccans had agreed to negotiate the pact on an equal footing with Muslims, something hailed by modern Western historians as a master stroke of diplomacy on Muhammad's part. In 7 A.H./late 628 C.E., Khaybar was conquered but Jews there were allowed to stay on the land on a 50-50 sharecropping basis.

In 8 A.H./630 C.E. Mecca fell to Islam, thus fulfilling the central aim of the Prophet's policy in Medina. The Meccans had been fighting a tribe with which the Muslims had a pact of mutual help. When the Muslim army arrived outside Mecca, the city surrendered without bloodshed. Muhammad entered the city, his head bowed in humility and prayer. A general amnesty was declared, Meccans embraced Islam, and the idols in the Ka'ba were dislodged from their places. Tribal delegations from all over Arabia arrived and converted to Islam. In 10 A.H./632 C.E. the Prophet made his last pilgrimage to Mecca, where he delivered a moving sermon, celebrated in history, that emphasized the brotherhood of Muslims, the equality of mankind irrespective of color and ethnicity ("You are all children of Adam and Adam was from dust"), and substituted the bond of faith for that of tribal blood kinship (the community for the tribe). It summed up his moral, socioeconomic, and religious reforms. Upon his return to Medina, he fell ill and died in 10 A.H./632 C.E.

HISTORICAL PERCEPTIONS OF THE PROPHET

Because of the complexity of Muhammad's character, he has been much misunderstood and maligned by Western writers, and it is only recently that a more positive appreciation of both his character and his performance has developed. Muslim tradition, on the other hand, has tended to mythify his person and life with elements borrowed from a variety of sources, particularly Christian ones. Thus, while the Qur'an denies that Muhammad performed any miracles except that of receiving the Qur'an (11:13; 2:23; 6:33-35; 17:59), Muslim tradition attributes numerous miracles to him, apparently in competition with other religious traditions.

Certain verses of the Qur'an (17:1; 53:5-18; 81:19-24) speak of a series of spiritual experiences of the Prophet in which his self expanded and became identified with the whole range of reality. Muslim tradition fused all these into one single locomotive experience, the ascension of the Prophet to the heavens, most probably in competition with the Christian belief in the ascension of Jesus. Muslim tradition also contends that Muhammad was illiterate, thereby seeking to strengthen the genuineness of his revelation. Although there is no direct evidence to prove or disprove his literacy, some indirect evidence points to his being literate—for example, the fact that he was a trader and managed his first wife's business. What is certain is that he had no direct acquaintance with Jewish and Christian Scriptures.

The Western difficulty in understanding the Prophet, apart from inherited prejudice, springs mainly from viewing his Meccan and Medinan careers as two separate—indeed, disparate—phases. In Mecca, he appears to Western writers as a genuinely inspired personality, a suffering and oppressed prophet. He approaches the Christian image of Jesus. In Medina, however, he wages battles, legislates, judges, and rules. He also marries a multiplicity of wives, becoming an ordinary person in Western eyes. This dual picture is belied not only by the Qur'an, which was revealed to Muhammad in Mecca and Medina with the same sincerity and force, but also by a closer study of the spiritual history of the Prophet himself.

Although he was an inspired personality in Mecca, he was at the same time a realist who dispassionately searched for ways and means to implement his teaching. His cool, self-controlled, and statesmanlike behavior is strikingly brought out by the way he conducted negotiations with the Medinese and concluded the Pact of Aqaba in connection with the hijra. In Medina, while the affairs of society and state occupied him much of the time, he never claimed the status of a ruler, a general, or a lawgiver; he was only God's messenger, as he had been in Mecca. Nor is there any evidence of a change in Muhammad's character based on the intensity of Qur'anic revelation: "If We had sent this Qur'an down upon a mountain," says a Medinese verse, "You would have seen it humbled and split asunder through fear of God" (59:21).

As for his marriages, although there is no denying the fact that he liked women, there is absolutely no evidence of any impropriety. Nor does sex appear to have been a prominent feature of his marriages; Ayisha was the only virgin wife he married. The reasons for the plurality of his marriages were the ones that characterized that society generally: an abundance of war widows who needed economic protection, and marriage as a means of establishing tribal alliances.

For Muslims, Muhammad was not only the greatest prophet but also the last of the series of divine messengers. This belief rests on the words "Seal of the Prophets" used in the Qur'an (33:40).

THE MESSAGE

The teaching of Islam is embodied principally in the Qur'an, which for Muslims is the Word of God in the literal sense. (The second source of Islam, the *sunna,* or model of behavior of the Prophet, will be treated in Chapter 3.) The Qur'anic revelation began with three major themes: monotheism, socioeconomic justice, and the Last Day (the final accountability of man).

First in importance is belief in a unique, all-powerful, merciful, and purposeful God. God alone is infinite, and all His attributes—power, will, mercy, knowledge—are as infinite as His being. The creation of the universe is due to His primordial mercy. This is why there exists the plenitude of being rather than the pure emptiness of nothing. Because of His literal infinitude, He encompasses all, and no other being can share in His divinity. He has created the universe as a cosmos rather than as chaos. There are no gaps and dislocations in nature because God has ingrained in everything its measure or the laws of its behavior.

To accept or conform to the laws of God is islam, which means to surrender to God's law. According to the Qur'an, therefore, the entire universe is *muslim* (the active participle of islam or that which submits)—that is, the universe conforms to the laws of God ingrained within it. Since nature has no free will nor choice, it is automatically muslim. God wanted to create a being with choice and free will who would be his vice-regent on earth and who would surrender to God's law—that is, would be muslim by choice. In the case of man, the "is" of nature would be replaced by "ought," and the natural law by moral law.

Second, we come to man, his nature, and his destiny. Adam was created from baked clay. When his carnal frame had been built, God breathed his own Spirit into him. When God was about to create Adam as His vice-regent, the angels did not take kindly to the idea and said to God, "Will You put therein [that is, on the earth] one who will sow corruption therein and will shed blood, while we carry out Your commands and sing Your glories?" (2:30). In His reply, God did not deny these charges but said, "I know what you know not." He then brought the angels and Adam together and asked them to name things. The angels could not, while Adam was able to do so—that is, Adam proved himself capable of creative knowledge. Because of this, he voluntarily bore the trust of moral responsibility that no other creature was able to accept (33:72). Yet the Qur'an persistently complains that, despite man's great potential for knowledge, he has, to date, not been able to fulfill this primordial trust of moral responsibility. Where does the trouble lie?

We said above that monotheism, socioeconomic justice, and belief in the Last Day were the earliest themes of the Qur'an's message. For the Qur'an, the basic weakness of man lies in his pettiness, his narrow-mindedness, and his smallness of heart:

> Man is by nature unstable: When evil touches him, he panics, but when good things come his way, he prevents them from reaching others. (70:19-21)

This narrowness of man is at the root of all his troubles. His polytheism prevents him from rising to one universal God and confines his vision to small goals, and his selfishness prevents him from reaching out to others in self-giving and active goodness:

> Say [O, Muhammad!], if you were to possess all the treasures of the merciful bounty of my Lord, you would still sit upon them fearful of spending [them]. (17:100)

The remedy, then, is to rise above this satanic condition of pettiness and to give generously "the best parts of your wealth" for the welfare of the poor.

The Qur'an aims at creating a kind of human with a keen moral insight who can distinguish between right and wrong (this state of mind is called *taqwa,* protecting oneself from moral destruction), for the greatest trouble with man is that, because of his smallness and shortsighted vision, he identifies his wishful thinking with objective truth, his short-range goals with true moral goodness. It is this tendency to self-deception that prevents him from correctly evaluating his deeds:

> Say [O, Muhammad!], shall we tell you who are the greatest losers in terms of their deeds? Those whose whole effect has got lost in the lower pursuits of this world but who think they have performed prodigies. (18:103-04)

This is why belief in the Last Day becomes central to the Qur'anic teaching. When "deeds shall be weighed" and their true worth determined, the deeds of those who acted from a myopic vision, living from hour to hour and day to day, will have to be separated from those of people who acted with the end in view.

The Qur'an, then, envisages the establishment of a social order on earth based on a viable ethical foundation. It decisively rejects ethnicity, color, tongue, or territory as a valid base for defining

human organization, and unequivocally declares the consubstan-
tiality of the entire human race. Virtue is the only valid basis for
true human worth. To this end, the Qur'an established a brotherhood or community of Muslims whose members were expected to
be imbued with that kind of virtue. The function of this community
was "to be median"—that is, to avoid and smooth out extremes—
and, above all, "to command good and prohibit evil" in order to "reform the earth and uproot corruption therefrom"—morally, socially, politically, and economically. Hence, it follows that no separation nor compartmentalization of life is recognized in Islam between the private and the public spheres, between a personal religion and collective political or social institutions. There are thus
such things as an Islamic state and Islamic law just as there is an Islamic personal faith.

While this mission was laid upon the shoulders of the community, the Qur'an gave the community no assurance that it would automatically be God's darling. On the contrary, the Qur'an clearly
tells Muslims:

> If you neglect [this teaching], God will bring another people in
> your place who will not be like you. (47:28; cf. 9:39)

The Qur'an, therefore, squarely repudiates all claims of all communities to "proprietorship" over God's truth and guidance, including the doctrine of election. God's guidance has been universal; He has left no nation, no people, without guidance sent
through His messengers. Further, although a particular messenger
may come to a people to deliver the Message "in their tongue," the
Message nevertheless is universal and must be believed by all
human beings. This is why Muslims are required by the Qur'an to
believe in all prophets, and Muhammad is made to declare in the
Qur'an, "Say I believe in any book God may have revealed" (42:15).
Prophethood, therefore, is an indivisible office, and the Qur'an
sternly condemns divisions among separate religions, "every group
[that is, community] rejoices in what it itself possesses" (23:53;
30:32). Basically, all messengers have been calling people to one
God and to obey Him, and Him alone. Nevertheless, there has been
an evolution in religious consciousness, which is why a community
from a distant past cannot be judged by the standards of the Book
of a more advanced community.

Besides the Last Judgment, the Qur'an developed the doctrine of the Judgment of History. While the Last Judgment will be concerned with the performance of individuals, the Judgment of History is visited upon nations, peoples, and communities on the basis of their collective performance. Because the Qur'an was immediately concerned with changing the attitudes of the Arabs—particularly Meccans—as a society, from the start it cited stories of earlier peoples and communities that met their doom because of their persistence in evil ways and their rejection of the call of their prophets. In the Qur'anic prophetology, two names from ancient Arabia, Hud of the tribe of Ad and Sabih of Thamud, are added to those of the Old and New Testaments. These two tribes, along with the people of Noah, Lot, and Pharaoh and his army, among others, are constantly held up as examples of God's vindication of truth and destruction of evil. Noah was saved from the flood, Abraham from fire, Moses from Pharaoh, and Jesus from the Jews. (The Qur'an rejects the story of the crucifixion of Jesus.) This attitude strongly imbues the Qur'anic teaching with the idea of the eventual vindication and success of the truth; Muhammad and his message must, therefore, be successful, despite heavy odds, since this is God's design.

While basically the Qur'an is a document of ethical guidance—it calls itself guidance for mankind—it also contains a certain amount of legislation. An important part of this legislation consists of the rites of worship: daily prayers, fasting during the month of Ramadan, and the annual pilgrimage to Mecca that is incumbent upon every adult Muslim once in a lifetime, provided he or she can afford it and is in good health. Then there is the zakat, which is incumbent upon every Muslim and due on such wealth as he or she has possessed for one year.

The Qur'an also has certain penal laws—the law of retribution for murder (although forgiveness on the part of the injured party is also emphasized), cutting off a hand for theft (theft in a tribal society was considered not just an economic crime but primarily a crime against the honor of a person), 100 lashes for adultery, and 80 lashes for bringing a false charge of adultery. The Qur'an also has detailed inheritance laws that are essentially supplementary to the existing laws of the Arabs. The basic change lies in the allotment of shares to women (who were previously deprived of inheritance rights): the share of a female is fixed at 50 percent of that of a male.

Also introduced was a category of inheritance known as "the womb's share," whereby relatives on the female side may inherit. Pre-Islamic inheritance could be claimed only by relatives on the father's side.

The Qur'an made a general and sustained effort to strengthen and ameliorate the condition of the weaker segments of society: the have-nots, orphans, slaves, and women. For the have-nots and those in pecuniary difficulties in general (for example, chronic debtors), zakat funds were made available. The institution of usury, whereby debts unpaid within a prescribed time were doubled and kept on doubling, so that debtors could never hope to get rid of their debts, was abolished at one stroke. Those who resorted to usury were threatened with "war from God and His Prophet" (2:279). Tribes bound in usury to other, more economically powerful tribes were thereby immediately released from their bondage. The emancipation of slaves was not only encouraged in general terms but slave owners were asked specifically to execute freedom contracts with their slaves and to "spend of your own wealth that God has given you upon them" (24:33). Because of socioeconomic considerations, however, slavery was not abolished. On the contrary, it worsened as a result of early Muslim conquests and a huge influx of war captives.

On the subject of women, the Qur'an undoubtedly took a great leap forward. It was noted above that women were allotted shares of inheritance. Capricious divorce of women was condemned. Kind and generous treatment of women was recurrently emphasized, and even in case of divorce, "If you have given a wife a heap of gold [as a gift], take back nothing from it—will you take it back as an awesome calumny and a clear sin?" (4:20). The general equality of men and women was affirmed: "The rights of women [against their husbands] are commensurate with their duties toward them" (2:228), except that "man is a degree higher" because he is made financially responsible for women by earning through his strength (4:38).

Regarding polygamy, the Qur'an restricted the number of simultaneous wives to four. The classical passage for this is sura 4:3. It appears that the intent of the Qur'an, as is clear from the context, was to allow up to four marriages to orphan wards, for in 4:2 and 4:12 the Qur'an accuses the custodians of these orphan girls of improperly consuming their properties, of being unwilling to return their properties to them when they came of age, and of marrying them to enjoy their properties permanently. But, for reasons that are not clear, this permission for polygamy was taken out of context and made general. Sura 4:3 reads:

> If you fear you will be dishonest with regard to [the properties] of these orphan [girls], then you may marry [cf. 4:127] from among [them] one, two, three, or four; but if you fear you will not be able to do justice [among co-wives], then marry only one.

And sura 4:129 explicitly states, "You shall never be able to do justice among women, no matter how much you desire." The law of general permission for up to four wives, therefore, does not seem to square either with the letter or, indeed, with the spirit of the Qur'an. For this reason, contemporary reformers in most Muslim countries have enacted laws severely restricting permission for a second marriage to certain special grounds: for instance, if the first wife is an invalid or barren. Tunisia has totally prohibited polygamy.

THE QUR'ANIC TEXT

The Qur'an is the collection of those passages (usually consisting of a dozen or more verses—but in very few cases whole chapters or suras) that were revealed to the Prophet from time to time over a period of about 22 years (610 C.E.-632 C.E.). These passages were arranged into suras of very different lengths. Although this is not certain, there are some reports that the Prophet himself directed what passages should be put in what suras. It is now widely held by modern scholars that probably the whole Qur'an was written down on various materials—parchments, shoulder bones, leaves—during the lifetime of the Prophet. The primary method of preserving the Qur'an, however, was through recitation from memory on various occasions, particularly daily prayers. (The incredibly prodigious memory of the Arabs, who had very little written literature, is well established.)

The first written codex was, according to Muslim tradition, prepared by the first *caliph* (the temporal successor of the Prophet), Abu Bakr, a year or so after the Prophet's death. Many

who had preserved the entirety of the Holy Book in their memory
had lost their lives in battles against various tribes who had lapsed
back into tribal sovereignty after the Prophet's death. Today's accepted text dates from the reign of the third caliph, Uthman (d. 35
A.H./656 C.E.), who set up a committee of six persons to produce
an authoritative text. This committee used Abu Bakr's codex. A
great many variant readings have been recorded by Qur'anic commentators but, as scholars agree, they do not materially affect the
meaning of the Qur'an except in a very small number of relatively
unimportant points of ritual.

The Qur'an is divided into 114 suras that are arranged according to length, with the longest at the beginning and the shortest at
the end. Generally speaking, the chronological order is exactly the
opposite: the earliest suras were short and characterized by an ab-
rupt, staccato style, like sudden volcanic outbursts. But as the
Qur'an proceeded with its unfolding of theological arguments and
formulation of rituals and laws for the nascent Muslim community,
the style eased up and became more fluent. From the first to the
last, however, the Qur'anic language is characterized by a numinous quality that is at once powerful, graceful, and awe-inspiring.
For this reason, it is essentially untranslatable, as held both by Muslims and non-Muslim scholars: no matter how skillful and inspired
a translation may be, it cannot capture the incredibly subtle
nuances and shades of meaning—and, of course, the beauty, the
grandeur, and the splendor of the original.

The Qur'an is very consciously an "Arab Qur'an" given in
"clear Arabic tongue."

> If we had made this Qur'an a non-Arab one, they [the oppo-
> nents of Muhammad] would have said, Why are its verses not
> eloquently set out? (41:44; also 26:198)

As previously pointed out, the Qur'an was the only "miracle" of the
Prophet for its numinous language and untranslatability. For this
reason, Muslim orthodoxy has resolutely prohibited any publication of the Qur'an in translation unaccompanied by the Arabic text.
When Muslim children all over the world learn to read the Qur'an,
they do so in Arabic, regardless of their native tongue and of
whether they can understand Arabic. Later they read it in translation in their own language accompanied by the original Arabic.

As was also previously mentioned, the Qur'an was originally intended to be recited. Muslims have developed a whole science of the recitation of the Qur'an. On the occasion of the Friday service, marriage, death, or any other celebration or special event, the Qur'an is solemnly recited or slowly chanted according to the rules of this science. This recitation, whether the listener understands Arabic or not, is extraordinarily effective and moving. Because Islamic orthodoxy banned music from very early times, there was all the more reason for Muslims to develop the art of Qur'anic recitation. Very recently, several Western scholars have studied this art and its effect on the audience. The number of Muslims, both male and female, who have the entire Qur'an actively in memory most probably runs well over a million.

On the basis of its style and of claims within the Qur'an that "its like cannot be produced" by humans, there developed in the early history of Islam the dogma of the inimitability of the Qur'an. This dogma, which was accepted by all Muslim schools of thought and all sects, regarded the language, style, and ideas of the Qur'an as miraculous and not reproducible by a human agency. In the later Middle Ages, there developed a branch of learning, called the science of rhetoric and eloquence, whose source of inspiration was primarily the Qur'an, not the Greek science of rhetoric formulated by Aristotle (who had been translated into Arabic in the third/ninth century A.H./C.E.). From the thirteenth through the nineteenth centuries C.E., this science of rhetoric overshadowed other substantive disciplines in the Islamic seats of learning and militated against the appearance of original works in intellectual and scientific fields. The majority of the commentaries on the Qur'an produced in this period are characterized by their obsession with rhetoric and grammar. There exists, for example, an eighteenth-century Qur'anic commentary by the Egyptian al-Khaffaji in which the well-known formula that opens the Qur'an ("In the name of God, the Merciful, the Compassionate") is analyzed, on more than 100 oversize pages in fine print, in terms of rhetoric and grammar, and which brings out the linguistic nuances and insuperable excellence of the Qur'anic language.

INTERPRETING THE QUR'AN

Without an understanding of the Qur'an in its broad chronological development, it is not possible to understand its message adequately and effectively. It is, of course, not possible to reconstruct the Qur'an chronologically passage by passage, but it is certainly possible to do so in broad outline. The most helpful method is to trace the emergence and development of the Qur'anic themes historically. This method is further aided by the fact that the issues that the Qur'an addresses existed in a known historical context. We have seen that in the beginning the Qur'an was a response to the polytheism and socioeconomic disparity in Mecca. The Qur'an is not a purely speculative document but a historical one in this sense: it is an answer to concrete developing situations in the Prophet's struggle. This is especially the case with the sociopolitical, ethical, and legal parts of the Qur'an, as distinguished from the purely theological portions.

The background information on the revelation of most of the Qur'an has been preserved in the Qur'anic commentaries and also in special works called Occasions of Revelation. There are undoubtedly problems with this literature and one finds inconsistencies in it; nevertheless, on the whole, it is very helpful in understanding the problems or at least the kinds of problems to which the revelation was a response. Additionally, the Qur'an itself, in making a legal or quasi-legal pronouncement, often gives the reason behind it along with the pronunciation itself. Using this information, one can adequately grasp the message of the Qur'an and its purpose.

Although all these materials have been preserved, their existence has rarely been used to achieve a chronological or developmental understanding of the Qur'an—which is absolutely essential for understanding the Qur'an as a whole and its real objectives. Modern Western Islamicists have made important contributions in this field. Yet, Western scholarship on the Qur'an to date has contributed little understanding the content of the Qur'an and its message. Instead, Western efforts have concentrated on establishing the chronological order per se, or on demonstrating the influence of Judaism and/or Christianity on the Qur'an. In fact, Jewish and Christian scholars have often competed with one another in their efforts toward that end. Thus, neither Muslim nor non-Muslim scholars have really grappled with the essential world view of the Qur'an. It has been atomistically understood by Muslims who have written commentaries on it verse by verse in a nonchronological order, while non-Muslims view the Qur'an extrinsically at best and are biased at worst.

Commentaries on the Qur'an started with the companions of the Prophet, after his death. During the first two centuries of Islam, certain principles had been formulated on the basis of which the Qur'an could be validly interpreted. This activity was undertaken particularly in connection with the derivation of law from the Qur'an. The intellectual tools considered necessary for this purpose were the following:

1. A good knowledge of the Arabic language and especially of the literature (primarily poetry) of pre-Islamic times and of that period contemporary with the Prophet, because such knowledge facilitated understanding the idiom of the Qur'an.
2. A knowledge of the Occasions of Revelation
3. A knowledge of abrogating and abrogated verses. The problem of inconsistency arose for commentators because of what seemed to be contradictions within the Qur'an. While it is true that on certain points the Qur'an modified or reversed an earlier stance or practice, those types of changes are very few in number. Generally speaking, apparent inconsistencies can be resolved by using the chronological approach for interpreting the verses in question
4. A knowledge of the verses that have general application and those that are applicable to a restricted situation. This is derived from the Occasions of Revelation materials, but is not uniformly used.

A general and lamentable flaw in the interpretation of the Qur'an has come about through the universal predilection of commentators and lawyers for taking the specific do's and don't's of the Qur'an very seriously while attaching considerably less importance to the general moral principles of the Holy Book and regarding them as recommendations rather than commands. Numerous examples of this can be given, but one example will illustrate the point.

The issue of polygamy and its conditions was discussed earlier. Commentators take literally the permission to marry up to four wives and give it legal force, regardless of the fact that in the next clause the Qur'an puts forth the rider of justice among co-wives as a necessary condition for polygamy, and a little later declares such justice impossible to achieve. Much of the orthodox commentary has, therefore, distorted the Qur'an's teaching on this and other issues. In modern commentaries, considerable attention has been paid to these issues, although even modern Muslim scholarship has yet to evolve a more adequate methodology for interpreting and understanding the Qur'an.

Still, imperfect though the orthodox methodology of Qur'anic interpretation has been, it has been in general sober and in conformity with the general ethos of the Qur'an. But it is a very different case with two other genres of commentaries—one resorting on a large scale to allegorical interpretation; and the other, to esoteric interpretation. The first type is exemplified by the Mu'tazilite school and the philosophical exegesis of the Qur'an, while the second is represented by the Shi'i and, in particular, certain Sufi schools of thought.

The Mu'tazilite rationalist school of theology developed certain beliefs that forced its members to interpret verses of the Qur'an that did not agree with these theses in allegorical, metaphorical, or other nonliteral terms. For example, one of their main theses was that, in the sphere of moral human actions, man has absolute free will, and any hindrance to the free exercise of that will comes not from God but from natural factors. This emphasis on absolute human free will followed from the belief that man, rather than God, is the source of injustice and evil. The Qur'an certainly and explicitly upholds freedom of will and choice on the part of man, but it equally insists on the omnipotence of God and declares that nothing occurs outside His will. The Mu'tazilites, however, interpret all verses of the latter type as metaphorical or allegorical expressions. The Qur'an does not recognize this as a problem to be solved, but as a tension with which one must live.

A far greater challenge for Islam was created by esoteric or symbolic interpretations of the Qur'an by certain extreme Shi'i groups (particularly the Isma'ilis) and Sufis. This kind of exegesis recognized no objective criteria nor principles for interpretation but was utterly subjective: anything could be made a symbol for anything. The most extreme examples of this type of exegesis are among the writings of the Shi'i al-Qummi (d. late third or early fourth century A.H./ninth century C.E.) and the Sufi ibn Arabi (d. 638 A.E./1240 C.E.).

Not recognizing any anchoring point for their exegesis, the esotericists felt free to let loose their unbridled imagination. Under pressure, however, from the sober schools of religious thought, which severely castigated esotericism as pure and irresponsible subjectivism, the esotericists generally attributed two levels of meaning to Qur'anic verses: an external or objective meaning (*tafsir,* exegesis) grounded in the language, background, and context of the Qur'anic verses, and an esoteric meaning (*ta'wil,* interpretation), which is valid for the person who can understand it in this particular way and for others to whom it may be appealing. Among the writings of sixteenth- through eighteenth-century Sufis it is not rare to find statements that read, "This is the tafsir meaning of this verse, while the ta'wil meaning is. . . ." Under the impact of modern rational ideas, esotericsm has been weakened greatly among both the Shi'is and the Sufis, although, since Sufism rests upon a life of inner experience, it cannot cut itself off entirely from some form of esotericism. In the hands of many modern Sufis, however, Sufism is increasingly subject to modern psychical research and parapsychology.

3

The Foundations of
State and Society

Roy P. Mottahedeh

Islam allowed little room for the compartmentalization or sep-aration of life into sacred and secular spheres, and hence little room for the dichotomy of church and state that has been such a familiar part of the Western Christian experience. Nevertheless, the practical historical experience of Muslims in trying to build an Islamic state did bring home to them that while there was a sphere of individual action for which one could be held accountable, there was also a sphere of collective action from which the individual might have in part to divorce himself or herself. This partial di-vorce arose because of disagreements about the nature and source of authority in the Islamic community after the death of the Prophet. Such a partial divorce of the individual Muslim from his government was always thought to be a temporary arrangement. But it proved to be a beneficial one, in that it has allowed Muslims to preserve a general sense of political community on an ideological level even though, on a practical level, the Muslim world has been divided among many governments for over a millenium.

Roughly two years before his death in 632 C.E., the Prophet Muhammad made his last pilgrimage to Mecca. On this occasion he gave a moving (and often quoted) address to his followers, in the course of which he said, according to one source, "God has given two safeguards to the world: His Book [the Qur'an] and the sunna [the example] of His Prophet [Muhammad]." According to

This chapter is adapted, with additions by the author, from his *Loy-alty and Leadership in an Early Islamic Society* (Princeton University Press, 1980), pp. 7-25. Reprinted by permission of Princeton University Press.

another source, Muhammad said: "God has given two safeguards to the world: His Book and the family of His Prophet." Taken together, these two statements contain all the basic ingredients of Muhammad's legacy for the future political life of the community: the Qur'an, the family of Muhammad, and the example of Muhammad. Yet the correct mix of these ingredients remained a subject of active (and sometimes bitter) disagreement.

Even before he led a political community, it had been clear to Muhammad that the moral vision of Islam had political implications. Islam was a religion in which public life was very much a collective responsibility of the community, and the Qur'an provided regulations according to which the community should discharge the responsibility. When, for the last 12 years of his life, Muhammad was the actual leader of a political community, the political aspect of Islamic belief was confirmed and extensively elaborated.

When Muhammad died, the Islamic community no longer had a divinely inspired leader, and quarrels over choosing a new leader immediately broke out. These quarrels have so preoccupied most historians, both Eastern and Western, that they have neglected the gradual emergence of a remarkable unanimity among Muslims on an issue even more fundamental than the choice of a successor to Muhammad: the consensus of Muslims in the original centers of Islam in Arabia that the community should have a single leader. They agreed that the community of believers should neither be divided into separate Muslim political communities (like the separate Christian and Jewish political communities), nor accept some form of collective leadership, such as a governing council. In the decade after Muhammad's death, the Muslims of the Hijaz thoroughly defeated separatist movements in Arabia, after which the great majority of Muslims everywhere and for centuries accepted the idea that the Muslim community (umma) should be politically unified under a single leader.

This unity of the umma and of its leadership was in perfect agreement with the character of the Islamic revelation. In the view of Muslims, God had revealed in Islam a moral law intended for all mankind, and the vehicle of this revelation was a single man (Muhammad) who lived a life of exemplary obedience to that law. Muhammad, the single vehicle of revelation and perfect example, had maintained a unified community under his sole leadership. After his death, Muslims quite naturally felt that his example of single leadership should be followed.

QUR'AN AND SUNNA

The Muslim community also agreed on the status of the Qur'an, the first "safeguard" that Muhammad had left for his community. The Qur'an is, in the belief of Muslims, the infallible word of God. The earlier revelations that are described in Jewish and Christian Scripture have been distorted through time, and were never intended to have the completeness of Islam. The Qur'an is the undistorted revelation in which, as God tells the believers in the Qur'an itself, "I have perfected your religion for you and completed My favor [or benefit] to you" (5:3). But the Qur'an discusses leadership in general terms. It gives no direct indication as to how a new leader should be chosen, although later commentators constructed many and conflicting interpretations of the implications of Qur'anic verses for this question.

If the agreement of the Islamic community on the status of the Qur'an did not solve the constitutional problem of succession to leadership, it did guarantee the central importance of the Qur'an for Islamic culture. The most complete revelation must have implicit in it something of relevance for every human situation, and most Muslim thinkers sought to make some connection between their ideas and the contents of the Qur'an.

The second safeguard left for the Muslim community was the sunna of the Prophet. If there was widespread agreement as to the importance of the sunna, there was equally widespread disagreement as to its contents. The word "sunna" means customary practice; and in the context of Muhammad's speech quoted above, it means the practice established by the example of Muhammad (and, to a lesser extent, by his closest companions, who were presumed to be most deeply influenced by him). The Qur'an may have been comparable with the Christian Logos in its role and its preternatural perfection; but the Qur'an did not directly legislate for all circumstances, and the Qur'an was a book, not a person. Muhammad was the perfect example of a Muslim; and his example, therefore, was a nearly indispensable guide to living the life of a Muslim and to making the implicit concepts of the Qur'an explicit.

This example was known to later generations through hadith. The word "hadith" is often translated "tradition," and is explained as a report of a saying or action of Muhammad. But hadith is more than this; it is the body of accounts of what Muhammad said and did, what was done in his presence and not forbidden by him, and even includes some of the sayings and doings of his close companions. It is, in effect, all the historical material available to establish the sunna. To draw another analogy with Christianity, from the point of view of many Muslims, the Gospels are a form of Christian hadith about Jesus.

The sunna, therefore, was very much a "safeguard" to the community. It gave the Islamic community a means for extending the teachings of Islam, and it assumed an underlying unity in these teachings. It assumed this unity not only because an extensive spiritual and ethical system needs some degree of harmony between its parts, but also because reverence for the sunna meant that such extensions would, if at all possible, be traced to a single historical source, the lives of the Prophet and his closest companions. The study of the Qur'an had primacy over the study of hadith, but anyone who has looked at the earliest extant Qur'anic commentaries knows that in the first two centuries of Islam, the greater part of such commentary consisted of hadith. Together, the study of Qur'an and hadith gave a further unity of focus for future Islamic cultures, because Arabic philology developed in large part out of a desire to understand the sometimes difficult and often elliptical language of Qur'an and hadith. As a result, wherever there were Muslim men of learning, they cultivated the "Arabic sciences" as an integral part of religious learning.

A body of material so important and so lacking in boundaries could not pass through history unmolested. Hadith appeared that were generally thought to be forgeries; and the "science" or "knowledge" of hadith, which studied the validity of hadith, developed gradually but with ever growing elaboration over the first four centuries of the Islamic era. Hadith was the central ingredient of religious "knowledge" (*ilm*) and, consequently, *ulama* ("knowers" of religious knowledge) were above all knowers of Qur'an and hadith. The knowledge or science of hadith involved a careful study of the chain (*isnad*) of transmitters through which a hadith had been handed down from a companion of Muhammad to the generation of the scholar; and gatherings to transmit hadith were probably the most common occasions on which ulama came together in formal meetings.

Only in the fifth century of Islam does the study of hadith seem to have decreased in importance among the religious sciences. By this time, isnads were becoming impossibly long, and there was increasing consensus as to which written hadith collections were reliable. Moreover, other religious sciences had been more fully elaborated. For example, the implications, or pseudo implications, of hadith for law had been distilled into law books; and however much early law and hadith may have been intertwined, scholars—especially if they wanted a career involving law—could hardly study their subject without making the law books their principal concern.

THE FAMILY OF MUHAMMAD AND SHI'ISM

The third "safeguard" was the family of Muhammad. Neither of the other two safeguards was the cause of so much disagreement as was this one. Some believed that Muhammad intended his family to succeed him in leadership of community, and saw in this safeguard the only correct understanding of Qur'an and sunna; for how could there be agreement in interpreting the Qur'an and the sunna without the (possibly infallible) leadership by a member of this family? Others saw in this legitimist attitude a denial of the whole rationale of the sunna. If the sunna was the example of Muhammad as reported by his close companions and confirmed by the subsequent actions of these companions, how could anyone claim that the reports and actions of these companions should be radically discounted unless confirmed by the interpretation and example of leaders from Muhammad's family?

At the death of Muhammad, the family-centered theory of leadership looked to Ali, Muhammad's cousin and son-in-law, as the obvious successor (*caliph*) to the Prophet. Ali had been one of the very earliest (possibly the earliest male) to accept Muhammad's message. He was, moreover, the adopted son of Muhammad and, through his marriage to Fatima, he was father of Muhammad's only grandsons to reach maturity, Hasan and Husayn. However, at the death of Muhammad, the majority of Muslims did not accept the family-centered theory. The advocates of the family said that because the other companions of Muhammad wanted the leadership, they chose to disregard the obvious claims of Ali and the expressed intention of Muhammad that the descendants of Ali should take over the leadership.

In contrast, the majority of Muslims did not believe that Muhammad had clearly designated Ali as his successor, or that Ali was a choice clearly superior to other close companions of Muhammad. Ali did not press his claims, but after the third caliph was killed, many Muslims accepted him as the new caliph. The death of Ali's predecessor, however, had marked the beginning of the first civil war in Islam; and Ali was swept into this civil war without being able to bring it to an end. He was killed in 661 C.E., and the caliphate passed away from his branch of Muhammad's family.

The descendants of Ali, the Alids, continued to play an important role in the Islamic world. Even those who rejected Ali's claim to be the appointed successor of Muhammad revered the Alids for the family ties that had distinguished their ancestors. In fact, because most of the Alids were descended from Hasan and Husayn, the sons of Ali and Fatima, they were, through their mother, lineal descendants of Muhammad himself. Most Muslims considered it a religious duty to show the Alids signs of their great respect, signs that sometimes included gifts of money. Therefore, even Alids who did not claim any special right to the caliphate had a certain advantage in seeking political power; and there have been many Alid kings in Islamic history, including the present King Hassan of Morocco and King Husayn of Jordan.

There were always Alids, however, who regarded the honor of their ancestry not as a possible focus for the reverence of other Muslims, but as a positive claim for their political allegiance. The supporters of these Alid claimants were called *shi'atu Ali* (the party of Ali); hence they became known to Muslims as Shi'is. Shi'ism was in the first instance based on a political claim; and for one branch of Shi'is, the Zaidis, the political claim continues to be the most important element of belief that distinguishes them from non-Shi'is. The Zaidis believe that any Alid who personally and militarily seeks the leadership of the Islamic community, and has the religious learning necessary for leadership, can be the caliph. The recent rulers of the northern Yemen, the Imams, are such leaders. The Zaidi theory recognizes that two or more Alids may make such a claim to leadership simultaneously. But the principle of unified rule is preserved in that, if the territories of two Zaidi leaders are close enough to be in effective contact, one of them must resign (or be forced to resign) leadership in favor of the other.

In the earliest Islamic period these political claims seem to have been the most important element in Shi'ism, but claims to spiritual leadership soon came to be of central importance to a large group of Shi'is. As was discussed above, such claims allowed the Shi'is to maintain a unified view of religious life by making a single Alid leader the authoritative standard for the interpretation of legal, political, metaphysical, and all other matters. It was also natural that some branches of Shi'ism should emphasize the spiritual leadership of their leaders because, in most cases, real political leadership remained in the hands of non-Shi'is. Many Shi'is, therefore, came to distinguish between caliphate—actual political leadership—and imamate—the theoretical right to leadership. Muslims in their collective daily prayer stand behind an imam who leads them and is the model for their movements; and where an imam is not officially appointed by the government, any group of Muslims is supposed to defer to the "best" among them as imam. The overall leader of authority and model for the Islamic community was, in the view of the Shi'is, an Alid, who was also called "imam" in this more particular sense. The shi'is held that the imam should also be caliph, though circumstances might prevent him from attaining this office. Even if he passed his life in unrelieved obscurity, the one God-given imam for any period was, in the view of his followers, the only real authority for the spiritual and political life of is age.

After a few generations, there were hundreds of descendants of Ali. If only one of them could be the imam (and, it was hoped, the caliph), which one should it be? As we have seen, the Zaidi answer was both clear and confusing—the imam was any learned Alid who was militarily successful in claiming leadership. But other Shi'is laid much more emphasis than the Zaidis on the imam's role as authoritative interpreter, and they therefore sought to explain the presence of this authority as the result of something more than individual initiative. Most Shi'is other than Zaidis felt that the Alid imam could be identified because he had directly inherited his station and/or had been specifically designated by his predecessor.

Neither of these principles, however, could induce agreement among the non-Zaidi Shi'is. Inheritance was essential to the overall claim of the Alids, and the line of imams most widely recognized by present-day Shi'is is a line in which the imamate usually passed to the eldest son. Yet the principle of primogeniture was never very strong in the Islamic Near East; and even in this widely recognized line, the imamate passed from Hasan (Ali's eldest son by Fatima, Muhammad's daughter) to Husayn (the second eldest son by this mother). Specific designation proved just as unreliable a means of guaranteeing an undisputed succession. Most non-Zaidi Alid claimants to the imamate kept such claims secret or, at least, were wise enough not to discuss them publicly, for these claims implied a challenge to the existing non-Shi'i leadership, especially to the non-Alid caliphs. Therefore, specific designation was almost never performed publicly, and the claims of any supposed designee were hard to establish. Since most such designations seem to have been made orally by the dying imam in his last hours, their authenticity was almost inevitably suspect to some of the followers who had not been present.

It is not surprising, then, that Shi'is often disagreed as to which Alid was the imam. It is also not surprising that frequently, after the apparent death of an imam, some of his followers held either that he had not really died, or that his successor was living in such perfect secrecy that even those close to him did not know of his station. Alid pretenders had been repeatedly defeated, and God had allowed their opponents to continue in power. Therefore, some Shi'is were not at all astonished to hear that their imam had not died, but disappeared, and would reappear in the fullness of time to become, with divine aid, the actual ruler of the Islamic community.

The most important instance of such an interruption to a line of visible imams took place in 873 C.E., when the eleventh imam in succession from Ali through his son Husayn died in Iraq. Some of his followers held that he was succeeded by his infant son, the twelfth imam, who had disappeared and would return as a messianic figure. The Shi'is who awaited the return of this twelfth imam were called Twelvers. The Twelvers changed their allegiance from a visible to an unseen imam at a juncture in Islamic history when divisions had forever destroyed the political unity of the Islamic umma, and the caliphs who still ruled the core of the former empire, Iraq and surrounding territories, were being murdered periodically by their Turkish palace guard. It was a good moment for the Twelvers to put aside their aspirations for worldly power. Moreover, non-Shi'i Muslims were willing to tolerate the Twelvers more than they did most other Shi'i groups, especially if the Twelvers had no immediately present candidate for the caliphate. At present the majority of the inhabitants of Iran and southern Iraq are Twelvers.

SUNNISM AND THE FIRST CALIPHS

While Shi'is, deprived of power, were evolving a variety of political theories, historical events were hammering out the political theory of the non-Shi'is. Later Muslims would look back and call these early non-Shi'i Muslims Sunnis, as most non-Shi'is came to be called in a later period. In the early Muslim world, the Shi'is had strongly held, definite positions on succession to the caliphate; but for most other Muslims, events moved faster than theory, and their theory was to a large extent an explanation of events and a reaction to the more exclusive political theories of the Shi'is. Only later did this initially less well-defined theory become the basis of conscious sectarian self-definition. Sunnism, the school of Islam espoused by the majority of present-day Muslims, was the historicist solution to the problems presented by Muhammad's death. In light of the hadith in which the Prophet had said his community would never "agree upon an error," the Sunnis could look back at the history of the Islamic community and, in retrospect, use the agreement of previous Muslims as a test for the validity of previous experiments by Muslims in creating a Muslim government. However, the formulation and the contents of this retrospective, historicist solution could (and did) emerge only after the Islamic community had lived through a fairly long historical experience.

On the day of Muhammad's death, after heated discussion, a large meeting in Muhammad's capital city of Medina chose Abu Bakr as his successor; and in token of their choice, each of them swore an oath of allegiance to him. Abu Bakr had a measure of authority among Muslims because of his very long and close association with Muhammad. He was, for example, Muhammad's father-in-law, and had been appointed by the Prophet to be the prayer leader (imam) in his place during his final illness. Just as important was Abu Bakr's membership in the tribe of Quraysh, which ruled the nearby city of Mecca. The next day, when the Meccans heard that a fellow Meccan of Quraysh had been chosen caliph, they accepted the choice. These historical events were later to become fundamental points of reference for Sunni political theory.

In Medina, several further choices of caliph by discussion and/or acclamation followed; it was a procedure familiar from the practice of Arab tribes before Islam, and sanctioned by a verse in the Qur'an that said, "[Better and more enduring is the reward of God] to those who obey their Lord, attend to their prayers, and conduct their affairs by consultation" (40:38). No clear precedent for the method of consultation emerged in these early choices of caliph, and the Islamic world was soon plunged into a civil war that ended, after the murder of Ali, with the victory of the Umayyads, a clan of Muhammad's tribe, the Quraysh. The Umayyads set up the first successful hereditary succession to the caliphate, though their right to this succession was not uncontested.

Finally, in 750 C.E., another family of the tribe of Quraysh, the descendants of Muhammad's uncle Abbas, defeated the Umayyads and assumed the dignity of the caliphate. From their capital in Baghdad, they ruled virtually all of the Islamic world except Spain, which passed into the hands of a descendant of the Umayyads. The Abbasids tried to win the support of the ulama by their extensive patronage of religious learning. Even if they did not claim the infallibility that was attributed to various Alid leaders, the Abbasids hoped to be accepted as the spiritual guides of the Islamic community. Despite the caliphs' vacillating support of conflicting views of orthodoxy, however, the great majority of Muslims refused to concede to the Abbasid caliphs any special authority to regulate such matters. Yet their patronage of learning and their ostentatious use of religious symbols made the Abbasid caliphate itself a religious symbol. Therefore, Muslims who had lost any desire to obey the Abbasids nevertheless defended the principle that the Abbasid caliphs should, even if deprived of executive power, be maintained as a symbol of legitimate government and of unity among Muslims.

That the Abbasids should lose actual control of an empire stretching from the Atlantic to Central Asia was hardly surprising. What is surprising is the frequency with which both the Abbasids and their usurpers agreed to cover each loss with the fiction that the caliphs had kept full theoretical sovereignty over any province while granting actual control to the usurper. In token of this sovereignty, the actual ruler (often called an *amir,* commander) had the name of the reigning Abbasid caliph mentioned in the Friday congregational prayer and on the coinage. By the tenth century, these amirs called themselves kings, a title that had rarely been used by rulers since the pre-Islamic period. Because of the pagan associations of kingship, the caliphs had always sought to disassociate themselves from this title, and kingship and caliphate continued to have separate existences. In exchange for the recognition offered by an amir, the Abbasid caliph often (but not invariably) sent a diploma investing the amir with the right to rule his territories. Among the many advantages offered by this exchange of formalities was that it recognized the continuing agreement of most Muslims to the principles that had prevailed after the selection of the first caliph, Abu Bakr, an agreement that there was not, nor could there be, a plurality of Islamic communities. There was one Islamic community, by definition a unity of all Muslims; and the symbol of its unity was the single leader: the caliph, the "successor" of the Prophet.

CONSENSUS

If the ruler was the personal symbol of the unity of the Islamic community, the principle that symbolized the will to unity was *ijma* (consensus or agreement). Both Shi'is and those groups who later came to be called Sunnis accepted the validity of the famous hadith that "my community [umma] will never agree upon an error." The theory of most Shi'i groups in some sense anticipated the basic political needs of the Islamic community, and provided a precise means for their complete fulfillment: the community needed an Alid leader chosen according to a definite principle, and considered this leader to be the most authoritative interpreter to Islam for his age. Most non-Shi'is believed that God had intended that the leader of the Islamic community be chosen by some sort of consultative process. Beyond that, they did not agree on the procedure to be used in this consultative process, or the scope of the authority of a leader so chosen. They believed in the historical mission of the community, which in the long term would not "agree upon an error."

The amazingly rapid territorial expansion of the Islamic state in the generation after the Prophet's death made it clear that from the start the community would perform this historical mission, not only in the confines of the Arabian peninsula but also on the stage of world history. It seems likely that the earliest caliphs, Abu Bakr and Umar, did not intend wars of conquest. But when their expeditions to subdue pro-Byzantine and pro-Persian Arabs revealed the weakness of the Byzantine and Persian empires, they showed great genius at organizing and controlling subsequent conquests, which within a few decades put the caliph in Medina in control of Iran, Iraq, Syria, Egypt, and areas beyond. What might have been an uncoordinated migration of militarily aggressive bedouin was, in fact, an ordery change of regimes in which much of the lower-level civil administration of the conquered areas was kept intact. In accord with the practice of Muhammad and the precept of the Qur'an, Jews and Christians, as "People of the Book"—that is, communities possessing revelations recognized by the Qur'an—were allowed not only to continue to practice their religion but also to retain some authority to run their own communities; and non-Muslims continued to constitute the majority of the inhabitants of the new Muslim state for well over two centuries.

While the rapidity of the conquests encouraged the tolerance of Christians and Jews, it also encouraged some discrimination on the part of the early Muslims. The first generation of Muslims was overwhelmingly Arab and, not surprisingly, some Arabs saw themselves as naturally superior, a ruling class with a proprietary right to interpret Islam. Many of the sectarian divisions of the first two centuries were sharpened by the social division between Arab and non-Arab Muslims. The rapidity of the conquests also gave emphasis to the military interpretation of jihad, "the struggle" for Islam, a term probably meant to denote the inner moral and spiritual struggle as much as the struggle in the outside world. Implicit in a monotheistic system in which revelation has brought a new system of law is the idea that God intends the government applying this legal system to be the government of all mankind. Hence, reinforced by their amazing conquests, early Muslims believed that it was God's intention that Muslims "struggle" to make Islamic government universal, although, as we have said, they had no intention of forcing the conversion of other monotheists like Christians and Jews. From this military interpretation of jihad grew the concept of dividing the world into the Dar al-Islam and Dar al-Harb, the latter the area yet to be conquered.

Early Muslims realized that the military achievement of the Islamic community was little short of miraculous. For some, the "miracle" of these successes must have been proof of the correctness of their leadership in this period. Even if it were not accepted as confirmation of this leadership, the military achievement seemed to many Muslims too valuable a gain to risk in uncertain struggles for new leadership. Therefore, both for practical reasons and to live within the religious injunction to consensus, they accepted leadership that was not necessarily the "best" that the Islamic community could provide. They felt that unity was more important than purity, and that no leader or other individual could by himself establish the norms of the Islamic community, since they were an extension of the norms of all of the close companions of Muhammad. It cannot have been clear to Muslims in the period immediately after Muhammad's death how they should treat variations in these extensions of the sunna. Gradually, however, it became clear that consensus was one way of judging such variation. Interpretations of Islam that did not allow themselves to be judged by consensus could not, of course, be accepted within this framework.

In general, consensus-minded Muslims were more prone to inclusion that exclusion, to postponement rather than haste, and remained close to the spirit of the famous saying of Thomas à Kempis that "man proposes but God disposes." In areas not unambiguously discussed in the Qur'an, men would act and suggest how other men should act according to their understanding of Islam; and the long-term judgment of the Islamic community would judge whether their actions and injunctions were appropriate models for future Muslims. The reception of moral principle was similar to the reception of hadith: anyone could elaborate the norms of Islam or transmit hadith, but only the collective judgment of the Islamic community could accept a hadith as genuine or accept that a principle was truly in the spirit of Islam.

For a long time, this attitude of consensus-minded Muslims corresponded with the shared political and economic interests of Muslims. For over two centuries, Muslims were a minority in their new empire. At first, their law and theology were far from being fully elaborated. More particularly, they had, as we have seen, only very general principles to guide them in developing a constitutional theory. Various legal and theological positions did, of course, appear in these early centuries. If factions had succeeded in persuading the majority of Muslims that they must choose a position and fight to impose this position on other Muslims, the Islamic empire might well have shrunk back to the wastes of Arabia from which it had sprung. However, the privileged Muslim minority did in fact recognize its shared interests well enough to stay and prosper.

Moreover, Islam, in the view of most of its followers, was more a religion of correct practice than of correct belief. Four of the five pillars of Islam, often listed as the fundamental principles of the Islamic faith, are things one should do, not ideas one should believe. To preserve a unified Islamic community, consensus-minded Muslims demanded considerable uniformity in the public acts required of Muslims in the Qur'an, and avoidance of open contradiction to the explicit teachings of the Qur'an. For the rest, they usually allowed variation and did not seek to anticipate the judgment of history.

Through the collective judgment of the Islamic community, and especially of the ulama, history did—slowly but ineluctably—render its judgment. There was not then, nor has there ever been since, a consensus even on the method for consensus. Was the ijma the consensus among the people of Medina, or among the ulama, or among all Muslims? The emergence of widely accepted views, in spite of the vagueness and variableness in the definition of ijma, shows how strongly Muslims were determined to maintain some degree of unity. Often this consensus was achieved by virtue of allowing that a limited variety of positions was acceptable on certain questions. Accordingly, differing schools of law arose that came (sometimes reluctantly) to accept each other.

The consensus-minded scholars were able to preserve the sense that they were working within a shared tradition only by continual backward glances at the particular strand of the tradition they were elaborating. Hence the strong piety of each school of elaboration toward its founders (often hadith scholars), and toward the companions of Muhammad whose practice became a common reference point for these schools. This piety had actually increased as the period of the companions receded into the remote paste, and as the study of hadith became more elaborately scientific in its attempts to link each hadith with a known companion.

Only after considerable historical experience could ijma create distinctive positions for the consensus-minded Muslims. Agreement on the canonical body of the hadith, the sunna in its strictest sense, was an essential element in the evolution of a defined Sunnism; but such agreement was slow in coming. For example, of the six books of hadith that are supposedly canonical to Sunnis, the *Sunan* of ibn Majah (d. 886 C.E.) began to be accepted as canonical only in the eleventh century. North African Muslims seem never to have accepted it as canonical, yet they remained Sunnis both in their own view and in the view of Near Eastern Muslims. In its treatment of hadith, as in so many other respects, the more clearly defined and sectarian Sunnism of later generations emerged only gradually.

A LIMITED PLURALISM

Another supposed mark of a defined Sunnism is the doctrine that there were four, and only four, schools of law acceptable to Sunnis. This doctrine is based on the contention that the individual right to bring new ideas into Islamic law by interpreting Qur'an and hadith ceased in the ninth century, when the founders of the four schools and a handful of their most important followers had died. In the classic phrase of the Muslim lawyers, the "gate" of individual interpretation had closed. While it is true that Muslim lawyers of the ninth century were increasingly persuaded that there was no more room for individual reasoning on the law, it is also true that they were not agreed as to which of the existing schools were "canonical," and would not agree for centuries.

There were, however, many reasons why there should be a constant movement toward tighter definition of what was or was not acceptable to the Sunnis. With the passage of time, Sunnism became rigid simply because the collective judgment of the Muslim community had established positions on a great number of issues. But the historical circumstances of the Muslim community were an even greater incentive to delimit a Sunni form of Islam. When the Abbasid caliphs lost actual control of vast provinces of the Islamic empire, it became clear that the Muslims could not rely on a central government to preserve a community of belief among Muslims. To confuse matters further, most of the new regimes of the tenth century were Shi'i. And most of them were founded by men from peripheral areas of the Near East, nomads or mountain dwellers, who had little interest in the fine points of the religion of their city-dwelling subjects. The Sunnis saw that in the presence of alien and occasionally hostile governments they had to rely largely on themselves to preserve the achievement of earlier consensus-minded Muslims, and to prevent deviant speculation from pulling the community in so many directions that it would be irretrievably rent. An increasing number of scholars therefore sought to find an inclusive but clear definition of the boundaries of Sunnism.

They were spurred on in this effort by the activities of the Isma'ili Shi'is and the Hanbali Sunnis. Other forms of Shi'ism were, compared with Isma'ilism, ideologically benign. Zaidi Shi'ism was in most respects similar to Sunni Islam, except that it reserved the imamate-caliphate for descendants of Ali. By claiming that its leader had disappeared, Twelver Shi'ism left the confused and dangerous field of ninth-century caliphal politics. The Isma'ili branch of the Shi'is, however, refused to bury its claim. A successful Isma'ili rebellion in Tunisia gave a living Alid control of an important segment of the Islamic world. In 969 C.E. his descendants conquered Egypt, where the Fatimids, as this Alid dynasty came to be known, ruled until the late twelfth century.

The Fatimids assumed the title of caliph, and claimed the doctrinal authority granted to the Alid Imam by most forms of Shi'ism. For the first time, this kind of Shi'ism had the support of a government; and law codes, works of theology, and other expressions of this interpretation of Islam poured forth from the pens of Fatimid supporters in Cairo. The Isma'ili Fatimids also had a carefully organized propaganda service; and their agents were amazingly successful in establishing clandestine groups of Isma'ilis throughout the Islamic Near East. (The Druze of modern Syria, Lebanon, and Israel are the spiritual descendants of a group of Isma'ilis who were converted by Fatimid missionaries in the eleventh century.) The elaborate definition of this form of Shi'ism; the direct challenge of its leader's assumption of the title caliph, in open opposition to the Abbasid caliphate, the symbol of consensus-minded Islam; and its successful missionary activity all forced the non-Shi'is to define their attitude toward the Shi'is, and so to become, in their own turn, more sectarian.

The Hanbalis were ready to answer this challenge even before the Fatimids appeared. Hanbalism is a school of law and of theology. The Hanbalis insisted on finding hadith solutions to questions whenever possible. Correspondingly, they insisted that the close companions of Muhammad were all to be respected, and Hanbalis were horrified that the Shi'is should denounce some of the companions while venerating Ali in what was, to their mind, a pagan spirit. In the seat of the caliphate, Baghdad, Hanbalism became a genuinely popular movement, in part because it seemed to offer a remedy for the decline of the Sunni caliphate and the related fortunes of its capital. Hanbalis felt that Muslims should take individual action to combat innovations introduced into the Islamic community since the time of the companions. In tenth-century Baghdad, the Hanbalis were the most active of all religious groups in mounting popular demonstrations that, since they were often directed against other religious groups, did a great deal to sharpen the boundaries between those groups.

Fear of sharpened boundaries and annoyance at Hanbali agitation drove the Abbasid caliph to compromise the inclusive spirit of consensus-minded Islam. In 934 C.E., because of "their imposing conditions on people" and causing unrest, he issued a rescript declaring that if the Hanbalis persisted, he would use fire and sword against them. Significantly, the decree accuses them of "ascribing unbelief and error to the party of the Prophet's family." The decree implicitly contrasts the Hanbalis with the great majority of Muslims, who called each other unbelievers only in extraordinary circumstances. Hanbali thinkers would probably have rejected the charge that they called Shi'is unbelievers, but their attitude to anything that they regarded as deviation from Islam was so severe that it may well have seemed to their victims that they had been treated as unbelievers.

In the long run, however, the inclusive spirit of consensus-minded Islam prevailed among most Hanbalis as well as among most of their opponents. The prevalence of consensus-mindedness and the inclusive spirit that accepted a certain pluralism of belief were reinforced by the political circumstances of Muslims after the disintegration of a universal Islamic government. The majority of Muslims, including a majority of the Shi'is, accepted the necessity of living in societies that were very imperfectly governed, however one interpreted the guidance Muhammad had offered in his speech during his farewell pilgrimage. Most Muslims understandably refrained from giving deep commitment to these imperfect governments and reserved such commitment for descriptions of ideal Islamic government, which they felt had existed in the past and might again be realized only in a remote, perhaps messianic period in the future.

This devotion to an ideal of Islamic government, together with an allowance of a degree of pluralism within the boundaries of orthodoxy, held the Islamic community as a whole together in the absence of any formal government or structure of state to bind its members. While there was still no separation of the sacred and the secular, most Muslims came to see the utility of a clear distinction between the actual and the ideal. They were willing to live with their actual, very imperfect governments as long as they could cherish their ideal. Devotion to this ideal may have stunted the growth of a political theory that dealt with necessarily imperfect institutions, but it had important practical consequences: it preserved a unified sense of the umma based on Islamic law that recognized the sanctity of contracts of all kinds across the borders created by kings and sultans. It had another consequence as well: it preserved a sense of community that could survive repeated changes of governments and conflicts of interest among Muslims. This sense of community, even in the face of the terrifically powerful and divisive force of modern nationalism, is very much alive today.

4

The Early Muslim Empires: Umayyads, Abbasids, Fatimids

Francis E. Peters

Societies are immortal. Unlike the human organism to which they are so often compared, they suffer neither death nor annihilation. It is their monuments, not the societies themselves, that turn to dust; their bones do not bleach in sandy fastness. Their true analogs live elsewhere, perhaps in the animal kingdom, in the creatures that shed their skins or shells or cocoons and emerge under new forms scarcely recognizable from the old. It is the old shells that we take for dead societies, while the butterflies flutter off with different markings and under a different name.

It is not certain that Islam was or is a society, though we can scarcely speak of it in any other way. It certainly was not a single people who spoke a single tongue or shared a single faith, nor did it have a single form of government. It had, it is true, a certain geopolitical shape. It was, as the Muslims themselves thought of it, the Dar al-Islam, the "Abode of Islam," that immense sprawl of lands from Spain to the Indus valley where Muslim political sovereignty prevailed. It is also true that for many centuries—down to the beginning of the twentieth, as a matter of fact—most Muslims in some sense acknowledged that that sovereignty rested in the hands of the caliph, the "successor of the Prophet of God," as the head of the community.

But prophets have no real "successors"; and the caliphate, for all its long life as an institution, for all its early imperial trappings and the unmistakable legitimacy that clung to the name, is one of history's great nominal offices: its tenant was a political leader who could neither make law nor define dogmas, a spiritual leader with no power to "loose or to bind" either in heaven or on earth. Only Muhammad, through whom God Himself spoke, had managed to hold together the polity that he had wrought, and within two or

73

three generations after him, real power, though not always its outward signs and esteem, had fled or been taken from the caliph's
hands and was held by other, more secular figures: princes, upstarts, usurpers, visionary revolutionaries, and Turkish soldiers
from Morocco to Afghanistan, the whole spectrum of potentates
summed up in the single eloquent Arabic word *sultan* (power).

CONQUEST, CONVERSION, ASSIMILATION

We may not always grasp the too easily assumed unity of Islamic society, but we can at least try to understand some small degree of its extraordinary variety. That variety did not begin with
the conquests. Those early Muslims were the heirs of two very large
and heterogeneous empires, the Byzantine and the Persian, each itself in a state of transition, though the spread of Muhammad's message over a large part of what was then called the "inhabited world"
undoubtedly accelerated the rate and extent of those changes.

At first the conquest seemed to make little difference to the
new subjects of this new regime. To start with what was probably
most important to the people who lived there, the taxes they paid to
their new Muslim masters were no heavier than those that had been
exacted by emperor or shah; and if we can detect a difference between the new tax as the tribute of the conquered to the conqueror
rather than as moneys claimed in the name of the common good,
that difference was not much remarked on by those who paid it.
Nor were the other changes any more notable. The new arrivals
spoke a language that was different but not uncommon to many in
the seventh-century Near East, Arabic, and professed what was to
the local populations a new but not a very alien faith, Islam.

We must proceed with common sense here. People do not
change either their language or their religious beliefs overnight,
particularly if there is no coercion to do so. If we take Persia as an
example, we can perhaps understand the dynamics of what was occurring under the new regime. The Persians were neither Arabs
nor even Semites; their language was a branch of the Indo-Euro-
pean family to which English and Greek belong, and their religion
was a state-supported, clergy-dominated, and not very vigorous
form of Zoroastrianism. In Persia, Islam made its most rapid and

widespread religious inroads but had little success in replacing the local language and literary tradition—or, to put it more directly, the Persians rapidly became Muslims but continued to speak and write in Persian.

In Syria and Iraq, on the other hand, the reverse occurred: the Christian population remained largely Christian for many centuries but soon began to speak the tongue of the new arrivals. Like Portuguese speakers adopting Spanish, they traded in their Aramaic dialects for Arabic, not necessarily a more engaging tongue but one in which business, commercial or political, could be conducted with profit. The principle is clear: where the local tradition was strong and resilient, it resisted the new; where it was feeble or moribund, it yielded.

The literature of the conquerors, the "Conquests of the Countries," does not speak of such things. It is far more concerned with the exploits of its heroes and, more to the point, with the terms of the capitulation treaties with the cities of what had shortly before been the Byzantine and Persian empires. They were curiously reticent conquerors, those Arab Muslims. They stayed out of the cities they had won—the problem of instant assimilation of the conquerors by the conquered was perhaps apparent—and they sought to impose neither their faith nor their customs on their new subjects.

Nor did they occupy the land in the usual sense. The Muslims helped themselves to both the booty and the tribute that followed upon the conquest, but they showed a notable reluctance to grant outright ownership of the land to their soldiers or their commanders. Perhaps they intended to live like subsidized military mandarins within their own encampments; if so, they badly, and fortunately, miscalculated the power of symbiosis, the attractiveness of Islam on the one hand and that of the carefully eschewed cities on the other.

Many parts of the Near East—Syria and northern Mesopotamia in particular—constituted a richly urbanized landscape long before the Muslims arrived from their Arabia of villages and oases. But unlike Muhammad, who was a townsman, those troopers collected in the name of Islam were for the most part bedouin, men of the steppe; and when they paused here and there in their headlong race across Iraq and Syria and Egypt and North Africa, they lived in rough camps on the margin between the steppe, whence they had come, and the sown land they had conquered. Those encampments—Kufa and Basra in Iraq, Jabiya at a day's march from Damascus, Fustat close upon the site of what was later Cairo, and Qayrawan in Tunisia—were all at first rude and unfinished places, tent cities collected around a central prayer and assembly hall called a mosque, with the commander's residence attached or nearby, and grazing grounds for the tribes' herds and mounts distributed round about.

Jabiya was the first to succumb to the pull of urban gravity. It was too close to Damascus either to compete with or to resist the attractions of that ancient and splendid city set in its rich oasis, fed with the waters of the Lebanon and turned into the showcase of Syria by Roman investment. Damascus, with its easy access to the steppe and all the cities of both inland Syria and the Mediterranean coast, drew the Muslims from Arab Jabiya into itself. First the military commander and then, after 661 C.E., the caliph dwelt and ruled in Damascus from a palace at the side of the Great Mosque, once the temple and precinct of Jupiter, and later the Church of Saint John the Baptist.

JERUSALEM

The conversion of the cathedral of Damascus into a mosque was a relatively rare event in Islamic history—the Muslims generally built their own places of prayer and left the Christian shrines untouched—and it draws us back to another urban project undertaken in the early days of the conquest. The Qur'an says nothing of Damascus, but it refers, in its oblique and allusive way, to another city in the "land of Sham," as Syria was called. That city was Jerusalem, and though it was holy to both the Jews and the Christians, it was to the biblical city, the place of Solomon's Temple, that the Qur'an returned more than once. Thus Jerusalem appears to have been known and sacred to the Muslims from the beginning, though perhaps only a few in the armies that rode the trails northward toward Palestine in the 630s had ever seen it. And when they took it without notable resistance in 638 C.E., they found not the city of David and Solomon but a Christian place filled with churches and shrines and pilgrims.

The Christians were left undisturbed in their churches, but, true to their Qur'an-inspired interests, that first generation of Muslims occupied the chief biblical site in Jerusalem, the field of ruins neglected by Christian rulers and faithful alike that marked the place of Solomon's Temple atop Mount Moriah. Indeed, there is strong evidence that the Jews were not only permitted to return to and live in Jerusalem, whence the Romans, both pagan and Christian, had banned them for five centuries, but that the Muslims allowed them to worship at their side on the Temple Mount, the Noble Sanctuary, as the Muslims called it.

At first the Muslims built only a small mosque for themselves, but then, perhaps within the next 50 years, they also began to erect at the center of Herod's old Temple platform what was, and is, the most splendid shrine in Islam, the Dome of the Rock. On the southern edge of the platform they rebuilt their first crude mosque in more splendid form and called it al-Aqsa—the Qur'an calls Jerusalem *al-masjid al-aqsa* (the distant shrine). Below it, at the foot of the southern end of that platform, they began work on a palace complex of imposing dimensions.

The sources are silent on whether the Muslims intended to rule the immense new Dar al-Islam from Jerusalem, the Qur'an's holy city. Palace and mosque and shrine, all unparalleled elsewhere in size and magnificence, speak of ambitions compounded equally of religious sentiment and the feel and grasp of empire. The caliph was in fact the successor to Byzantine emperor and Persian shah, and his portraits in the art of the time leave little doubt that he accepted and savored that role. And we think—there is no present way of demonstrating it—that the first choice of a setting for that dignity was Jerusalem. What changed the plan, if such there was, and why the first Islamic dynasty of the Umayyads in fact ruled from Damascus and a number of other lesser places rather than from the unfinished palace beneath the "Noble Sanctuary," the Haram al-Sharif in Jerusalem, we likewise cannot say.

THE FIRST MUSLIM DYNASTY: THE UMAYYADS OF DAMASCUS

Perhaps it was pragmatism. Damascus had commercial and strategic advantages that Jerusalem could never possess. It sat astride the major trade network in the Near East and at the same time it dominated, on its eastern side, where the steppe begins just beyond the edge of the city's oasis, the grasslands on which great bands of Islam's bedouin warriors had come to a restless halt. The Umayyad dynasty, whose claims to legitimacy were challenged by the family of Ali and their still embryonic "party," among others, had need of those bedouin troops, and Damascus was probably a better place than Jerusalem to control the fractious tribes. The Umayyad rulers would go into their midst to distribute gifts and display their new imperial elan at the small but sumptuous "chateaus" that they built out along the steppe line from near Amman up into middle Syria.

The Dome, the Aqsa, the Jerusalem palace (had it been completed), and the desert palaces were the first flowering of the visual side of the new Muslim culture. The world of word and idea, spiritual ideas and the high art-speech of the Arabic tongue, was already displayed—or, rather, engraved—in the heart of every one of that small band of Muslims. But here, on the land and in the cities that had already known and savored the high culture of the Greeks and Romans, a different kind of edifice had to be constructed. Here the Umayyads' objective was not, as was God's Word and the Prophet's voice in the Qur'an, to move the heart to compunction and the soul to spiritual submission. The goal was to announce and glorify Islam, to impress the still unconverted masses of Christians and Jews, to instill confidence in the followers of the new faith, and, to be sure, to indulge in the architectural self-flattery that has characterized every regime that has ever put hand to stone. How successful the Umayyad enterprise was in all its aspects is transparent to anyone, Muslim or not, who has ever stood on the Mount of Olives and gazed down upon the Noble Sanctuary of Jerusalem.

To some modern eyes—those of Westerners, for example, or some Arab nationalists—the Umayyad rule of the Dar al-Islam from 661 to 750 C.E. appears as a golden age. To many of their Muslim contemporaries, the Umayyads were worldly tyrants and nepotists, altogether too kingly and too secular to govern a community whose essential, and perhaps sole, bond was a shared submission to the will of God. In 750 the dynasty was overthrown, and rule passed to the Abbasids, who held the caliphal office first in Baghdad and then in Cairo until it was assumed by the Ottoman Turks in the sixteenth century. Unlike the Umayyads, who made little effort in that direction, the Abbasids were successful in cloaking themselves with at least the appearance of temporal and spiritual Islamic legitimacy.

Jesus said he had come to bring not peace but the sword. Muhammad promised neither but demanded, in God's name, submission to God's will. But promised or not, intended or not, the Prophet's followers brought peace: not always peace among themselves, surely—Sunnis and Shi'is battled savagely on occasion—but on a larger, international scale. The conquests destroyed little; what they did suppress were imperial rivalries and sectarian blood-letting among the newly subjected population. The Muslims tolerated Christianity but they disestablished it; henceforward Christian life and liturgy, its endowments, politics, and theology, would be a private and not a public affair. By an exquisite irony, Islam reduced the status of Christians to that which the Christians had earlier thrust upon the Jews, though with one difference. The reduction in Christian status was merely judicial; it was unaccompanied by either systematic persecution or a blood lust, and generally, though not everywhere and at all times, unmarred by vexatious behavior.

THE THOUSAND AND ONE NIGHTS OF ABBASID BAGHDAD

The Umayyads are celebrated only by their monuments; they did not survive long enough to leave their stamp upon either the historiographical or the literary tradition of Islam. The Abbasids, however, had the opportunity to design their own history. Their capital lies irretrievably buried beneath modern Baghdad, and their chief physical monument is the empty ruins of the grandiose and sour city of Samarra, to which they were forced to retreat in the ninth century with their Turkish guardsmen. We see all of early Islam as far back as the Prophet himself through their eyes. Whatever the monuments say, it is to the Abbasids that the glory of the Islamic tradition belongs, and nowhere more engagingly than in the celebrated *Thousand and One Nights,* in which the early Abbasids move through an Arthurian haze of benevolent wealth and easy but enlightened learning.

There is romance in the portrait, surely, and a great deal of accumulated nostalgia for a remote and vanished past, but there is truth there as well. Islam was at the height of its political power, and the reach of the caliph would never extend further. There was wealth and luxury in the early Abbasid Baghdad of Harun al-Rashid and his immediate successors, but there was something more, and none of Islam's provincial pretenders to the glory of Baghdad ever quite achieved it: the coming together of Muslim, Christian, and Jew in a brief but glorious exploration of what they saw, then and there and never perhaps again, as their common intellectual heritage.

Early medieval Baghdad was not a utopian republic of letters, surely, but despite the occasional charges of heresy or the frequent one of temerarious innovation, a number of Muslim scholars joined with equally daring Jewish and Christian contemporaries in the catholic atmosphere of tenth- and eleventh-century Baghdad and followed where the Greeks had led—and not merely as slavish imitators. In mathematics, astronomy, optics, medicine, and metaphysics, Muslim scholars were masters and not merely disciples. Without benefit of endowment or even a great deal of encouragement, they constructed intellectual edifices as elegant and impressive as the scrolled domes and glittering tiled minarets that rise above the rooftops of Cairo or Isfahan. They are most impressive, perhaps, if we look upon them as important stops in a continuing intellectual quest and not, like their architectural counterparts, as mere monuments and mausoleums.

THE PEOPLE OF THE BOOK

The condition of the Jews and Christians under Islam should not be idealized. They were political subjects, though the Christians were for a long time a majority in the polity, and Islam was the religion of the state. They were taxed as such, a head tax on all and a land tax on the free peasantry; the Muslims, on the other hand, tithed as a religious and not as a political obligation, for the benefit of "the poor, the orphan, the wayfarer." Those subject People of the Book, as the Muslims called them, enjoyed a protected status. By the terms of the original "contract" with the Muslim conquerors, their property, ecclesiastical or private, could not be confiscated. They were tried in their own courts, under their own laws. They could practice their religion within their own buildings, but they could not proselytize or scandalize the Muslims among whom they lived. So read the contract. The historical reality is that the Muslims clasped favored Christians and Jews to their bosoms in good times or when they needed them, and on occasion accused both groups of everything from arrogance or knavery to high treason. The theory was clear; it was only the practice that was, from time to time and place to place, uncertain.

The Muslim dependence on the Christian population was strongest at the outset, as we might expect of conquerors who had moved out of their own environment and into the high-culture habitat of others who were skilled in all the political and urban arts, from administration to architecture. Christian craftsmen adorned the Dome of the Rock, and Christian bureaucrats ran the chanceries in Syria and Egypt, and the caliph's own bureaus in Iraq. This non-Muslim administrative infrastructure was gradually, very gradually, disassembled, and in the end the divans (bureaus of the nascent Islamic state) were staffed with Muslims and their business conducted in Arabic. Throughout most of the Middle Ages one can still find Christians and Jews in high office and low, but more often than not they were ex-Christians or former Jews.

CITIES, WEALTH, TRADE

What they administered and how, we have already seen. Our vision is very imperfect, however, and it becomes even less certain when we descend to what was, by any standard of judgment, the basic unit of government in most of the medieval Muslim societies, the city. Neither the Qur'an nor the Islamic law derived from it says anything of corporate entities. It is silent on cities and citizens and magistrates, all of them notions from another culture. God alone ruled in the heavens, but not, be it noted, in some Augustinian City of God. Man answered to God in that same supernal domain, and was exhorted to act justly and mercifully toward his fellow Muslims here below. Where this engagement of mercy and justice took place did not much matter.

If God chose to dwell in eternity, men continued to prefer cities. And this religion of Islam, which was revealed in a caravan town in remote Arabia and taken up and swung about their heads by bedouin tribesmen who knew little of cities and despised what little they knew, built up or created afresh an urban culture of extraordinary vitality, prosperity, and allure. Ottoman Istanbul rivaled Byzantine Constantinople, and Muslim Damascus far overshadowed the Roman city that went before it. The great medieval metropolises of Isfahan, Cairo, Baghdad, Fez, and Samarkand had only villages as antecedents.

Most of these Islamic cities, like the larger of the Greco-Roman and Persian centers before them, were imperial showcases, the seat of a Muslim dynasty's power and thus the focus of its investment. But they had other, equally powerful incentives to growth, the wholesale and long-distance trade that crisscrossed the Dar al-Islam. The Pax Islamica brought more than peace. It threw down political frontiers and commercial barriers; it exploited new sources of precious metals in Africa and unloosed the hoarded wealth of churches and temples; it introduced a standardized bimetallic currency from one end of the empire to the other; and, unlike the Byzantines and Persians, it allowed the system to run itself. It was not yet a capitalist utopia: customs dues were exacted at major stops along the way, and every illegal entrepreneur, from imperial extortionist to highway robber, attempted to take his share. But it was, for all that, an open commercial climate, uninhibited by either moral or legal scruples about the life of commerce, and with a banking and credit system that operated effectively over a wide area.

That area reached far beyond the boundaries of the Dar al-Islam: eastward to India, the Spice Islands of Southeast Asia, and China, and westward into the Mediterranean basin. It was once thought that the Islamic conquests shattered the commercial as well as the political unity of what the Romans were accustomed to call "our sea." If that was so, it was only for a brief period, however, and a three-cornered trade among Byzantines, Muslims, and the entrepreneurs coming to the fore in the Italian cities managed to survive theological differences, changes of regime, and even overt political aggression.

There were disquieting elements in this commercial exchange almost from its beginning. The Byzantines and Europeans were most often consumers; the Muslims not so much the producers as the suppliers, middlemen in a commercial network that began in the Far East. And the transactions took place in the Near East: at piers where Italian ships were moored in Muslim ports, and then in the commercial hospices that the Western cities began to maintain for their own convenience in the Near Eastern emporiums. For most Muslims, Europe remained a remote and alien place, unknown and perhaps even uninteresting.

ISLAM AND EUROPE

The Europeans suffered no such disability. The Near East was for them a perennial landscape, real or imagined, spiritual or commercial, conned from the ancients or described by merchants or the stream of Christian pilgrims who never ceased, Islam or not, visiting the place that Constantine had converted into a Christian Holy Land. The trouble with Jerusalem, the Muslim Muqaddasi complained about his native city in the tenth century, was that it was always filled with Jews and Christians (as it still is). For Muqaddasi it was a source of irritation, and no more; and for the Christians and Jews and Muslims who lived there, Muslim sovereignty was a fact, as was the presence of the most notable churches of Christendom and the primary Jewish yeshiva of the Mediterranean world.

The actual tenth-century Palestinian city was neither a very prosperous nor, indeed, always a very safe place to live. It was in the center of a war zone between Egypt, where a new Shi'i dynasty called the Fatimids had come to power in 969 C.E., and the older strongholds of the caliph and his Turkish praetorians in Iraq. Like some ancient Belgium or Armenia, Palestine was often overrun by armies heading elsewhere, with the additional hazard that when the dust cleared, the predatory bedouin who infested the area often moved in to pick the bones.

The Muslims did not often visit Jerusalem in those days; indeed, they could scarcely defend the place. And when tyranny descended upon the land, it was usually all three communities that shared the oppression. For the Muslims that oppression was largely economic; for the Jews, and particularly the far more visible Christians, it frequently cast itself in religious raiment. Thus al-Hakim, the eleventh-century Fatimid ruler of Egypt whose memory is fragrant in no one's annals—Muslim, Jewish, or Christian—and who was disturbed, if not entirely deranged, had destroyed the Church of the Holy Sepulcher in 1009 C.E. It was a piece of senseless malice that unwittingly set in train events that are still unfolding.

When the Jews in Jerusalem found themselves in difficulty, they often turned to their richer and more influential fellows in other Islamic centers in Egypt or Iraq. Levers were pulled, money changed hands, an entire trans-Islamic apparatus of diplomacy could be set in motion. The Christians had additional resources; they could turn to political powers abroad, to the Christian Byzantine Empire or to one of the emerging Christian polities of Europe, and so engage the more thunderous mechanisms of international *Machtpolitik.*

It was not Jerusalem or its Christians that originally brought those powers into the Near East. Trade had already accomplished that, as we have seen; and the merchants of Amalfi early had a hospice in Jerusalem, as Charlemagne may have had two centuries earlier. The Latins were unmistakably present in the Near East, and their presence had little to do, in the first instance, with holy places.

What the holy places did provide was a point of leverage and a quasi-juridical instrument to focus and justify intervention. Trading privileges were precisely that, privileges, but concern for the Christian holy places within the Dar al-Islam was often perceived in the West not as a privilege but a right—indeed, an obligation. The Byzantines used the argument to rebuild the Church of the Holy Sepulcher after its destruction by al-Hakim's agents and got some special privileges for the Christians of Jerusalem in the bargain— their own walled quarter in the northwest corner of the city, among others. But in the tangle of eleventh-century politics, that was by no means the end of it. The Muslim Turks had broken into Anatolia and were marching on Constantinople. If the West was concerned with the fate of Christendom, let them begin by coming to the aid of Constantinople.

THE COMING OF THE CRUSADERS

That may have been the argument that the Byzantine Emperor Alexius used in the West in the last years of the eleventh century, and it may have been the same argument that planted the notion of a crusade in the mind of Pope Urban II. But the crusade—

not that crusade, at any rate—had nothing to do with Constantinople. In an extraordinary triumph of popular sentiment over both papal and imperial politics, the Crusaders turned directly and decisively toward Jerusalem. The idea of the Christian Holy City, which had rested quietly in the popular consciousness in the West over the centuries and had occasionally been nourished by accounts of pilgrims who continued to go there all through the Islamic era, suddenly burst into political bloom. "Deus le volt" was the popular Crusader cry in Europe. God may indeed have wished it, but there is certainly no evidence that the Christians of Jerusalem did, or that anything extraordinary was occurring to pilgrims there to prompt such a response at that moment in history.

There is no need to rehearse the First or Jerusalem Crusade—or, better, "the Pilgrimage," as those who were participants called it. The Western knights, most of them French, took Jerusalem in 1099 and slew the Muslim survivors down to the women and children. The fate of the Jewish community is less clear. Some were doubtless killed, but many others were ransomed by their coreligionists in Egypt and so found themselves in possession of a city that was filled with holy places but had no inhabitants except themselves. The Dome of the Rock was converted into a church, the Templum Domini; and the al-Aqsa mosque, renamed the Templum Solomonis, after a brief career as the palace of the Latin king was handed over to the new Order of the Knights Templars, who began to subdivide, enlarge, and adapt the building to their own uses. The Eastern Christians were lured back into the city, and eventually some Jews and Muslims must have made their tentative and modest reappearance in Jerusalem.

This extraordinary interlude in the history of Jerusalem and Islam lasted less than a century, from 1099 to 1187, when the Crusaders were driven out by the armies of Saladin. The fighting was savage once again, but this time there was no wholesale massacre in its wake. The Haram buildings were of course restored to Islam, but the Church of the Holy Sepulcher, which the Crusaders had extensively rebuilt, was left untouched, as were most of the other major Christian shrines in the city. Saladin did, however, convert the convent attached to the Church of Saint Anne into a law school, and part of the palace of the now departed Latin patriarch into a Sufi convent and hospice.

HOLY CITY, HOLY WAR

The law school and convent were relatively new institutions, not merely in Jerusalem but also in the Islamic world, and they are worth pausing over, since they say something of importance about Muslim intentions, then and afterward, toward Jerusalem, and reveal deeper strains of transformation and renewal in Islam in the twelfth century. Saladin's countercrusade was not simply a natural and angry impulse to strike out against infidels and foreigners in a city that had known many such. The notion of a holy war (jihad) was certainly present in Islam, but it is neither so omnipresent nor so easily invoked as many Westerners think. A jihad against the Franks did not spring immediately to the mind of every Muslim, from Fez to Bukhara, in the twelfth century; it was one of many competing items on a very full political agenda in Egypt and Syria.

The Crusade might indeed have passed as simply another occupation of that much-occupied city had not the Franks made it clear by their behavior and propaganda that they, at least, were engaged in a holy war over Jerusalem. That notion slowly took hold in Muslim minds, at least among the religious intelligentsia in Damascus and Aleppo, and eventually in the thinking of some of the political leaders as well. Muslims' consciousness of their own religious claims to Jerusalem began slowly to rise—hortatory writings on the "Merits of Jerusalem" appeared for the first time—and it was the genius of Saladin that he was able to convert this sentiment, neither so widespread nor so popular as the earlier Western enthusiasm for a "pilgrimage in arms" to Jerusalem, into effective political and military action.

Saladin had not merely taken Jerusalem back from the Franks; he had also recovered both it and Cairo for Sunnism from the heretical Shi'i dynasty of the Fatimids, who had ruled Jerusalem from Egypt before the Crusades. That was the point of the law schools, convents, and similar institutions that were constructed and endowed—building, staff, and students—in Jerusalem over the following centuries. They were the primary instruments for the propagation and sustenance of Sunni Islam against what was judged in the twelfth century to be a far greater threat than the Franks to the Islamic commonwealth: the rising tide of revolutionary, anti-caliphal Shi'ism. The Franks were politically dangerous;

the Shi'is, with their radical denial of the caliph's right to rule in the name of Islam, were subversive of Islam itself, as perhaps most Muslims then understood it. The Sunnis fought the Shi'is not only with their loyal Turkish troops but also with the new institutions of Sunni law and piety, not merely in Jerusalem, which was not particularly important in that struggle, but in the great centers of Baghdad, Damascus, and the former Fatimid capital of Cairo.

Saladin did not, of course, invent these institutions, but what he and other Turkish princes further east did was patronize them. Earlier Muslim rulers had built large "cathedral" mosques to testify to their piety; from the eleventh century on, the wealth of the regime went into making those mosques what they had perhaps once been in a Christian world: instruments of propaganda, now no longer turned outward toward the infidel but within, to cure the schismatic fissures that Shi'ism had introduced into the Sunni consensus. Saladin and countless other rulers around the Islamic world invested the wealth of their regimes in the services of Islam, Sunni Islam, whose needs had in the eleventh century been translated into institutions of Islamic learning and Islamic piety.

THE SUNNI REVIVAL

This struggle toward a new consensus within the Islamic community had little to do with the Crusades, except perhaps that the Crusades helped finance it. The Crusades, trailing off in the late Middle Ages, had established a complex network of association between Muslim East and European West, and as Christian enthusiasm for a "pilgrimage in arms" dissipated in its sheer hopelessness, there flowed along that same network a new commercial vitality that brought wealth and prosperity to both parties. Muslim and Christian were by the thirteenth century locked into a permanent trading partnership, and whatever its long-range inequities, which began to be felt only in the seventeenth century, it brought a new wealth into Islamic cities from Morocco to Iran.

The wealth from this trade poured into the cities, circulated through the wholesale network of *khans* (commercial hostels) and warehouses, thence into the retail bazaars, and finally into a rich lifestyle. Elegant and well-furnished private residences and public buildings were constructed. The latter, however, did not follow the Roman or the Persian tradition of palace, theater, or law court, but consisted of mosques, law schools, Sufi convents perhaps, or fountains to refresh passersby, funded by religious endowments designated for that purpose. Other endowments went directly into subsidies for the poor, the pilgrim, students, and teachers of the Qur'an and the Islamic law, muezzins, and preachers in the mosques.

This endowment mechanism, called *waqf* in Arabic, was one of the great social and economic institutions of medieval Islam. It was by means of this fiscal base that the great institutional achievements of the post-Crusade generations of public leaders and private citizens built the edifices and supported the institutions that typify medieval Islam. By this endowment the donor surrendered ownership of some income-producing property in his possession: the property in effect belonged thereafter to God, and its income after expenses was dedicated to some purpose stipulated by the donor. Agricultural land became waqf, as did shops, baths, bazaars, rental properties, and entire villages; and from their profits were built most of the public buildings that still fill the eye in a traditional Muslim city or quarter. And from these same sources spread the less visible network of Islamic philanthropy and, in the name of that philanthropy, a great deal of employment and subsidy in an Islamic city.

We are well informed on waqf—on how it worked, at least, if not its full extension into every corner of the Dar al-Islam—because it was a formal legal procedure, and we have endowment contracts that go back to the ninth century and became increasingly plentiful from the thirteenth century on. They spell out the terms: the precise limits of the donated properties; the recipients of the endowment—the holy places in Mecca, Medina, and Jerusalem were principal beneficiaries, as might be expected; and the mechanism of administration. All were to operate, without let or change, "until God shall inherit the earth."

THE ISLAMIC CITY

What we do not know a great deal about, however, precisely because they were not legal entities, were the institutions that governed, or at least regulated or administered, the cities, with their profusion of public religious buildings. The distant caliph or sultan claimed sovereignty, with the governor his local agent. The latter was usually a military man and, as time went on, often a foreigner— Turks and Kurds or Berbers were generally the military backbone of whatever regime ruled in the Islamic world. The governor possessed the citadel, but he could hardly be said to have possessed the city.

The medieval Islamic city was a very heterogeneous organism, and sometimes an unruly one. The chief or "cathedral" mosque normally sat at its center, and along the main streets that led from the center to the main gates were the commercial bazaars, where wholesale and retail trade was conducted. These same streets, which had no residential function, likewise separated the city into quarters, each with its own mosque (or church or synagogue), its own neighborhood bazaar of the grocery-store variety, its own bakery, and perhaps its own bath.

But the quarter of an Islamic city was no mere neighborhood. It was in the later Middle Ages a sequestered enclave, often with limited physical access and often, too, with a self-regulating, homogeneous population. The dwellers in cities sorted themselves out by ethnic and even village origins; by religious affiliation or, if that category was too gross or too uncomfortable, by sect or rite. There were Shi'i quarters, Armenian Christian quarters, Turkoman quarters, and so on.

The quarter, with its own chief or headman, was probably the most important element in the decentralization of the Islamic city, but it was not the only one. Jews and a great variety of Christian groups had their own courts and justice, and so constituted an almost separate jurisdiction under the chief rabbi or bishop. The military answered only to their commander, the Muslim clerics to the grand mufti or chief judge, the Sufis to the shaykh of their brotherhood or order, guild members to their chief. The Islamic city was not so much a headless organism as a conglomerate of sometimes conflicting—occasionally violently conflicting—sometimes cooperating interest groups, each with a clear-eyed investment in its survival and prosperity. The marvel is that it worked; as with all informal, invisible, and unspoken arrangements, we only wish we knew better how it worked.

ISLAMIC SOCIETY IN THE MIDDLE AGES

As in most preindustrial societies, the bulk of the population in the Dar al-Islam was engaged in agriculture—village farming, for the most part, without the benefit of large-scale slave labor. Slaves there assuredly were—Islamic law did not forbid or encourage enslavement, though it certainly commended manumission—but they were found in domestic and small industry services within the city or, most surprisingly to us, with our own perceptions of slavery, as the professional soldiers of Islam. Even more oddly, slavery, particularly military slavery, was likely the single most effective means of upward mobility in Islamic society. A peasant could aspire to little or nothing, as in most societies; an artisan, to prosperity; a merchant, to riches; and a Sufi or a religious scholar, to high prestige; but the military slave, the *mamluk* (possession), as he was called, might aspire to the effective rule of the Dar al-Islam.

Medieval Muslim society was not caste-ridden, but it knew and enjoyed a great variety of distinctions. The People of the Book (Christians and Jews) aside, in many circles it was a matter of distinction to be of Arab blood; and if that were coupled with descent from the Prophet and his family, the cachet was considerable, if not always unimpeachably authentic. Racial stereotypes abounded, which the Persians gleefully applied to the boastful Arabs and both groups applied to the overbearing Turks and the too-pale northerners and too-dark southerners.

This is the stuff of all human societies, of course; what is probably more genuinely Islamic are the elite classes that developed within the cities. Above the slaves, the menials and the manual workers, the artisans and small merchants, stood a triple hierarchy of power, wealth, and religious prestige. One group was the military *amirs,* professional soldiers for the most part bought as slaves outside the Dar al-Islam (it was forbidden by Islamic law for one Muslim to enslave another), converted to Islam, and then reared in sequestered circumstances to serve as an armed base for the twin columns of Sunnism and sultan. Their rewards were land—or, rather, the income from large estates that they held by a kind of deed of fief and over which they exercised rights that only the most acute of lawyers could distinguish from true ownership.

THE RELIGIOUS INTELLIGENTSIA

At the side of the military amirs were two other groups whose power was not so nakedly displayed, perhaps, but was nonetheless real: the great merchants, whose wealth derived from the lucrative wholesale trade of the Islamic world, and the clerics, almost an Islamic rabbinate, trained in the law in the *madrasas* (schools) that are such a consistent feature of the Islamic cityscape from the twelfth century on. Though the ulama, as the clerics were called, were generally not wealthy—both their education and their later income were supplied out of waqf endowments—they enjoyed the prestige of close association with the religious law that set much of the tone and direction of the private and personal side of Islamic society. The ulama did not traffic in dogma like their Christian episcopal counterparts, but, as Jewish history copiously shows, the teachers of the law, who are also its chief exegetes, needed no ex cathedra voice to shape the conscience and mores of a community. "Islam," that global term that we use to describe the faith and practice of Muslims even to this day, was largely, though not entirely, the creation of the ulama.

The ulama were formed in madrasas, law schools with remarkably similar curricula, from Morocco to India. The madrasa has been compared with the Western medieval university, a comparison that is true only if we note that the same scholastic method was used in both and, more important, if we imagine the European institution without its faculty of arts. The madrasa was first, foremost, and almost exclusively a school for the study of the religious law of Islam, and the more profane arts and sciences were not represented in its curriculum. The study of physics had no place there, nor literature, nor that crown upon the arts, philosophy.

Muslims who followed the more secular pursuits of philosophy or science had to do so elsewhere, usually under private tutorship, since both the subjects and some of the conclusions that might be drawn from them were regarded by the more conservative ulama as inimical to faith. The rise of a law-school-educated clerisy in Islam in the eleventh and twelfth centuries corresponds almost exactly to the end of the most productive period of investigation in what were called, significantly, "the foreign sciences." The ulama were, of course, correct in their assessment of that rival learning.

One cannot follow either Plato or Aristotle to the end of the line of their inquiries and still remain a believing Muslim—or, for that matter, a Christian or a Jew—and the uneasy ulama had plenty of company among the clerics of those latter communions.

Most of the Islamic intelligentsia, from the Middle Ages down to the beginning of modern times, passed through the madrasa system, a fact that created a certain uniformity in their religious formation and that of the society as a whole, but in no way converted Islam into a society of lawyers. Lawyers there were, and in large numbers, among the educated classes; but there was a remarkable heterogeneity of profession and avocation in a culture with such a uniform formation. The association between law and history was close, far closer than in most Western cultures, and Islamic society was chronicled in a quite remarkable way. Historians and biographers abounded, and both the obligation of pilgrimage to Mecca and the wide reach of its commerce loosed across the face of the Abode of Islam a great flood of travelers who described the length and breadth of that empire, and the manners and customs of the people who lived there. Others turned to the more profane art of poetry—the deeply layered symbolism of the poetry gives a certain profane dimension to even the most religious of poems—or to the science of the heart that is called Sufism.

The ulama stood at the center of the Islamic law; the Sufis experimented with its outer, affective edges. There was a tension between those two postures, as there always is between heavenward-looking mystic and earthbound canon lawyer, between Talmudic rabbi and Hasidic enthusiast, but there was much exchange and mutual instruction as well. On the scales of Islamic orthodoxy, it was surely the ulama who counted more heavily, since it was chiefly they who defined and measured orthodoxy, and thus more successfully exemplified it. But the Sufis called to a higher, more mysterious, and therefore more dangerous enterprise: the pursuit of God and the contemplation of His ineffable name. And in Islam, as elsewhere, the lawyers' concern with the letter of the law had in the end to yield, soften, and adapt to the Sufis' cultivation of its spirit.

However one wishes to read these political and spiritual currents, the Abbasid caliph in Baghdad had little to do, for good or ill, with any of them. By the eleventh century he had neither an army of his own to send against a Frankish invasion nor the wealth to subsidize the intellectual and spiritual renewal that followed it. The dominant political figures of the era were not the shadow caliphs who sat in Baghdad but two of their subjects: the pious and energetic Kurdish general Saladin, who ruled Syria and Egypt; and the learned Persian Nizam al-Mulk, who served the Turkish sultans in Baghdad as their *vizier* (administrative official). Both were wealthy and admired men who committed their prestige and their wealth to the institutional support of what a scholar of the time called "the re-vitalization of the sciences of religion." And it was they, not the caliphs, who bore the name, who saved the medieval Islamic legacy that is called Abbasid.

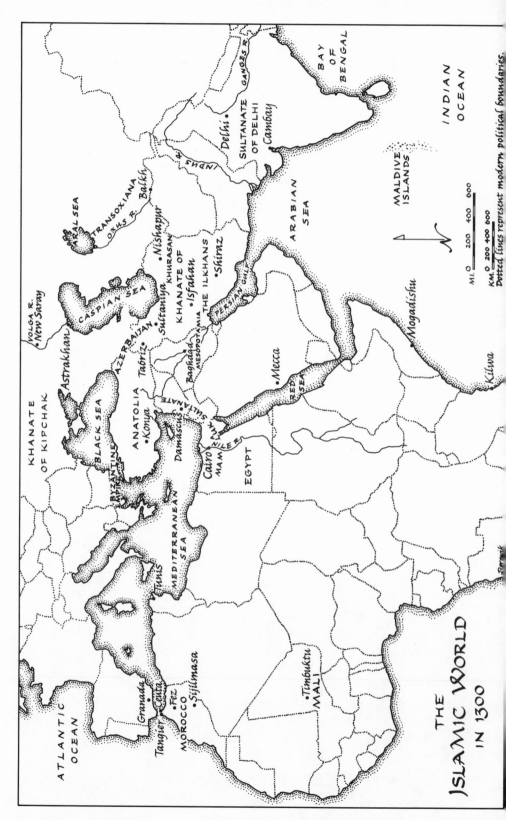

THE
ISLAMIC WORLD
IN 1300

ATLANTIC OCEAN

INDIAN OCEAN

BAY OF BENGAL

ARABIAN SEA

MEDITERRANEAN SEA

BLACK SEA

CASPIAN SEA

ARAL SEA

RED SEA

PERSIAN GULF

KHANATE OF KIPCHAK

KHANATE OF THE ILKHANS

SULTANATE OF DELHI

TRANSOXIANA

KHURASAN

AZERBAIJAN

ANATOLIA

BYZANTINE

MAMLUK SULTANATE

EGYPT

MOROCCO

MALI

MESOPOTAMIA

•New Saray
VOLGA R.

•Astrakhan

•Balkh
OXUS R.

•Nishapur

•Sultaniya

•Tabriz

•Konya

•Shiraz

•Isfahan

•Baghdad

•Damascus

•Cairo
NILE R.

•Mecca

•Delhi
INDUS R.
GANGES R.

•Cambay

•Mogadishu

•Kilwa

•Tunis

•Granada

•Tangier
•Ceuta
•Fez

•Sijilmasa

•Timbuktu

MALDIVE ISLANDS

MI. 0   200 400 600
KM. 0 200 400 600

Dotted lines represent modern political boundaries.

Berawi

94

5

Islamic Universalism in
the Later Middle Ages

Ross E. Dunn

For 500 years following the disintegration of the Abbasid empire, Islam as a religious and cultural system came to dominate a far larger share of the eastern hemisphere than any rival civilization. By the fourteenth century Muslim sultans and princes were the rulers of a chain of states stretching from Morocco and Senegal in the west to the Strait of Malacca in the east. Sufi preachers, legal scholars, theologians, and merchants were introducing Islam in the rain forests of West Africa, the tropical coast lands of Tanganyika, the steppes of the Ukraine, and China. Literate Muslims possessed a cosmopolitan ideal approaching a more universalist vision of mankind than any other civilization before them had achieved. In the later Middle Ages (eleventh-fifteenth centuries), they were collectively the only group of people on earth whose world view included the inhabited Afro-Eurasian region taken almost as a whole.

A FOURTEENTH-CENTURY COSMOPOLITE

The career of Abu Abdallah Muhammad ibn Battuta (1304-1368 C.E.), a Moroccan legal scholar who spent three decades of his life traveling throughout most of the Afro-Eurasian world, strikingly exemplifies the cosmopolitan ideals of educated Muslims. Raised in the port city of Tangier and given an advanced education in the religious and juridical sciences, he left home as a young man in 1325 (the year after Marco Polo died) to make the pilgrimage to Mecca and, as aspiring young scholars of North African countries did, to undertake a study tour of Cairo, Damascus, and other great intellectual centers of the Islamic heartland.

Prompted by a desire to acquire the wisdom and holy blessings of the great teachers and Sufi masters of Islam, to share in the patronage that Muslim rulers customarily bestowed on pious and learned men, and simply to see the world, he set out from Mecca on a series of journeys that took him to Persia, East Africa, Asia Minor, Byzantium, Central Asia, and India (where he spent the years 1334-41 serving as a judge in the sultanate of Delhi). He then continued his travels to south India, the Maldive Islands, and—depending on whether one accepts the veracity of his narrative—to Southeast Asia and China. In 1349 he returned to his homeland but soon set forth again, first to the Muslim kingdom of Granada in Spain, then by camel caravan across the Sahara to the empire of Mali. At the end of his traveling days and before retiring to a provincial judgeship in Morocco, he dictated the accounts of his travels to a fellow scholar, who worked them into a coherent literary narrative.

The significance of Ibn Battuta's cosmopolitan adventure is not that he made his way through numerous alien and exotic lands and somehow survived but, on the contrary, that he was traveling most of the time within an interregional network of cities whose literate inhabitants shared not only a religious confession but also the same moral values, legal norms, cultural standards, and social manners. The sacred law, the educational system, and the rituals of public orthodoxy together provided a universalist and astonishingly resilient base for a homogeneous ordering of urban life over an immense area.

Most of the cities Ibn Battuta visited were clustered within the belt of agrarian lands that extended, west to east, from the Mediterranean basin through the Middle East and India to China, the zone of intense intercommunication where all the major civilizations had sprung up. At the time of his career, moreover, peripheral areas to the north or south of the intercommunicating zone—Sudanic Africa, the East African coast, the islands of the East Indies, the steppes of inner Asia, and Europe north of the Alps—were being incorporated into the urban nexus through trade, migration, conquest, and cultural diffusion. Except, notably, for Europe, Muslim soldiers, merchants, scholars, and holy men were the principal intermediaries between these areas and the high civilization of the central agrarian lands. Thus Ibn Battuta found himself perfectly at home among the ruling and lettered classes not only in Tunis,

Cairo, Isfahan, and Delhi, but also in Mogadishu, Kilwa, Astrakhan, and Timbuktu.

Ibn Battuta was preeminently a man of the city, and his narrative tells us far less than we might like to know about life in the countryside. The expansion of Islam in the post-Abbasid centuries, however, was by no means confined to the urban districts. Merchants, wandering Sufi preachers, and Muslim herding folk migrating from one grazing ground to another were converting millions of rural people to the faith of Muhammad. Lacking any centrally directed hierarchy of clerics to insist on ecclesiastical conformity, Islam wove itself rather easily into the belief systems and everyday rituals of Indian peasants, Berber highlanders, and Anatolian farmers.

At the same time, the myriad local traditions within the Islamic sphere by no means totally surrendered to the values and tastes of Muslim high culture, which was derived mainly from the Arabo-Persian core of civilization in Abbasid times. The cosmopolitan model of civilization that men like Ibn Battuta exemplified did not come near to homogenizing Islamic peoples as a whole. Rather, Islam left wide scope for local social customs, arts, and languages to flourish. Mosque and minaret, for example, were symbols of the allegiance to the Dar al-Islam that all Muslims shared, yet building materials, architectural devices, and decorations varied as widely from one part of Africa or Asia to another as did the regional traditions they reflected.

AN AGE OF TURKISH POWER

If the enduring style of Islamic civilization, including its universalist values, was established in the Middle East core area under the protecting dome of the unitary Abbasid empire, the further advance of Islam into Africa and Asia was accomplished under conditions of repeated shifts and changes in the patterns of political boundaries and regimes. Traveling from Morocco to India between 1325 and 1333, Ibn Battuta passed through the territories of something like 22 independent or autonomous Muslim polities. By the time he returned from the Far East, a little over a decade later, the political map had changed substantially.

Political instability in the heartland of Islam in the Middle Ages was in large measure a consequence of the dynamic relationship between the settled and urbanized peoples of the central agrarian lands and the horse- or camel-riding barbarians inhabiting the adjacent arid regions to the south (Sahara and Arabian deserts) or north (Central Asian steppes and the Gobi). Indeed, the history of the eastern hemisphere taken as a whole from very ancient times to about 1400 C.E. may be conveniently organized around a single macro theme: the recurring surges of nomads, as migrants and conquerors, into the agrarian zones.

One of these movements occurred in the seventh century, when bedouin armies flying the green flag of Muhammad burst from the Arabian desert and overran the Middle East and North Africa. Arabia, however, was far too barren of population and resources to produce such an explosion very often. Much heavier concentrations of mounted tribespeople inhabited the Central Asian steppes to the north. There the enduring climatic fact, that rain falls more often and grass grows taller as one moves west or southwest, encouraged over the millennia the repeated building up of barbarian pressures against the Middle East by way of the easy, open routes through Persia.

During the period 1000-1400, pony-riding nomads advanced into the Islamic core region in two major migrations, seriously disrupting political and social patterns as they had been worked out under the caliphate. The first crisis occurred in the late tenth and eleventh centuries, when Turkish-speaking warrior tribes, moving in successive waves south across the Oxus River, overran Persia and Mesopotamia. A Turkish dynasty, the Seljuks, held together for a few decades a state spanning most of the Arabo-Persian zone, but over the long term these alien war captains proved incapable of creating an imperial structure on the Abbasid model.

The early disintegration of the Seljuk empire set the political pattern that would endure until about 1500: a fragmenting of the hub region of Islam into a number of military kingdoms, each ruled by a sultan or prince of Central Asian origin who imposed law and order with a corps of professional horse soldiers personally loyal to him. Over the greater part of the region this ruling class constituted an ethnically tiny minority of the population, a military caste commanding its Arab, Persian, and other native subjects from the social seclusion of its barracks and citadels.

In the northern part of the agrarian zone, however, Turkish warrior clans, with their families and great herds of horses and sheep, were migrating in the eleventh and twelfth centuries along a belt of territory running from Afghanistan through Khurasan and Azerbaijan to Asia Minor (Anatolia). In much of this area pastoralism gained an ascendancy over settled agriculture, and Turkish culture and language gradually became dominant in the countryside.

These rude folk brought to Islam a new expansive energy. The Turkish upstarts who took political control of the Middle East were already Sunni Muslims when they arrived, having converted to Islam as a result of earlier contact with traders and wandering proselytizers along the northern fringe of Abbasid civilization. Between the eleventh and thirteenth centuries, Turkish armies extended the frontiers of the Dar al-Islam spectacularly in two directions. To the west great, roisterous bands of horsemen, called *ghazis* (fighters in the holy war), pushed steadily across Greek Anatolia. By the fourteenth century the Byzantine emperor was clinging feebly to a tiny corner of Asia Minor, and the population of almost the entire region between the Black Sea and the Mediterranean was being converted from Christianity to Islam and from Greek to Turkish culture. To the east other ghazi cavalry defeated the Hindu Rajput kings of north India and established Muslim rulership over the rich Indo-Gangetic plain. In the thirteenth and early fourteenth centuries the Turkish sultans of Delhi annexed or at least plundered almost the entire subcontinent. In India, however, no major influx of Muslim population occurred, and the great majority of the population remained attached to their ancient Hindu traditions.

Turkish captains under the leadership of the Kurdish hero Saladin seized Egypt in 1171, defeating the Shi'i Fatimids and returning the Nile valley to Sunni Islam. In the post-Abbasid states the core of the sultan's army was usually made up of professional soldiers having the status of military slaves, or mamluks. In Egypt a corps of them seized power in 1250 and founded the Mamluk sultanate, which subsequently conquered Greater Syria and the upper Nile valley, drove the last of the Frankish crusaders from the Levantine coast, and ultimately endured longer than any other Turkish state until the rise of the Ottoman Empire.

The new military masters of the central lands, ignorant and unpolished though they were, eagerly supported Islamic high civilization and its cosmopolitan tendencies. The governing style of the sultans and their commanders (amirs) was personal, arbitrary, and often brutal. Public subordination was ensured through a growing body of administrative and penal laws having no foundation in Islamic law and sometimes in gross contradiction to it. Yet in order to govern densely populated agrarian lands and guarantee the flow of tax revenues to their treasury, the rulers were obliged from the start to come to a general understanding with the local Arabic- or Persian-speaking jurists and theologians (ulama), as well as the families experienced in administration and finance.

The ulama and other lettered men of the cities were the guardians and exponents of the sacred law (shari'a) and the arbiters of cultural standards. In return for their cooperation they insisted that the shari'a be respected and applied in religious matters and civil disputes among Muslims. They also insisted on the ideal of a higher allegiance to the Dar al-Islam as a whole. The Turkish lords agreed freely. Sons and grandsons of barbarians, they could hardly offer an alternative model of urban civilization. On the contrary, they looked to the scholars, poets, and divines assembled at their courts to teach them proper civilized behavior and the value of a cosmopolitan outlook.

As alien, socially insular elites, the new masters were the antithesis of nation builders. The states they erected were de facto arrangements for preserving a rough-edged civil order and exploiting the productive labor of the peasants. The internationally minded savants and merchants who traveled routinely from one distant city to another depended absolutely on the amirs for intellectual patronage and commercial security, but for the literate classes the Abode of Islam was an effective reality transcending any secular kingdom in moral and juristic importance. The Turks themselves, in order to enhance their legitimacy with the learned spokesmen of the sacred law, were willing to make a purely formal submission to the Abbasid caliph, who was in fact, from the tenth century on, either a titular leader under the supervision of military strongmen or, at best, the king of a modest territory centered on Baghdad. By continuing to pay homage to the institution of the caliphate, Turkish usurpers gave recognition to the ideal of Islam as a political and legal order greater than any mere sultanate.

THE MONGOL IRRUPTION

Then, suddenly, the prevailing drift of Islamic civilization was again disturbed, this time by the invasions of the pagan Mongols, the second great nomadic movement of the Middle Ages and the last one in history. Though the Turkish incursions of the eleventh century had involved much bloodshed and disruption of settled life, the Mongol assault on the Islamic heartland was a nightmare of violence and destruction. The armies of Genghis Khan wreaked death and ruin wherever they rode, from north China to the plains of Hungary, but nowhere more so than in Greater Persia, where most of the cities of the north were demolished and their inhabitants annihilated between 1220 and 1223. "With one stroke," wrote the Persian historian Juvayhi of the Mongol invasion of Khurasan, "a world which billowed with fertility was laid desolate, and the regions thereof became a desert, and the greater part of the living dead, and their skin and bones crumbling dust." In 1258 Hulagu, Genghis Khan's grandson, invaded Mesopotamia, sacked Baghdad, and had the last of the Abbasid caliphs rolled up in a carpet and trampled to death.

This grotesquely symbolic victory over Islam befitted the Mongols' grand objective to conquer the world through tactical brilliance and the psychology of mass terror. The Turkish amirs now defending civilization, however, could ride and shoot too. In the west the Mamluk cavalry prevented a Mongol invasion of Egypt by defeating them in Palestine in 1260, though Syria was not militarily secure until well into the fourteenth century. In the east the sultans of Delhi repeatedly beat back Mongol armies over the course of about a century to defend the Indo-Gangetic plain.

A general trend of decline in population and agricultural production, along with retrogression or at least stasis in agrarian technology, appears to have been occurring in the Middle East between the eleventh and thirteenth centuries for reasons not yet fully understood. The Mongol calamity undermined still further the economic foundations of the older centers of Islamic high culture. More agricultural land was lost to Mongol and Turkish herds, irrigation works deteriorated further, and some celebrated cities of art and intellect, such as Balkh and Nishapur, never recovered from barbarian demolition. Yet the longer-term effect of the age of

Mongol dominance in Eurasia, extending from the death of Genghis Khan to about the mid-fourteenth century, was to stimulate further Islamic expansion and reinforce the general cultural patterns of the previous two centuries.

One reason for this was that the explosion of the Mongol bomb in Greater Persia produced a significant emigration of scholars, craftsmen, rich merchants, and divines—men with the money or connections to escape in time—to cities beyond the reach of the barbarians. Taking their skills and knowledge with them, they added richly to the urban life of Egypt, Anatolia, and India. Cairo, already a sophisticated capital under the Fatimids in the eleventh and twelfth centuries, succeeded gutted, depopulated Baghdad as the center of Islamic craft and letters of specifically Arab expression. Indeed, Cairo was the largest and intellectually most lively metropolis of the Islamic world during Ibn Battuta's time. Learned refugees from Khurasan and Transoxiana also traveled west over the Armenian mountains to Anatolia, where they contributed to the Persian-style Islamic high culture that was already flourishing in the Turkish kingdoms there. A similar process took place in India under the sultans of Delhi.

Another reason for the explosion and reinforcement of Islamic culture was that Genghis and his successors had incorporated into their war machine numerous Turkish clans of Khurasan and Central Asia. The majority of the warriors and field officers in the Mongol armies that attacked Persia were in fact Turks, many of them already Islamized. Thus the Mongol migration into the Middle East was in a sense a second Turkish one in disguise. The Mongol nobles depended on their Turkish allies to provide them with skilled clerks and officials to do much of the work of creating the new imperial government. Thus Muslims held positions of power and influence in the empire from the outset.

Having conquered Iran and Iraq, the Mongols suddenly found themselves the proprietors of an edifice of civilization far more complex and luxuriant than anything they had known before. Soon after Hulagu founded an autonomous Mongol state in Iran, known as the khanate of the Ilkhans (1258-1335), the mass carnage came to an end, towns dug themselves out, trade resumed, and the circulation of people was restored between the heartland and the prosperous Muslim cities around the fringe. Like their Seljuk predecessors in the eleventh century, the house of Genghis was quick to enlist the help of the Persian lettered elite, some of whom returned from abroad, to run the administration and collect taxes with efficiency. By the end of the thirteenth century, the Mongol rulers of Persia had converted to Islam and were successfully covering over their own work of mass contamination with new urban buildings and patronage of Islamic law and refined culture.

No single Persian city rivaled Cairo in the fourteenth century. But Tabriz, the Ilkhanid capital in Azerbaijan, arose as an important center of Persian crafts and international trade. In Sultaniyya, Shiraz, and several other towns, the Mongol period saw an effusion of creative production in architecture, textiles, ceramics, and miniature painting. The world of letters thrived again. It was under Ilkhanid patronage that Rashid al-Din, a Jewish convert to Islam and minister of state, completed, early in the fourteenth century, a work that must be regarded as the first truly universal history of mankind from genesis to the Mongol age: it embraced not only the whole of the Islamic world but also China, Byzantium, and even the recently civilized Frankish kingdoms of Europe.

Besides India and Asia Minor, the frontiers of the Dar al-Islam were being extended into the valley of the Volga River and the steppe lands north of the Black Sea through the conversion, early in the fourteenth century, of the khans of Kipchak, the Mongol successor kingdom later known as the Golden Horde. When, in the early 1330s, Ibn Battuta visited New Saray, the Kipchak capital on the Volga, he found a flourishing circle of Muslim jurists, Sufi mystics, physicians, and merchants. He counted 13 congregational mosques and numerous smaller ones. Another important center of Muslim faith and culture, already established before the Mongol Age, was at Bulghar, 800 miles up the river on the fringe of the Russian forests.

Neither Mongol nor Turkish power extended west of Egypt before 1500, but in North Africa (the Maghrib) the political pattern was not entirely different. There, in Ibn Battuta's time, Berber warrior aristocracies of Atlas Mountain or north Saharan origin ruled three kingdoms corresponding roughly in territory to the three modern states of Morocco, Algeria, and Tunisia. North of the Strait of Gibraltar, the little Muslim kingdom of Granada held out precariously against the powerful Christian states of Castille and Aragon. Indeed, the Iberian peninsula was the only region in the later Middle Ages where Islam was decidedly in retreat before a rival civilization.

As in the central lands, the Berber ruling classes of North Africa patronized Islamic learning and refined taste in the larger towns, whose prosperity rested on hinterland agriculture as well as the long-distance caravan trade running north and south between the Mediterranean and the gold fields of West Africa. In the fourteenth century Tunis and Fez were the most luminous centers of art and letters. Ibn Battuta would never have composed a book about his globetrotting experiences were it not for the insistent patronage of Abu Inan, a sultan of the Marinid dynasty who helped make Fez the leading intellectual center of western Islamdom.

THE CITY NETWORK

Most of Ibn Battuta's traveling took place during the twilight of the Pax Mongolica, when, despite the lingering economic effects of the barbarian storm, the movement of Muslims over immense distances was unusually intense. Newly civilized Mongol or Turkish rulers in the central lands stimulated travel by encouraging international trade and by luring famous scholars and craftsmen to their courts. Kings and princes in ruder, more peripheral areas of the Dar al-Islam worked even harder to attract to their capitals religious and literary personalities who would enhance their legitimacy and respect as defenders of the sacred law and proper civilized standards.

Ibn Battuta was a legal scholar of rather modest qualifications, but he was a member of the gentlemanly and learned class nonetheless. Therefore he traveled most of the time in comfort and style by accepting honors, gifts, and hospitality from Muslim rulers eager to display their sophistication and generosity to people of his status. It was common in that age for men with juridical, administrative, and literary skills to live in several different capitals over the span of their careers, holding well-paying positions as ministerial officials, judges, and courtiers. When Ibn Battuta visited Delhi in the 1330s, for example, the Turkish emperor of India was filling almost all senior governmental and religious posts with foreign Persian- or Arabic-speaking notables. Ibn Battuta was employed as a judge for about eight years and amassed considerable wealth in stipends and gifts.

The great physical mobility of Muslims was also a consequence of the political and legal character of cities. In Christian Europe in the Middle Ages, the ideal of town organization was to secure for its inhabitants special rights and obligations as against other towns, and especially to provide legal protection against arbitrary actions of the state. Towns aimed to become corporate entities in which people would cultivate exclusivist civic loyalties. In Islam, by contrast, the ideal was to have legal arrangements and social relations in all cities conform, insofar as possible, to the universalist norms of the shari'a. A visitor or a new resident should have essentially the same expectations about his personal status in one town as in another, no matter in which kingdom he happened to be.

The military governments of Muslim cities, whose job it was to maintain civil order and ensure tax collections, rarely invested more than the minimum in civic improvements. The task of making medieval towns reasonably livable was left to pious foundations, craft guilds, and voluntary associations, which supervised education, charities, and much public building. Lacking corporate legal protection, cities were extremely vulnerable to capricious, despotic treatment by unenlightened or greedy amirs. This political environment did not encourage long-term capital investment in industrial or agricultural technology. But because of their openness and the relative uniformity of legal and social norms, Muslim cities were well-suited to serve as the points for the exchange of goods, ideas, and skills from one end of the Afro-Eurasian intercommunicating zone to the other.

Cosmopolitan life was centered in three key urban institutions: the colleges (madrasas), Sufi centers (*khanqahs* or *zawiyas*), and the commercial hostels and warehouses (khans). The theological, legal, and linguistic curriculum of the madrasas was conservative, in the sense that the learned professors did not aim to sharpen the critical wits of students or to equip them to push the frontiers of knowledge beyond the limits of their elders but, rather, to transmit to the coming generation the spiritual truths, moral values, and social codes of the past—which, after all, appeared to be validated by the astounding success of Islam as both a religion and a system of social order. We should not, however, underestimate the extent of inquiry in the later Middle Ages into such fields as mathematics, astronomy, and medicine, which was often carried on privately or in institutions such as hospitals or observatories.

The most celebrated urban madrasas were international institutions, their classrooms and dormitories filled with teachers and pupils from far-flung places. In Islamic education the authority of the teacher who expounded a particular theological, juridical, or mystical text rested on the authenticity of the chain of learned masters extending back through time and linking him ultimately to the author of the text, or even to the Prophet. The ethnic or national origin of the teacher counted for very little. Kings, amirs, and rich merchants frequently founded colleges as pious endowments and then tried to attract to them reputable teachers from far and wide. Young scholars in search of advanced learning traveled to wherever the most celebrated masters were currently teaching.

The leading intellectual cities of the fourteenth century—Cairo, Damascus, Tunis, Mecca, and others—had dozens of madrasas. Everywhere, however, the curriculum was essentially the same, so that an African scholar from Timbuktu would find himself on familiar intellectual ground at a college in Konya, Anatolia, or Cambay, India. In that age almost all advanced teaching was done either in Arabic or in Persian, depending on the subject and the region. A traveling scholar armed with those two languages (Ibn Battuta was an Arabic speaker but picked up some Persian while living in Delhi) could make his way comfortably in refined circles anywhere between Gibraltar and the Bay of Bengal. It was through the madrasa system more than any other institution that literate Muslims developed their sharp consciousness of being citizens of the Dar al-Islam.

By Ibn Battuta's time Sufism was fully integrated into Sunni Islam as the mystical and speculative dimension of the faith. Sufi masters were often great theologians or jurists in their own right, but their primary mission was to offer the disciples who gathered around them the esoteric knowledge and ritual devotions by which they might eventually achieve a conscious personal unity with the Godhead. Though books on mysticism were taught in the madrasas, the centers of Sufi life were the khanqahs, where a *shaykh* (master) resided and where his adepts devoted themselves to his mystical "path" to God through prayer, study, ritual recitations, and feats of asceticism. A khanqah was also normally a charitable institution, feeding the poor and giving rest to wayfarers.

Ibn Battuta's century was the period when Sufi organization was becoming more formalized through the founding of associations of mystics, each grouped around a chain of master divines extending back to the founder. Several of the brotherhoods developed networks of khanqahs extending over wide areas of the Dar al-Islam. An individual might travel from one end of the Islamic world to the other, finding his supper and a bed almost every night in a Sufi lodge, whether a rustic hilltop hermitage or a grandly appointed urban khanqah. Ibn Battuta was an eminently worldy man, not at all inclined to a life of self-denial. He visited scores of Sufi centers in the course of his travels, however, and on occasion took time out, as members of the scholarly and official classes often did, to spend a month or so in contemplation and study with some well-known Sufi sage.

Any Muslim town on a trade route had a khan, or facility where merchants might stay and store or exchange their goods. In major cities, or sometimes even in the countryside, these hostels might be huge and splendidly decorated structures built around a central courtyard, with rooms on the ground floor for housing wares and animals and rooms upstairs for lodging merchants. For example, a khan in Cairo for Syrian merchants had 360 sleeping rooms and enough space for 4,000 guests at a time. When Ibn Battuta traveled across the rural interior of Anatolia in the early 1330s, he had the pleasure of lodging in grand, comfortable caravansaries built at government expense to facilitate both military administration and trade. The most elaborate of these khans had massive, ornately carved portals, great covered halls, facilities for bathing, and in some cases a small mosque.

Dominating the center of the Afro-Eurasian intercommunicating zone, the core cities of Islam were the entrepôts in the ever more complex long-distance trade ultimately linking Western Europe and the Mediterranean basin with China. Islam's command of the great trunk lines that passed through the Middle East, together with its moral rejection of fixed social statuses and legalized inequalities, produced a highly cosmopolitan outlook among the merchants, caravanners, and ship's captains who frequented the khans. Such men often ranged over great distances to buy and sell. Ibn Battuta reports that when he visited China, he met a merchant-scholar who had come there from Ceuta, a Moroccan port on the Mediterranean. A few years later, while passing through Sijilmasa on the northern fringe of the Sahara, he made the acquaintance of the man's brother.

In the overland trade Muslim merchants controlled a web of routes that began in the gold and ivory emporiums of Sudanic West Africa and extended across North Africa and the Middle East to the Chinese frontiers of inner Asia. For a time the Mongol holocaust disrupted long-distance traffic on the famous "silk road" across Central Asia. But even as Genghis Khan and his successors destroyed cities to achieve their immediate military objectives, they promoted trade through their domains as soon as the fighting was over. Moreover, they allowed merchants of all nations to move more freely across Asia than was the case either earlier or later.

Western education has conventionally taught that the Polo family and other intrepid Italians were the principal beneficiaries of this policy—indeed, that they in some way "opened" Asia. In fact, Muslim traders took even greater advantage of Mongol internationalism to extend their business deeper into the steppe lands and to the agrarian towns of northern China. When the great Mongol states disintegrated about the middle of the fourteenth century, Muslim overland operations remained largely in place east of the Black Sea, while Frankish traders were once again shut out.

Between the eleventh and thirteenth centuries, however, European shipping and navies invaded the Mediterranean and Black seas and achieved almost total commercial dominance. This seaborne offensive took place within the wider context of Europe's spectacular economic revival, the rise of the Italian city-states, and the long, unsuccessful assault of Frankish crusader-knights on Palestine. The drastic retreat of the fighting galleys and trading vessels of Muslim powers from the Mediterranean may be explained ultimately by a fact of nature: dwindling forest lands along the southern and eastern rim of the sea produced a chronic shortage of timber for shipbuilding, whereas the European states of the northern shore had unlimited supplies. (Western hegemony was temporary, however, for the Ottoman Turks regained naval superiority in the eastern Mediterranean in the later fifteenth century, drawing on timber supplies from Anatolia and the Black Sea rim.)

Muslim traders dominated the Indian Ocean, especially the western half, throughout the Middle Ages. Their ascendancy there from Abbasid times is partly to be explained by Eurasian geography—the central position of the Middle East in funneling goods between the Mediterranean and the spice and silk lands by way of either the Red Sea or the Persian Gulf. But equally important was the ease with which Muslim merchants set themselves up in alien territories from the East Indies to the coast of Mozambique. The shari'a, the legal foundation on which they erected their communities and mercantile enterprises, traveled with them wherever they want, irrespective of any particular political or bureaucratic authority. Moreover, a place in the commercial community of the Indian Ocean was open to any young man of ambition and intelligence, whatever his ethnic identity, as long as he was first willing to declare for God and the Prophet.

In the Abbasid era, Arab and Iranian Sindbads had carried on direct sea trade in lateen-rigged ships between the Persian Gulf and the south coast of China. By Ibn Battuta's time, however, growth in the volume and variety of southern seas trade had given rise to an interlocking network of multinational, cooperative associations of Muslim merchants—not only Arabs and Persians but also East Africans, Gujaratis, south Indians, Bengalis, and Malays—that relayed goods along sea routes that ultimately linked China with the coastlands of the North Sea.

No kingdom or commercial corporation, however, made a sustained attempt to seize control of sea-lanes and ports through armed force, as the Portuguese would do in the sixteenth century. The navies of the Muslim seafaring states rimming the ocean were small and employed mainly in defending shipping against pirates. The fluid, informal, relatively peaceful character of commercial interchange encouraged the spread of a shared cosmopolitan outlook among the inhabitants of almost all the busy ports from the Strait of Malacca west. In largely non-Muslim areas—Malaysia, south India, and East Africa—substantial conversions took place in coastal towns, and Sufis and men of letters extended their own webs of international affiliation throughout the trading region.

THE CONTINUITY OF ISLAMIC EXPANSION

Ibn Battuta was lucky to have returned home to retirement when he did, for the second half of the fourteenth century was a time of troubles for most of the Islamic lands. Political instability among Turkish and Berber ruling classes became much more evident. The Mongol states contracted or, in Persia and China, collapsed altogether. The region from Iraq to India experienced a new period of state fragmentation and kaleidoscopic political change. Between 1346 and 1350 the Black Death, a darker consequence of the ease and intensity of interregional communication, spread across the Afro-Eurasian agrarian zone from China to Europe, killing millions. Cairo, for example, may have lost 200,000 souls out of a total population of around 500,000 in the space of several months in 1348-49. Killing far more people than the Mongols did even in the years of their worst excesses, the plague appears to have accelerated the long-term economic contraction of the Islamic heartland and exacerbated the problems of political and social stability. The century ended on an equally woeful note when Tamerlane (Timur the Lame), the last of the great steppe captains, attempted to re-create a Mongol Empire by leading his armies on a rampage of destruction through the Middle East and India. His imperial dream quickly foundered, but not before he had dealt urban life in the core region another ruinous blow.

Yet Islam came out of the catastrophes of the later fourteenth century with the expansionary energies of Ibn Battuta's time undiminished. On the fringes of the Dar al-Islam, notably in the East Indies and the savanna lands south of the Sahara, the small establishments of Muslim merchants, scholars, and Sufis continued in the fifteenth century to introduce to Africans and Malaysians not only a new set of devotions but also the full range of institutions—mosques, colleges, law codes, and Sufi khanqahs—through which the Islamic model of civilization gradually became dominant. By the time of the European overseas explorations of the sixteenth century, both of these regions were on their way to being fully incorporated into the Dar al-Islam and the faith was continuing to make headway in such areas as East Africa, Central Asia, Bengal, and the southern Philippines.

In the central lands Tamerlane may have signaled the end of the era of steppe conquests, but the Age of the Turk was far from over. Indeed, Turkish military power entered a new phase in the fifteenth century when the Ottoman state, a modest Muslim principality of western Anatolia when Ibn Battuta saw it in the 1330s, succeeded in defeating all rival sultanates, incorporated them under a centralized administration, and organized Turkish cavalrymen to an unprecedented level of efficiency. Adopting firearms technology, building a navy, and employing bureaucratic methods in both government and army that were far removed from the tribal traditions of the steppe, the Ottomans went on to defeat and extinguish the Byzantine Empire (1453), expand into the Balkans, and reassert Muslim naval supremacy in the Black and Aegean seas. Thus the fifteenth century saw a continuation in mightier form of the Turkish expansionary drive that began with the Seljuks in the eleventh century.

After 1500, Turko-Mongol elites in Iran and India would follow the Ottoman example, pursuing innovations in armaments and administration to create two new empires, the Safavid and the Mughal, respectively. This tripartite consolidation of the entire Islamic region from the eastern Mediterranean to the Bay of Bengal brought to an end a century and a half of political fragmentation and flux in the central lands, and set the stage for a new prospering of Islamic trade, industry, urban life, and refined culture, paralleling in time Europe's portentous entry into the wider Afro-Eurasian scene.

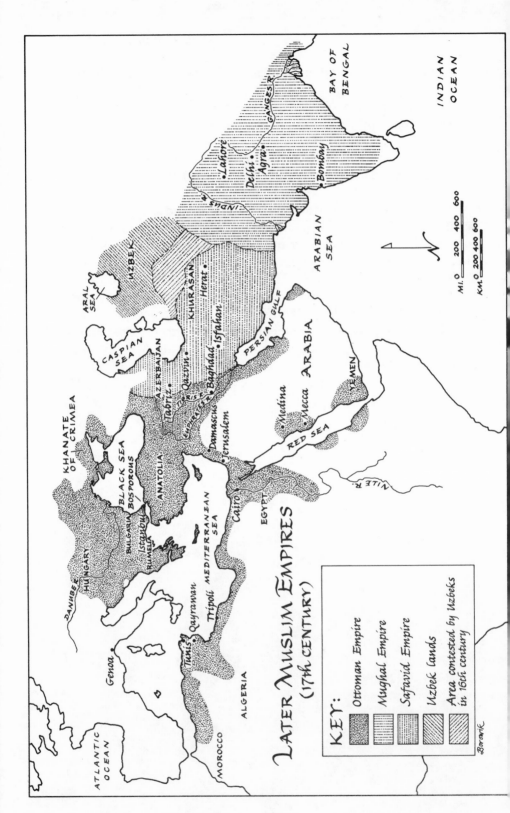

LATER MUSLIM EMPIRES
(17th CENTURY)

KEY:

Ottoman Empire

Mughal Empire

Safavid Empire

Uzbek Lands

Area contested by Uzbeks
in 16th century

Boravik

ATLANTIC
OCEAN

MOROCCO

ALGERIA

Genoa

Tunis

Qayrawan

Tripoli

MEDITERRANEAN
SEA

HUNGARY

DANUBE

BULGARIA

Istanbul

RUMELIA

BOSPORUS

BLACK SEA

ANATOLIA

KHANATE
OF CRIMEA

CASPIAN
SEA

ARAL
SEA

UZBEK

Tabriz

Qazvin

AZERBAIJAN

TIGRIS R.

EUPHRATES

Baghdad

Isfahan

KHURASAN

Herat

Damascus

Jerusalem

Cairo

EGYPT

NILE R.

RED SEA

Medina

Mecca

ARABIA

YEMEN

ARABIAN
SEA

PERSIAN GULF

Delhi

Agra

Lahore

INDUS

INDIA

GANGES R.

Bombay

BAY OF
BENGAL

INDIAN
OCEAN

MI. 0   200 400 600

KM. 0 200 400 600

N

112

6

The Later Muslim Empires: Ottomans, Safavids, Mughals

I. Metin Kunt

BEGINNINGS OF MODERN HISTORY

In terms of the history of Europe, the turn of the sixteenth century is a period of quickened change that signified the end of medieval society and the emergence of the modern age. This was a multifaceted transformation: the renaissance in culture and the reformation in Christianity were accompanied by new political, social, and economic arrangements. The feudal order of the Middle Ages gave way to relatively centralized kingdoms in England, France, and Spain, and in the Hapsburg domains in Central Europe. The new scientific spirit and technological outlook that emerged during the transformation facilitated, in turn, the medieval breakdown, as Gutenberg's printing press educated the burghers, merchants, and the king's bureaucrats, and as the newly fashioned cannon helped kings' armies batter feudal fortresses. Indeed, what made the age truly revolutionary was that each aspect of the transformation reinforced the others and was itself sustained by them.

Had this transformation been a purely European affair, mention of it would not have opened this discussion of Islamic history in the early modern period. But an integral aspect of the Renaissance in Europe was the voyages of maritime exploration and discovery. Financed by monarchs and merchants, these voyages were undertaken by captains sure in their belief in a spherical world, armed with the compass and other instruments of navigation as well as cannons and muskets, and commanding seaworthy vessels able to withstand the dangers of the mighty oceans. In the space of a few decades at the turn of the sixteenth century, the seamen of Atlantic Europe found a way to reach south Asia around Africa, stumbled

113

upon the continent they named America, and achieved the tremendous feat of circumnavigating the globe. In some lands, such as Africa and America, these seamen and soldiers, clad in armor and brandishing muskets, found their way to plunder and colonize. Elsewhere, in most parts of Asia, they had to be more circumspect. They were by and large content to establish trading posts; nevertheless, they also attempted to disrupt existing mercantile arrangements and to divert a growing portion of interregional trade to the oceanic routes they discovered and patrolled.

This was not the first attempt on the part of the Europeans to cross their boundaries. Medieval Europeans, too, made remarkable attempts to conquer and colonize that involved enormous numbers of people. Massive Crusader armies marched to the Holy Land from the eleventh to the thirteenth centuries; the Teutonic Knights, who also took part in the Crusading effort, staged a new push toward Eastern Europe in the thirteenth century; Italian sailors, the predecessors of Christopher Columbus of Genoa, honed their skills in the Mediterranean and the Black Sea from the eleventh century on. Such medieval attempts at expansion, however, met with only limited success, if not failure. In contrast, European oceanic exploits led to even greater involvement with the rest of the world in the succeeding centuries. Thus, the passage of Europe from its medieval past also marked a worldwide modern age. To be sure, it was only after the Industrial Revolution, at the turn of the nineteenth century, that European maritime contact with Asian polities turned to domination and the great colonial age began. Nevertheless, the sixteenth-century European voyages marked the beginning of a world united by means of a network of oceanic routes managed by Europeans with their cannon-bearing galleons. In this sense modern history is truly universal history.

The three centuries from the voyages of Vasco da Gama, Christopher Columbus, and Magellan to the American and French revolutions and the dawn of the industrial-technological age, a span of time termed the early modern period, is one during which Islam, too, flourished. Indeed, the turn of the sixteenth century marks a fresh start, a realignment of social and political forces within the Islamic world, although this new Muslim age did not prove as revolutionary as the contemporary European transformation. The theme of this chapter is this internal reorganization of Muslim societies. We shall see that the major preoccupation of Muslim powers of the early modern period was perceived in their own terms, involving a reconciliation of their different heritages within new imperial polities. In other words, the rise of European power and the European maritime network was a secondary consideration, except perhaps in the case of the Ottoman Empire. However, by the end of our period of study, all Muslim polities were to experience internal difficulties of varying degrees of gravity. In the late eighteenth century it was these internally weakened Muslim states that had to face an ever stronger Europe determined to impose its order on the rest of the world. Thereafter, the policies of Muslim rulers of necessity took on the character of responses to European encroachment.

TURKO-MONGOL DOMINATION OF MUSLIM LANDS

The fourteenth-century world through which Ibn Battuta, the indefatigable and observant Maghribi traveler, roamed was one united by the common Muslim heritage: a learned man like Ibn Battuta could tour the length and breadth of it and sojourn in various parts without a sense of cultural and social alienation. Politically, however, it was a fragmented society. The ideal of a coextensive Muslim state and society, approached in the days of the Abbasid universal caliphate, had been abandoned, even in theory, after the Mongol irruption. Political authority in all parts of the world of Islam, except in Ibn Battuta's homeland in the far west and in the sultanates of Southeast Asia, was in the hands of the descendants of the Turco-Mongol invaders of the Arab-Persian heartlands. Turks were already Muslims when they arrived in western Asia; Mongols in Islamic lands had converted by the turn of the fourteenth century. Furthermore, these new Muslim powers had extended the boundaries of Islam into the Ukraine, into Anatolia and the Balkan peninsula, and into India. In their conversion to Islam, however, they had retained a separate identity, bringing with them inner Asian notions of political and military organization.

In the steppes of Eurasia the Turks and the Mongols had been nomads: the states they formed had been confederations of clans gathered around a warrior leader. Sometimes, when the steppe people were united under an exceptionally capable leader, he would be able to direct the energies of his followers toward domination over neighboring sedentary societies. Such a world conqueror was graced, in Asian eyes, with heaven's mandate for universal rule. Following the example of the Huns and the Turks of earlier times, Genghis Khan's Mongol Empire of the thirteenth century was the steppe's last attempt at world domination.

An instability inherent in the steppe political conception led to a disintegration almost as swift as the creation of such empires. The ruler's whole family shared political authority: brothers and sons were assigned portions of the territory as appanages. At the ruler's death, succession to his position was by acclamation of the leading clan aristocrats; any able member of the family could aspire to the throne. Often the ambitious family members had difficulty accepting the choice of the confederation assembly. The newly elected khan then had to bring the dissenters back to the fold by force of arms. Even when the khan was able to reunite his followers, success, after virtual civil war, was costly. Often the result was a permanent rupture, with several rival khans vying for supreme succession.

Genghis Khan's huge empire, enlarged in succeeding generations, was soon divided into four major sections. Of the original four sections, the Golden Horde in western Eurasia, the Chagatay khanate in central Asia, and the Ilkhans in southwest Asia became Muslim and linguistically Turkified, while the fourth ruled the original homeland in Mongolia as well as China, as the increasingly sinified Yuan dynasty. In the thirteenth century Kublai Khan in Peking was the great khan, and the Ilkhans of Iran paid him their respects. In the following century, however, the four portions of the great empire were totally separate and the regional Ilkhans, too, underwent disintegration in their turn.

In the late fourteenth century there arose a new warrior leader at Samarkand in Turkestan: this was Tamerlane (Timur, in Turkish), with a claim to descent, through marriage, from the illustrious Genghis Khan and a mission to re-create his predecessor's world empire on an Islamic basis. Through his conquests Tamerlane united the former territories of the Chagatays and the Ilkhans; he further campaigned into Muslim (northern) India and into Golden Horde domains. At his death in 1405, he was planning the conquest of China. He was a worthy successor to Genghis Khan's ideal of world domination; nevertheless, the fate of his empire was no different. In the course of the fifteenth century there emerged various states in the Muslim world, from India to the Balkans, all with a Turkic military ruling group. These were regional states, successful for a limited time and with limited scope, alluding neither to the Islamic ideal of the political unity of the umma, the community of Muslims, nor to the steppe ideal of universal domination.

What makes the early sixteenth century significant in terms of Muslim history is that at that point, we can discern the emergence of a new stability, a new alignment of durable political organizations that lasted for some centuries. During this time the major regions of Islam were divided among the vast Ottoman Empire in the west, the Safavid Empire in the middle, and the Mughal Empire in India. A similar polity existed in Central Asia, ruled by the Uzbeks, descendants of the Golden Horde. Otherwise there were indigenous dynasties in Morocco and in the petty sultanates of Southeast Asia. Our present focus will be on the great empires that ruled over the overwhelming majority of Muslims.

THE RISE OF THE MUSLIM EMPIRES

The great Muslim empires of the early modern period and the Uzbek state shared certain characteristics and predicaments. At the same time each exhibited a new and different synthesis of their common Turco-Mongol political heritage and the Arabo-Persian cultural and religious milieu of Islam. Also, each joined Europe in the use of gunpowder and firearms by their armies, with the similar results that gunpowder armies both necessitated and facilitated the development of centralized power. The Uzbek state in Central Asia remained closest to the steppe heritage geographically, and therefore also culturally and politically, so that a strong central bureaucracy never developed. After 1600, Uzbek power was divided among rival khanates of Bukhara, Khokand, and Khiva. The Ottomans and the Mughals both ruled over large non-Muslim populations. The secular regulations of state (*qanun*) and the impartial justice of the dynasty in both empires appealed to Muslim as well as non-Muslim subjects. An articulated bureaucracy was created in each to extend the power of the state throughout the realm.

In contrast, the Safavid problem lay in achieving the harmonious coexistence of the mostly Persian-speaking sedentary subjects and the large groups of Turkic nomadic horsemen who supplied the dynasty's military might. The divisions in Safavid society were thus in language and life-style, not religion. The solution devised by the Safavid dynasty was unity in Shi'ism, personified by the shah and installed as the official state religion. The Safavid state thus not only attempted internal integration of its social components, but also distinguished itself from its Sunni neighbors: the Ottomans, Uzbeks, and Mughals.

A further element distinguished the Ottomans from the other Muslim powers. By virtue of its position in Asia, Europe, and Africa, the Ottoman Empire was European and Mediterranean as much as it was Asian and Muslim. The traditional land-based steppe military organization that had already become more centralized with the use of muskets and artillery needed, in the case of the Ottomans, to be augmented with a navy in order to be able to control the Black Sea and to vie for supremacy in the Mediterranean, and even in the Indian Ocean, with European navies. In Europe, Ottoman power extended as far as Hungary. Ottoman policy influenced both economic life in Central Europe, through trade relations, and the course of the Reformation, by aiding the rise of Protestantism. Ottomans encouraged Protestant movements in Transylvania, an area under their suzerainty, and in the Netherlands; they also welcomed closer ties with England. In all cases Ottoman policy was guided by a desire to counter Catholic Hapsburg power in Spain and Austria. The Ottoman Empire thus was involved in European affairs and diplomacy, and was open to the effects of the great European transformation to a much greater degree than were the other Muslim powers. The similarities and contrasts that have been sketched here very briefly will become clearer as we trace the careers of the Ottomans, the Safavids, and the Mughals in the following sections.

OTTOMAN CONQUESTS

The Ottoman state was the oldest of the three empires, and the longest-lived. It was also, in contrast with the others, established in western Anatolia and southeast Europe, an area newly gained for Islam. Conquest of non-Muslim territories remained its major policy and a source of pride. The state took its name from the first independent leader, Osman Bey, who, at the turn of the fourteenth century, gathered under his banner a band of frontiersmen on the Seljuk-Byzantine borderlands in northwestern Anatolia. His companions and followers included Turkoman tribesmen, Byzantine captains and lords, Muslim-Turkish and Christian peasants. Taking advantage of the weakness of the Byzantines and protected by the distance from the centers of Ilkhan power in Azerbaijan, though mindful of Mongol power, Osman Bey expanded his tiny territory to include nearby villages and towns. As his rule was extended, the number of his followers increased—and thus emerged the "nation of Osman."

The Ottomans were only one of a dozen or so frontier principalities that emerged with the influx of Turkish nomads and Mongols into Anatolia. What distinguished them from their peers was that by the middle of the fourteenth century, they controlled the shores of the Dardanelles, and thus the passage across this narrow body of water to Europe. The ghazi frontiersmen of Anatolia joined the Ottoman enterprise in ever greater numbers as new conquests pushed the frontier toward the Danube, across Bulgaria, Macedonia, and Greece. By the end of the century, the Ottomans ruled over most of the Balkan peninsula as well as Anatolia, where other Turkish ghazi principalities joined them. They had conquered almost the whole of the Byzantine Empire and, to signify their claim to succession to the emperor's position, they styled themselves "Sultans of Rum," rulers of the lands of the Romans.

Mehmet II, the seventh Ottoman ruler, came to be known by his subjects and throughout the Islamic world as "the Conqueror" after Constantinople, the capital of the Byzantines, succumbed to Ottoman might in 1453. This was an accomplishment that had eluded the early Muslim caliphs and the all-conquering armies of Islam. It had remained, since the seventh century, a dream to be fulfilled by "a glorious commander and his auspicious troops," in words attributed to Muhammad.

The conquest of Constantinople, called colloquially Istanbul by both Greeks and Turks, supplied the Ottomans with a natural capital uniting the European and Anatolian halves of their state. Istanbul stands at the junction of Europe and Asia, separated by the Bosporus. In Ottoman times elegant rowing boats ferried Istanbulis from one continent to the other. (Since 1973 a graceful suspension bridge has united the two parts of the city as well as the European and Asian cultural worlds.) Istanbul also had a superb natural harbor in the fabled Golden Horn, a deep inlet that divided the European part of the city. Istanbul proper, with the majestic St. Sophia and the sublime Topkapi Palace, lay south of the Golden Horn, while the northern shore was the realm of European trading communities. As the city joined two continents, so the Bosporus flowed from the Black Sea through the Sea of Marmara and the Dardanelles toward the Mediterranean. With their mastery over the city, the Ottomans were destined to become a naval power. The strategic significance of the city is reflected in one of the epithets of the sultans, "the lord of two lands and of two seas."

The feat of the conquest itself indicates something of the enterprising spirit of Mehmet II and his armies. To batter the walls of Constantinople, the greatest cannon the world had known were cast under the supervision of a Hungarian master in Ottoman employ. The Byzantine defenders had stretched an enormous chain across the entrance of the Golden Horn to prevent Ottoman shipborne cannon from attacking the weaker sea walls. Mehmet the Conqueror countered by carrying his ships overland one night. It was with such determination, competence, and ingenuity that this epochal event was accomplished.

In 1453 the old Byzantine capital was a mere shadow of its former glorious self. It had never fully recovered from the plunder of the Crusaders in 1204. To restore its grandeur and majesty, Mehmet II undertook the settlement of Turkish, Greek, Armenian, and Jewish subjects from his other cities. The sultan and his chief ministers established pious foundations in all quarters of the city, with mosques, colleges, alms kitchens, baths, shops, and stores to revive the social, cultural, and economic life of the new capital. These buildings, in the distinct and new Ottoman style of architecture developed in the earlier capitals, Bursa and Edirne, gave the city a definitely Islamic and Ottoman flavor. The most famous scholars and artists of Islam were invited and encouraged with lavish largess to make their homes in Istanbul. The sultan's cultural horizon included Renaissance Europe as well: Gentile Bellini came from Italy to paint a portrait of Mehmet the Conqueror and to train palace painters in the new Italian techniques. There was word that Leonardo da Vinci might come to build a bridge across the Golden Horn. Istanbul was thus once again becoming a magnificent imperial city, famed in the East and West.

Mehmet II's successors added their own edifices to their capital to give it one of the most celebrated skylines in the world today, a harmony of high cupolas punctuated by graceful minarets reaching to the sky. Istanbul, with a population of more than 500,000, was the largest city in Europe in the sixteenth century (when London and Paris were both below 200,000), and it ruled territories from Budapest in Hungary to Baghdad in Iraq, from Algiers in North Africa to the Caspian Sea. Ottoman armies besieged Vienna in 1529 and made conquests in Europe as well as in Asia. Ottoman fleets patrolled the Black Sea and the Red Sea, defeated an allied European navy in the Mediterranean in 1534 at the Battle of Preveza, and vied with the Portuguese in the Indian Ocean. It was thus already a power with worldwide branches when its Muslim rivals were emerging in the early sixteenth century.

THE SAFAVID SYNTHESIS

The Safavid state sprang from very different origins. The Ottoman state and dynasty were named after Osman Bey, a leader of ghazi frontiersmen. The Safavid name refers to Shaykh Safi, a contemporary of Osman Bey and a Sufi leader who established a mystic brotherhood in Azerbaijan near the Caspian shore in the early years of the fourteenth century. For almost 200 years, while the Ottomans grew into a significant state, the Safavids prospered as a Sufi order. As leaders of the brotherhood, the descendants of Shaykh Safi were particularly revered by the Turkish tribesmen in Azerbaijan and eastern Anatolia. After Tamerlane's empire had disintegrated, several Turkoman dynasties had attempted to establish their rule in its former territories.

The Safavid Sufi shaykhs were related by marriage to the Akkoyunlu, the most prominent of such Turkoman states, in western Iran and eastern Anatolia. The great Akkoyunlu leader Hasan Padishah (or Uzun Hasan, his sobriquet) challenged the Ottomans in 1473 but, in spite of his superb cavalry force, he was defeated by superior Ottoman firearms. After Hasan Padishah returned to his domains in disgrace, and as his successors battled each other in steppe fashion, the Safavid shaykhs turned decidedly political. Resolved to capture the Akkoyunlu throne for themselves, they issued appeals to their followers to incite them to action under Safavid saintly leadership.

Akkoyunlu attempts to contain the politicization of the brotherhood and to keep the family leaders under surveillance eventually failed. Safavid followers, kept alert by a network of Sufi propagandists, rushed to join their leader, the young Shaykh Isma'il. After routing an Akkoyunlu army in Azerbaijan in 1501, Isma'il went on swiftly to conquer all of Iran, Iraq, and the rest of the Akkoyunlu lands in eastern Anatolia. With Isma'il, the Safavid skaykhs became shahs of Iran.

The Safavid appeal to Turkish tribesmen was an impassioned one: Shah Isma'il was venerated as a saintly, almost godlike, figure. Especially to the proud tribesmen living under Ottoman rule in Anatolia or Mamluk rule in Syria, subjected to restrictions, regulations, and tax assessments, Shah Isma'il appeared almost as a savior. He held out the promise of a new order in which the tribesmen would once again be the honored mainstays of the state. Many Turks from Anatolia and Syria joined him and proudly wore the traditional Turkoman red cap, which had become the Safavid symbol, under their turbans. Called *qizilbash* (red heads) with derision and contempt by the Ottomans, such adherents of the new shah threatened to undermine the stability and integrity of Ottoman Anatolia.

To protect his domains from the inroads of Safavid propagandists, the Ottoman Sultan Selim I rounded up all suspected Safavid sympathizers and had them executed as heretics, then marched against the Safavid cavalry massed in eastern Anatolia. At Chaldiran in 1514, Shah Isma'il's valiant horsemen were routed by the well-ordered and well-trained Ottoman troops using muskets and field artillery. This was a defensive victory for the Ottomans: the Safavid capital, Tabriz, was entered but could not be held; the Ottoman army returned to its base in Istanbul; the Safavid danger had been contained but not destroyed.

The Safavid-Ottoman duel continued for more than a century, but the borders were drawn fairly early in the struggle and remained quite constant: Tabriz and Azerbaijan remained in Safavid hands; the Ottomans held eastern Anatolia and Iraq, including Baghdad and Basra. While Ottoman conquest turned to Syria and Egypt (1517), and later to Europe again, the Safavids were engaged in another rivalry in Khurasan and Turkestan against the Uzbek khans.

Once Shah Isma'il formed a new Turkoman state, he had to face the internal problem, a constant in Iran since the establishment of the Seljuk state in the eleventh century, of achieving the integration of his qizilbash tribal followers and the Farsi (Persian)-speaking population of his cities and villages. The solution was the swift and forceful installation of Shi'ism as the Safavid state religion. In the eyes of the "red head" Turkomans, Shah Isma'il was a saintly and valiant leader of the Sufi brotherhood to which they all belonged. In brotherhoods such as the Safavid and the Bektashi, widespread in Ottoman lands from Anatolia to the Balkans, with an appeal primarily to Turkish tribesmen and peasants (in contrast with such urban and high-culture brotherhoods as the Mevlevi), Ali, the fourth caliph and the first Imam of Shi'ism, had a special place and significance. Many other typically Shi'i ideas and practices had also permeated the ceremonies and hymns of such brotherhoods. Shah Isma'il claimed descent from the caliph Ali and the Prophet; in other words, he asserted a spiritual dimension to his leadership that would also be meaningful to his Persian subjects, forcibly converted to Shi'ism.

Before the establishment of the Safavid state, Shi'ism had been the minority belief in Iran as elsewhere in the Islamic world. The conversion of Safavid subjects was rapid and remarkably effective. To this day Shi'ism remains the strongest bond that unifies the people of Iran, whatever their ethnic, linguistic, and social backgrounds may be. Indeed, in the modern age of nationalism, Iranian nationalism is of necessity defined in terms of Shi'ism, with obvious implications for present-day Iran. Nevertheless, the dichotomy between the qizilbash Sufi followers of the Safavid shahs and the Shi'i subjects also remained a source of friction that was gradually resolved in the seventeenth century when the Shi'i ulama definitely gained the upper hand vis-à-vis the Sufi propagandists of the brotherhood. This development seems to have been connected with the deliberate attempt during the reign of Shah Abbas the Great (r. 1588-1629) to strengthen the central institutions of the state (an important subject to which we shall return).

The center of the Safavid brotherhood was in Ardabil, a small town in eastern Azerbaijan near the Caspian Sea. Ardabil remained the spiritual center for the qizilbash but Shah Isma'il's political capital was Tabriz, the greatest city in Azerbaijan. However, Tabriz was not only dangerously close to Ottoman territories but also was far from the other centers of the Safavid realm. Later in the sixteenth century, after Tabriz had been sacked twice by the Ottomans, Qazvin, southeast of Tabriz, became the capital. It was still close to the original power base of the dynasty but somewhat removed from immediate Ottoman threat. Shah Abbas I moved the capital once again, this time to Isfahan in the central plateau.

Culturally and artistically the Safavids were heirs to the brilliance of the Timuri court in Herat. During the sixteenth century Safavid court artists in Tabriz elevated the arts of the book, miniature painting, and calligraphy to unsurpassed levels. The achievements of Safavid miniature painters in intellectual conception, refinement of execution, and brilliance of color were also admired in Ottoman and Mughal domains. When Shah Tahmasp sent an embassy to Istanbul in 1574 to congratulate Murad III on his accession, among all his priceless gifts the one considered the most valuable by the Ottomans was a beautifully illustrated *Shahname (Book of Kings,* the greatest Persian epic). Safavid artists sometimes accepted employment in Indian and Ottoman courts and influenced the course of artistic development there as well.

Isfahan painters at the court of Shah Abbas further developed the tradition of the great Tabriz school in new directions. Perhaps even more important than the arts of the book during the great shah's reign was his architectural program aimed at elevating his new capital to the ranks of the greatest cities of the world. An enormous space in the center of the city served as public park, polo fields, and parade grounds. Along one side was the imperial palace; two major mosques and a great covered bazaar also faced on the park. The brilliantly colored and intricately designed ceramic tile decorations of the facades and the domes of these edifices dazzled visitors and merchants from Europe as well as from the world of Islam.

THE MUGHAL GRANDEUR

The Ottomans represent a polity based on continued conquest of non-Muslim territory, though along the way they also extended their rule over older Muslim lands of the Mediterranean basin. The Safavids achieved a new synthesis of the Muslim population of the heartlands. As for the Mughal Empire, it was established in northern India, where Arab, Turkish, and Afghan Muslim conquerors had already held sway for centuries. The new emperors went on to unite almost the whole of the subcontinent under their rule. Giving a significant role in their administration to Hindus as well as Muslims, they established an efficient and effective government that was able to extend justice and prosperity to all its subjects. The cultural and material richness of India in this period was so impressive that the name of the dynasty, in the slightly altered form "mogul," became a byword for power and splendor.

Mughal rule was first established in the 1520s by Babur, a descendant of the great Tamerlane; but the struggle to wrest control from the previous Muslim and Rajput (Hindu) lords of India in fact went on for some decades and occupied all of his son Humayun's troubled reign. The third ruler of the dynasty, Akbar, finally succeeded in defeating all rivals and installed, during his long reign (1556-1605), the foundations of the stable government of his realm.

Before the coming of Babur and his family to Delhi, northern India had been ruled by several Turkish and Afghan dynasties since the eleventh century. The Muslim conquerors, however, had remained aloof from the Hindu population they ruled, almost as a new caste of conquering rulers in the layered society of India. It was only in the fourteenth century, more than 300 years after the first Muslim administration had been installed, that a Hindu general achieved the rank of commander in this "caste" of Turkish warriors.

Akbar's task was to extend his unified rule over an area much greater than had ever been conquered by a Muslim state in India and to achieve a much higher degree of social and political integration between his Hindu subjects and Muslim commanders. After uniting the lands already under Muslim rule in northern India, Akbar turned his military and diplomatic skills to the belt of territory in the hands of Rajput lords, Hindu warrior-princes. Many Rajputs joined Akbar's entourage as trusted and honored generals. In exchange for giving up independence in an insignificant domain, they gained the prestige reflected from the glory of the great emperor. For Akbar's part, his gain in including unconverted Hindu commanders among the ranks of his Muslim officers was the extension of his rule.

In an attempt to achieve the highest degree of dynastic justice toward all his subjects, Akbar went so far as to abolish the *jizya*, the personal tax paid by non-Muslim subjects, so that his Hindu and Muslim subjects were now equal in their obligations to the state. Following procedures established by an earlier Muslim ruler who had been his father's rival, Akbar also regularized and standardized the subjects' tax obligations. The state's dues were not necessarily light but they were predictable, not arbitrary; furthermore, collection was lenient, for it took into consideration acts of nature that might affect the peasants' ability to pay.

In addition to the village and the army camp, the emperor's court was a means of integration. The dominant intellectual currents in Akbar's palace favored harmony between Hindus and Muslims, not only in social and political terms but in purely religious ones as well. In Indian Islam, as in Ottoman and Safavid domains, Sufism rather than a strict ulama interpretation was prevalent. Again as in the Ottoman experience, Sufi teachers with their tolerant outlook facilitated conversion of non-Muslims. At Akbar's court the universal spirit of Sufism tended to transcend religious differences, to promote greater understanding of the beliefs of different groups. Akbar was deeply interested in religious issues and heard the views of learned men of various traditions, apparently with the conviction that God's Way is one though its manifestations may be different.

This syncretic spirit was not popular with all Muslims, nor with all Sufis. The Naqshbandi Brotherhood, especially, was of a much more conservative outlook. For them the question was not so much coexistence or harmony with Hindus but the creation of a self-consciously and deliberately Islamic state and society. The dominance of Islam required that non-Muslims be relegated to a secondary place in society, not treated as equals in the councils of state or in the army camp. In the course of the seventeenth century such orthodox notions gradually gained ground, as they did in the other Muslim empires. The broad base of Akbar's regime eroded during the reigns of his successors. Even as the Mughal Empire reached its territorial zenith under Avrangzib (r. 1658-1707), it became an empire ruled by Muslims. The jizya was reintroduced; this time it was collected even from Hindus in the emperor's armies.

Perhaps because of the tolerant spirit developed under Akbar and continued until the reign of Avrangzib, the highest expressions of Mughal art were secular in character. Even in architecture the grandest and most brilliant examples were not mosques but forts, palaces, and imperial cities. The most famous edifice of Mughal architecture, the Taj Mahal, may resemble a mosque in conception, but it is the tomb of the beloved wife of Shah Jahan, Akbar's grandson. It is a monument to courtly love and, ultimately, to man's glory.

In addition to the tension between the two different approaches to the place of religion in the polity and the extent to which a strict Islam should define the basis of society, the Mughal Empire endured the stress between the desire to effect a strong centralized government and the need to allow a degree of authority in provincial administration. But these polarities were endemic in all three Muslim empires and should be studied from a comparative perspective.

MUSLIM IMPERIAL POWER: LAW AND THE ROYAL HOUSEHOLD

It was in the Ottoman state, two centuries older than the rival Muslim empires of the sixteenth century, that the power of the ruler and of his central government was most firmly established. In ideological terms the Safavid Shah, both as Sufi shaykh of the qizilbash and as descendant of the Prophet, had perhaps the strongest claim to leadership in his polity. Nevertheless, both the Ottoman and the Mughal *padishahs* (emperors) could assert leadership in Islamic terms as caliphs—not in the universal sense of the Abbasid caliphate, but as upright and just sovereigns who respected the shari'a. In fact, sixteenth-century Ottoman intellectuals argued, following earlier Islamic scholars, that while any law-abiding Muslim ruler (with the obvious exception of the "heretical" Safavids) could be termed a caliph, the Ottoman padishahs should be known as the greatest caliphs because they did more than any others to extend the rule of Islam and because they paid proper homage to the shari'a and to its guardians, the ulama.

There was also secular theoretical justification for the exalted position of the Muslim emperors. In Islamic political philosophy, following Greek and Iranian precedents, society was seen to consist of four components, corresponding to the four basic elements (earth, air, fire, water) in the makeup of the universe and to the four humors (fluids) in the human body. The emperor was to the body politic as the physician was to his patient: he ensured good health by keeping the four elements in balance and in harmonious existence. The four social groups were warriors, men of learning, merchants, and peasants; it was the emperor's function to keep them in check and to prevent any one group from oppressing, injuring, or cheating the others. The padishah was the crucial central figure also in the "circle of equity," a further theoretical formulation on the functioning of society: the padishah needed an army to establish his authority; subjects supplied, through taxes, the padishah's treasury to maintain his army; the prosperity of the subjects depended on law and justice; justice could come only through the padishah's authority.

In the three great Muslim empires of the early modern period, justice was not only Islamic, based on the shari'a: since the days of the Seljuks, and especially since the Mongol-Ilkhanid Empire, secular, customary law had been reinforced and its sphere expanded. It was the padishah who proclaimed such dynastic law—qanun, as it was called—to regulate state organization and relations between the state and its subjects. Qanun even encroached upon the areas of criminal and commercial law, which in earlier times had been more firmly within the purview of the shari'a. In Islamic conception the greatest emperor was he who showed greatest concern for law in his realm. The glorious Ottoman Sultan Suleiman I, known as "the Magnificent" in Europe, was called "Qanuni" (the Lawgiver) by his subjects.

Qanun was typically applied by officers of the state and not by the ulama. Padishahs, however, tried to influence the ulama as well and not let them be totally independent of the government. In all three empires, heads of the ulama were appointed by the padishah and worked at the imperial court, in close proximity. The Ottomans, however, strayed from the norm: they left the application of qanun in the hands of the ulama. If this practice strengthened the official position of the ulama, it also made them functionaries of the state and undermined their independent social leadership role. Ottoman ulama were thus bureaucratized and identified with the state. The Ottoman padishah willingly gave them a share in government and in return received their total support.

As extensions of his imperial self, the padishah maintained a sumptuous household and a standing army, his personal troops.

The ruler's troops ideally were composed of select, highly trained individuals who owed total loyalty to their master. In earlier Islamic states it was the practice to have purchased slaves or war captives from beyond the boundaries of the realm fill this role: they were displaced, and therefore had neither kith nor kin to share their allegiance. Furthermore, they could be trained from youth in special barracks without the yearnings for family and friends that free-born soldiers would have. Thus in almost all Muslim states the core of the military was made up of the ruler's personal slaves or servants who occupied the highest positions of command in the realm.

The Ottomans practiced this system to its fullest extent, and introduced a new element by recruiting the sons of their non-Muslim subjects for training for high military and administrative office. It was this feature of Ottoman government, common in other Islamic states, that most impressed and fascinated European observers in the fifteenth and sixteenth centuries. While in Europe blood nobility claimed all the highest positions, reported Busbecq, a Hapsburg ambassador to Istanbul, a shepherd boy in the sultan's domains could become a *vizier,* the highest rank in the empire, depending solely on his personal qualities and achievements.

After the gunpowder revolution, the size and significance of the padishah's household troops increased even more. Making and maintaining cannon and muskets, providing gunpowder, and training troops in the effective employment of firearms were activities so costly that only the sovereign could afford a gunpowder army. Furthermore, once an army wielding firearms was trained and deployed, resistance by smaller, regional powers was difficult. The more gunpowder came to be used in warfare, the stronger central authority grew.

With their proximity to European centers where firearms were developed, and facing modern European armies, the Ottomans were quick to embrace the gunpowder revolution. While the Safavids and Mughals, too, used the new weapons from the early sixteenth century, they lagged behind. Indeed, throughout the Islamic world, from Morocco to India and even to the sultanates of Sumatra and Malaya, Ottoman firearms experts were in high demand.

A major element in the reorganization of the Safavid state in the time of Shah Abbas was the strengthening of central authority on the Ottoman model. The shah's household troops were expanded to become a full-size force, and they were armed with muskets. A corps of cannoneers was also instituted. Shah Abbas' centralization was aimed at curbing the power of the qizilbash cavalry and their leaders, the tribal aristocracy, in control in the provinces. The tension between the emperor and his household troops versus provincial forces was one that appeared in all three empires.

PROVINCIAL ADMINISTRATION: REVENUE GRANTS

The seventeenth-century "Sun King" of France, Louis XIV, proclaimed that he was the state. His contemporaries, the great Muslim emperors, were more modest: they were only the rulers of a military-administrative elite that was properly considered the "state." In all three empires the main dividing line, as opposed to the theoretical four components of society, was between the functionaries of the state and the subjects. The subjects, Muslim and non-Muslim, whether peasants or townsmen, from the poorest farmer to the richest merchant, paid the state taxes on persons, production, and trade. The padishah and his palace servants, his household troops, other military groups, bureaucrats, and ulama, were totally exempt from taxes. *They* were the state; they shared the state's revenues as their livelihood.

All state income was apportioned among the members of the ruling elite, whether warriors or learned men. With his personal revenues each administrator, military or civilian, maintained his own household, his own slaves and servants. The governments of the Muslim empires we have been studying consisted of the sum of all these households, from the padishah's palace of thousands of men to a provincial cavalryman's handful of retainers. Each household, from the most sumptuous to the most modest, was equally a part of the state.

This system of apportioning state revenues directly to state functionaires has been compared with medieval feudalism. European feudalism and Muslim revenue grants may have developed for similar reasons: a relative scarcity of precious metals, and therefore of coin, and the consequent difficulty of collecting taxes taken in kind (that is, not in cash). Obviously a bushel of wheat received as tax payment, or a few sheep taken from a nomad's herd, would cost more to transport to the center than they were worth. They must be consumed, by the state or its representatives, on the spot, near where they were collected. There the similarity to feudalism ends; the rest of the system is in strong contrast with the political-economic arrangement of medieval Europe. The Muslim revenue grants were specific to office; they were not inherited, nor were they for life. The central government could reassign them and shift the officials at its discretion.

These revenue grants were called by different names in the three empires: *dirlik* (livelihood) or *timar* in the Ottoman Empire, *tiyul* in the Safavid domains, and *jagir* in Mughal India. While the terms were different, the system was essentially the same in all cases. All members of government, from the padishah to the bureaucrats and provincial cavalrymen, were assigned revenues commensurate with their rank. The official paid for his own household; the number of his retainers was determined by the size of his timar or jagir.

These premodern empires were agrarian societies, though they also had lively urban centers with important trading and manufacturing. Tax payments of the peasants and of the animal breeders were mostly in kind; urban folk, on the other hand, were living in a relatively monetized setting, so they provided most of the taxes in cash. It follows from these considerations that rural revenues should be assigned to the provincial military, while town and city taxes should be allocated to higher-ranking officials, court functionaries, and the padishah's person.

Revenues included fines levied against criminals as well as trade and production taxes. Thus, in the process of collecting revenues granted to him, an officer or a cavalryman also maintained public order in his area in collaboration with the *qadi* s magistrates of shari'a and of qanun, who heard the cases and passed sentence. This feature of the system meant that the military and the judicial officials of the state, though they represented separate traditions, had to work in close cooperation, and provided a check on the power of each other. The provincial revenue grant system, in sum, performed three functions for the state: it was a method of tax collection; it provided local security and law enforcement; it supported an army of provincial cavalrymen who paid all their own expenses on campaign.

The padishah, his viziers and ministers at court, high officers and commanders, governors of provinces and of districts needed to receive at least part of their revenues in cash. Therefore highly concentrated sources of revenue, such as mines and important trading centers and port cities with large customs duty collections, were reserved for such high personages. Revenues held for the padishah were termed *khasse* (*khalisa* in Mughal usage), meaning imperial demesne. The padishah and, for that matter, ministers and other high officers appointed members of their own households to the various localities in their demesnes to collect the revenues, convert payments in kind to cash at the nearby markets, and transmit the cash collection to the holder of the demesne.

The imperial army was made up of the revenue grant holders in the provinces and their retinues. In addition the padishah, out of his own revenues, maintained his personal household troops, the central army. In battle order, the padishah's household troops occupied the center with their cannon and muskets; the swift provincial cavalry formed the wings. We should note that as firearms and gunpowder became increasingly important in warfare, especially in the case of the Ottomans fighting European foes, the padishah's need for more khasse revenues also grew.

Padishahs always gave great importance to the unhindered flow of trade in and through their domains. Lively trade made for a prosperous economy; but from the discussion on the composition of khasse revenues it should be clear that trade was especially vital to the padishah's personal treasury. It was for this reason, as well as for the economic well-being of the populace in general, that rulers sought to make their lands safe and attractive for merchant caravans and trading vessels by building caravansaries, inns, and storehouses, and by patrolling trade routes, on land and at sea, to keep them free of bandits and pirates. Whether it was the Turkish or Mongol states of inner Asia on the silk route from China, or the west Asian states astride the spice route from the Indian Ocean to the Mediterranean, all polities actively encouraged and enticed merchants.

INTERNAL STRESS AND EXTERNAL CHALLENGES

With these considerations in mind, we should return to the opening section of this chapter, to the dawn of early modern history and the important role of European discovery, invention, and expansion in world history. Obviously it was the Ottoman Empire that was most directly affected by this European resurgence, and that resisted European encroachment. Indeed, for Safavid Iran and Mughal India the arrival of European traders was, in this early period, a positive development. If the trade of India and Iran was carried by Portuguese, Dutch, British, or French vessels instead of by caravans through Ottoman territories, this was not necessarily a loss to the Safavids or the Mughals. In fact, Europeans increased the volume of trade with Iran and India. The Ottomans, however, as well as earlier trade centers such as Venice, Genoa, and Ragusa, would be directly harmed if trade through west Asia and the Mediterranean were to be diverted from the Indian Ocean to the Atlantic.

In the fifteenth century the Ottomans had already developed a navy. After their conquest, early in the sixteenth century, of Mamluk Syria and Egypt, and of Basra around the middle of the century, they established naval bases in the Red Sea and in the Persian Gulf, in an effort to prevent a Portuguese blockade. In this aim they were successful. Nevertheless, wresting the Indian Ocean trade from European navies was beyond their abilities. The Ottomans were satisfied, in the end, to keep their share of the Asian trade at accustomed levels.

The seventeenth century brought a new development that was welcomed by the Ottomans: Dutch and British vessels, encouraged by the padishah because they were Protestants, and the merchants of Catholic France (a strategic friend and sometimes even an ally of the Ottomans in common enmity to the Hapsburgs) came to frequent Ottoman ports in increasing numbers. Their interest was not so much in the traditional transit trade of western Asia as in Ottoman products. Vessels full of silver from America came to purchase Ottoman grain, foodstuffs, and other agricultural goods. Showing something of a bullionist sensibility of their own, Ottoman writers of the seventeenth century commented favorably on this turn of events, and contrasted it with Ottoman trade with lands to the north and the east. The bullion that Europeans brought to Ottoman lands, they complained, went out again to Russia for furs and to Iran and India for fine shawls, delicate textiles, jewels, and other luxury items. Ottoman commentators could not be expected to foresee that eventually the Europeans were going to exchange their manufactured goods for Ottoman primary exports, and that the trade balance was going to tip in Europe's favor in the following centuries.

The stimulus from increased European trade helped sovereigns in all Muslim empires. However, in all three the padishah's need to augment his khasse revenues continued as each attempted a greater degree of central control. In the case of the Ottomans, because of the changing nature of warfare in Europe, the provincial cavalry became increasingly obsolete and there was a corresponding need to increase the size of the central army, the padishah's household troops. This increase implied diverting the central treasury revenues previously allocated to timar grants. Such a diversion, in turn, necessitated the greater involvement and cooperation of provincial notables in the collection of taxes and their conversion to cash. While the padishah's revenues increased, so did the role and power of local elites through the collecting and transmitting of these revenues. On the surface this was a process of centralization but, paradoxically, it carried the seeds of decentralization that matured in time.

In the Safavid and Mughal empires, too, there were similar developments in the seventeenth century. Shah Abbas started the process of enlarging central administration and extending khasse crown lands; this remained the main policy of his successors as well. In India, Akbar had even experimented with centralizing all revenue collection, including revenues granted to officials as jagirs; grant holders would be paid salaries from the central treasury. This experiment failed because the economy was not sufficiently monetarized. But in Avrangzib's reign most newly conquered land in the south was kept for the padishah as khalisa, despite the fact that the ranks of officers had swollen and there was therefore a great need for additional jagir grants. Safavid and Mughal centralization suited neither the qizilbash commanders, who saw that their power was eroded, nor the Mughal officers, who had to wait longer and work harder for revenue grants. The delicate balance between imperial authority and the prestige of its servants was disturbed; consequently the solidarity of the ruling group declined.

In the eighteenth century, trying to close the growing technological gap with Europe, the Ottomans were able to hold their own. By the end of the century, however, both Russia and Austria had repeatedly defeated the Ottoman Empire; the frontiers of the once mighty empire were gradually contracting. More seriously, the internal stability and balance of the state had been unsettled. In many parts local or regional upstarts had usurped imperial authority; and Ottoman justice, pride of the padishahs, was failing to satisfy the demands of the populace. Especially for the non-Muslim subjects in the Balkans, the glory of the old Pax Ottomanica had faded; the revolutionary Europe of 1800, industrializing and with attractive ideas on national society and polity, was beckoning.

For the Safavids and Mughals the impact of Europe was not yet serious; Iran and India suffered from a decline, not in relation to Europe, as in the case of the Ottomans, but in relation to earlier times of grandeur. In addition to the deterioration of relations between Muslims and Hindus on the one hand, and between the center and provinces on the other, the Mughal Empire suffered from struggles over the throne that accompanied each succession. The long reign of Aurangzib (1658-1707) seemed to signal the height of the empire in its expansion; nevertheless, the war of succession that followed his death was a particularly severe blow to central authority. In its aftermath various regional interests under Muslim and non-Muslim leadership, which had been suppressed by Aurangzib, reemerged ever more forcefully. Hindus in the south, who had barely been subdued, rose up against Mughal rule and pushed their way north.

An even more severe setback to Mughal power was an invasion in 1739 from Iran, led by Nadir Shah, that left the state vulnerable to successive invasions by Afghans. By the second half of the century, French and British penetration along the southeast coast and in Bengal had reached such proportions that, in addition to Afghans and various local lords, the Europeans became active elements in the struggle for power. Controlling only a small territory around Agra and Delhi, the Mughal dynasty was reduced to a mere shadow of its earlier glory, just one piece among many on the Indian chessboard.

The Ottoman dynasty continued until after World War I; even the Mughals lasted until 1857, albeit as British puppets. The Safavids of Iran, on the other hand, totally lost control, and were ousted in 1736. Already in the earlier decades of the century, Isfahan, resented by provincial commanders, had been unable to stop the growing Afghan power on the eastern frontier. By 1722 the Safavid shah was no longer in control, even in his capital: Isfahan was besieged and captured by the Afghan forces that had taken advantage of the disunity of Iran. Thereafter, several Safavid pretenders kept the dynastic name alive in various parts of the country in spite of the invasion.

Finally Nadir Khan, a qizilbash commander of the Afshar tribe in northern Khurasan, beat back the Afghans and declared himself shah in 1736. Iran was reunited during Nadir Shah's reign; he even undertook successful invasions of Mughal and Ottoman territories. At his death in 1747, however, the political integrity of Iran was completely shattered, not to be restored by a new dynasty, the Qajars, until the very end of the century.

We can conclude from this brief survey of the fortunes of the great Muslim empires that, with the arguable exception of the Ottomans, their fall was not primarily at the hands of Europeans. Rather, internal stresses, both political and social, eventually led to breakdown. But this setback to stability in Muslim lands coincided with the definitive rise of European technological and industrial power. In the nineteenth century all the Ottomans and the Qajars of Iran could hope to do, to avoid the fate of the Mughals, was to westernize: to learn from the new Europe and to use its weapons in self-defense. Their endeavors in pursuing this aim form the subject of later chapters of Muslim history.

7

The Colonial Period

Arthur Goldschmidt, Jr.

It has never been easy for Muslims to submit to the rule of a non-Muslim, or to countenance the loss of lands where Islam had once prevailed. The era of European imperialism evokes bitter memories for Muslims. Islam is a system of government and a way of life, not just a theology and a set of ethical principles. The shari'a purports to cover all aspects of human behavior. The Muslim ruler, no matter what his title or his means of gaining power, must make sure that his subjects can live according to the shari'a and prepare for the life to come. But what if some Muslims should fall under the rule of a non-Muslim? In the early centuries of Islam, when its realm was expanding, this seldom happened. In rare cases, like the thirteenth-century Mongol invasion of southwest Asia, Islamic jurists called for resistance and, if that failed, they advised Muslims to flee to a country that still had a Muslim ruler. But this problem afflicted relatively few Muslims up to the eighteenth century.

In the colonial period not only were Muslims forced to submit to non-Muslim rule but the conquerors were Christian Europeans. Fierce rivalry between Christendom and Islam had begun in the seventh century, when Muslims had taken the lands where Christianity was born. Although Islam spread in all directions, Europeans in the seventh and eighth centuries had been alarmed by the rapid conquest of North Africa and Spain, followed by Muslim thrusts into France, Sicily, and Italy. The Muslim duty to wage jihad, the struggle to expand the lands under Islam, was often misconstrued to mean the forcible conversion of Christians. By the same token, Muslims had learned about the "church militant" through the Crusades, which led at times to the despoliation of mosques, the theft of art objects and manuscripts, and the forced conversion of some Muslims and the massacre of others. Memories such as these assured a deep and often bitter antagonism between the two religions.

EARLY EUROPEAN COLONIALISM

The Christian country whose expansion marked the beginning of the colonial period was Portugal, whose sailors ventured ever farther from home ports in search of fishing and trading opportunities. In the fifteenth and early sixteenth centuries, Portuguese traders set up colonies at port cities in the Muslim areas of western and eastern Africa, on the Persian Gulf, in India, and on various islands of what is now Indonesia. Their example was followed in the sixteenth and seventeenth centuries by Spanish, Dutch, Danish, English, and French mariners. These Christian outposts, far from hemming in the lands of Islam, affected few Muslims directly. This was the era of the great Muslim states: the Ottoman Empire, the Safavid dynasty in Iran, the Uzbeks of Central Asia, the Mughals of India, plus the Songhay and Kanem-Bornu in western Africa. Muslims were not menaced by Christian sailors and traders. Rather, the Christians felt the threat of Ottoman expansion into Central Europe.

As long as these great empires remained strong, European colonialism barely dented the Muslim world. As their power ebbed, however, the rising Western states probed and attacked. The Ottoman Empire lost Hungary to the Austrian Hapsburgs by 1699 and the lands north of the Black Sea to Russia, starting in 1774. Meanwhile, the British were chipping away at Mughal India. The Russians moved south into the Caucasus Mountains, taking lands once under the Safavids, who had given way to a succession of Iranian dynasties. Even in those Muslim lands where Christians made no pretense of ruling, European residents and traders often enjoyed the protection of special treaties. In the case of the Ottoman Empire, these treaties were known as capitulations. They enabled subjects of the European signatory states to live and to trade in the Ottoman Empire, immune from local laws and taxes. This gave foreign merchants, or the chartered trading companies for which they commonly worked, a great competitive edge over local Ottoman merchants and artisans. Gradually, European manufactures became—or at least came to be viewed as—better than the local products.

Western imperialism tended at first to be economic; only later did it become overtly political. To many seventeenth- and eighteenth-century governments, foreign trade was a political instrument. Prevalent among the European states was a policy called mercantilism, which aimed to achieve a surplus of exports over imports. Setting up foreign colonies was a means of attaining this trade surplus. The colony was supposed to supply raw materials and primary products, and to purchase the colonizer's manufactured goods. Mercantilism led to intense competition among the strongest European kingdoms during the seventeenth and eighteenth centuries. Each tried to extend its sway throughout the world. Each encouraged its merchants and trading companies to spread beyond the lands that it ruled.

The colonizing powers differed in their means and their ends. Some European states, like Portugal, Holland, and England, had strong navies and commercial fleets. They colonized lands far from home, including parts of India and southeast Asia, for trade and settlement. Other colonizers, like Austria and Russia, were landlocked dynastic empires. Their great armies invaded adjacent areas and annexed them. Although they, too, sought trade and land for colonization, their stated motives were religious. Hapsburg Austria viewed itself as the major Catholic kingdom, the Holy Roman Empire, sweeping back the Muslim tide in southeastern Europe. Tsarist Russia, formerly ruled by Islamized Tatars and Mongols, saw itself as a crusader for Greek Orthodox Christianity and a protector of its correligionists under Muslim rule. Both challenged the Ottoman Empire in the Balkans, but usually they neutralized each other. France had both commercial and religious aims, and its means of expansion were naval as well as military. But its strongest motive was its "civilizing mission" to spread the French language, schools, laws, governmental institutions, consumer products, and culture to other parts of the world. (The Table at the end of the chapter lists today's predominantly Muslim countries and indicates which European powers ruled them.)

NINETEENTH-CENTURY COLONIALISM

Historians used to split Europe's colonial expansion into two main phases. The first opened with the Portuguese and Spanish voyages of exploration in the fifteenth century and closed with the American War for Independence. The second period, from 1870 to 1920, encompassed the European countries' scramble for colonies in Africa and their equally competitive encroachments in China, Iran, and the Ottoman Empire. Around 1900 Germany, Italy, Japan, and the United States joined the older colonial powers in this new contest. During this time many European banks, companies, and individuals went abroad to invest money, sell manufactured goods, or purchase food or raw materials. These two colonial eras, according to this traditional account, were separated by a "slack period."

From the Muslim viewpoint, though, Western colonialism never abated. During that "slack period" Russia conquered more lands around the Black Sea, taking from Iran's ineffectual Qajar dynasty Georgia, Armenia, and northern Azerbaijan. Napoleon occupied the Ottoman province of Egypt in 1798. Unable to withstand Anglo-Ottoman opposition, France later formed strong ties with Egypt's ambitious governor, Muhammad Ali (1769-1849), and his heirs. A French engineer directed the construction of the Suez Canal, which was formally opened in 1869. France began in 1830 to conquer and colonize Algeria. Somewhat later, it started moving inland from its coastal colony of Senegal, to take control of what would become French West Africa.

Meanwhile, the British strengthened their hold on India, completing their conquest by suppressing a military uprising, the Sepoy Mutiny, in 1857. By then their interest in securing the overland routes to India had led the British to sign treaties with the Arab amirs and shaykhs around the Persian Gulf. They also established colonies at Singapore in 1819 and Aden in 1839 that proved strategically important in controlling nearby Muslim lands. Even when the British, French, and Russians aided the Greeks in their war for independence from the Ottoman Empire during the 1820s, their aim was to increase their own power in the eastern Mediterranean.

Europe's encroachments on the lands of Islam and the colonial competition intensified after 1870. Russia pushed farther into Central Asia and vied with Britain for paramountcy in Iran and Afghanistan. Russian propaganda among Balkan peoples, stressing their Orthodox Christian and Slavic ties, sparked several uprisings in 1875-76. In the ensuing Russo-Turkish war, Russian troops captured eastern Anatolia and occupied Balkan lands to within a few miles of Istanbul, the Ottoman capital. France occupied Tunisia in 1881, and most of western and equatorial Africa by 1898. This nearly led to a confrontation with Britain, which had occupied Egypt in 1882, when France failed to do so. Because France had long enjoyed commercial and cultural paramountcy in Egypt, it resented the British occupation and hoped to terminate it by gaining control of the upper Nile. A largely Egyptian army, trained and equipped by the British, conquered the Sudan between 1896 and 1898, when it confronted a French force coming from West Africa. For a few weeks France and Britain stood at the brink of a colonial war for control of the Sudan, but the French force finally withdrew.

EARLY TWENTIETH-CENTURY COLONIALISM

Rivalries among European powers sometimes blunted their expansion, just as treaties and "understandings" aided them. British and German pressure during the 1878 Congress of Berlin made Russia give up most of the Balkan lands it had just conquered. For the next 30 years, the Ottoman Empire managed to thwart the imperial aims of both Hapsburg Austria and Tsarist Russia—as well as the national aspirations of its Christian subjects—in the Balkans. Only the 1908 Young Turk revolution broke the logjam. Austria promptly annexed Bosnia, a heavily Muslim area of what is now northern Yugoslavia. Bulgaria, which had a large Muslim population, declared its independence. Soon Crete, and then Albania, rebelled against the Ottomans. Many Europeans applauded what they viewed as nationalist uprisings against Turkish imperialism, but soon their own imperialist aims became evident. In 1911 Italy invaded Libya. The next year Russia incited the independent Balkan states to attack the Ottoman Empire in order to capture and divide Macedonia. By 1913 the Ottoman Empire had lost all its European lands except for the area around Istanbul.

Aside from the Ottoman Empire, every Muslim country still independent at the dawn of the twentieth century—Iran, Afghanistan, and Morocco—was threatened with annexation or partition. Qajar Iran was honeycombed with European traders and investors, who were buying commercial concessions from a weak, money-starved shah. Popular resistance sometimes blocked concessions, and by 1906 the Iranian nationalists were able to demand a constitution. But in the following year Britain and Russia recognized each other's claims to spheres of influence in Iran. Russian troops occupied northern Iran and effectively stifled the Iranian nationalists. Afghanistan was thrice invaded by British troops coming from India, either to support a local ruler or to keep Russia from taking control of the country. The Sharifian Empire of Morocco, the only Arabic-speaking country that never fell under Ottoman rule, became the subject of some complicated diplomatic maneuvers. Britain, for example, recognized France's primary interest in Morocco in exchange for France's acceptance of an indefinite British occupation of Egypt. France assumed a protectorate over most of Morocco in 1912, but Spain got a small enclave in the north, and an international government was set up in the port city of Tangier.

The Young Turks' decision to enter World War I on the German side sealed the fate of the Ottoman Empire. In a series of secret treaties signed in 1915-16, Britain, France, and Russia agreed to divide Ottoman lands if they won the war. Their aims were mainly strategic. Russia was to take Istanbul, the Bosporus, and the Dardanelles, thus assuring its access to the Mediterranean. France, already an established Mediterranean power, would get the Syrian coast and parts of western Anatolia. Britain would gain a sphere of influence over an arc of land between Egypt (over which it had declared a protectorate in 1914) and the Persian Gulf. In 1917, though, the Bolshevik Revolution caused Russia to leave the war. The new Communist leaders renounced the imperialist claims of the government they had toppled and tried to embarrass Britain and France by publishing the secret treaties. Nevertheless, when the war ended in 1918, Britain was the supreme power in the Middle East. British imperial forces patrolled Istanbul, Damascus, Jerusalem, and Baghdad, and even such remote lands as Azerbaijan and the Hijaz. King George V had become, de facto, the ruler of more Muslims than any caliph in history.

COLONIALISM AFTER WORLD WAR I

In their postwar deliberations Britain and France agreed to divide the Arabic-speaking Ottoman lands: Syria and Lebanon went to France; Iraq and Palestine, to Britain. Keep in mind that these now familiar place names were unknown up to 1920. The local inhabitants, mostly Arabs, wanted unity and independence. Some had taken up arms against the Ottoman Turks during World War I, in the Arab revolt led by Husayn, the Meccan leader of the Hashimites (the family of the Prophet Muhammad). An American commission of inquiry toured Syria and Palestine in 1919 and learned that most Arab inhabitants wanted the Hashimites, not the French or the British, to rule over them. Its findings were ignored. The modern Fertile Crescent states—Israel, Jordan, Lebanon, Syria, and Iraq—can trace their existence to the postwar machinations of the colonial powers whose rule they would later reject.

Egypt's history was separate from that of the Fertile Crescent. Legally a semiautonomous province up to 1914, its viceroys (called khedives) were nominally subject to the Ottoman sultan. Its real rulers after 1882 were Britain's diplomatic representatives in Cairo, backed by a small occupation army and a growing corps of British advisers in the various departments of Egypt's government. This "veiled protectorate" satisfied Egypt's European creditors, investors, and immigrants, but it also faced mounting nationalist opposition. Egyptians felt that the British neglected education and systematically excluded them from any positions of responsibility in the government. Most Western countries accepted British rule because it promoted Egypt's financial and political stability. As soon as the Ottoman Empire took Germany's side in 1914, the British government abolished Egypt's vestigial Ottoman ties, dethroned the reigning khedive, and declared a protectorate over the country. A nationwide revolt after the war pushed Britain into awarding Egypt the shadow but not the substance of independence in 1922. As late as World War II, Britain could still intervene to control Egypt's political life. The Sudan, nominally an Anglo-Egyptian condominium from 1899 to 1956, was ruled almost entirely by the British.

Seeing Britain's paramount position elsewhere in the Middle East, Iran's reigning Qajar shah in 1919 signed a treaty that would have put his country under a British protectorate. This treaty was nullified by popular opposition and by the 1921 coup that brought Reza Khan (later Reza Shah Pahlavi) to power. British primacy in Iran was maintained by the influential Anglo-Iranian Oil Company, which was developing Iran's petroleum in the southwestern part of the country. As late as 1941 Britain, together with Soviet Russia, could occupy Iran and force Reza Shah to abdicate.

World War I strengthened France's hold over Morocco, Algeria, and Tunisia, as well as French West Africa. In part as a result of a policy of cultural assimilation that envisaged turning educated African Muslims into brown- or black-skinned Frenchmen, France's colonial legacy lasted longer than Britain's. Political independence came only after 1955, and French intellectual and cultural influence remains strong in Muslim Africa even now. On the other hand, the most protracted and bitter struggle ever fought between a Muslim nation and a European colonizing power took place in Algeria between 1954 and 1962. This was partly due to the preponderant political and economic role played by over a million European settlers, one-tenth of Algeria's population.

After suppressing a religious and tribal rebellion at great cost in lives and money, Italy established its rule over Libya, a loose federation of three sparsely settled provinces: Cyrenaica, Tripolitania, and the Fezzan. The British captured Libya during World War II and ruled it under a United Nations trusteeship until 1951, when it became the first new African country to gain its independence.

Russia's Muslims enjoyed a respite from colonialism following the 1917 Bolshevik Revolution, but Communist factions gradually gained the upper hand in the successor republics, all of which joined the Union of Soviet Socialist Republics during the early 1920s. Although Lenin and his successors stressed the multinational quality of the new Communist state, their opposition to the formal observance of religion caused great resentment among the Muslims of the Caucasus Mountains and Central Asia. But so far no visible Muslim separatist movement has arisen, probably because the Soviet leaders would not tolerate it.

The Dutch tended to relax their rule in the islands of Borneo, Sumatra, and Java in the early twentieth century, but there was a large settler population and a growing emphasis on the development of rubber plantations. The Japanese conquered the islands during World War II. Although the victorious Allies restored them to the Netherlands, a series of nationalist revolts after the war effectively undermined Dutch control, and so the islands became independent as the Republic of Indonesia in 1949. British rule in India, Ceylon, Burma, and the Malay states also lasted until after World War II, although their subjects, both Muslim and non-Muslim, had become restive during the interwar years.

It is often forgotten that much of the inspiration for the nationalist movements in Muslim Asia and Africa came from the

Turkish-speaking remnant of the Ottoman Empire. Virtually prostrate at the end of World War I, Ottoman Turkey seemed ready for partition among the victorious Allies. British and French troops occupied its capital and guarded the Straits. Encouraged by Britain, Greece launched a massive invasion of western Anatolia, while the Allies were seriously considering an American mandate for Armenia, if not the whole of Anatolia. Only a heroic resistance led by Mustafa Kemal (Ataturk) saved what we now call Turkey from Western colonialism. The 1920 Treaty of Sèvres, imposed by the Allies on the defeated Ottoman government, was resented by Turkey's Muslims (and hence by their correligionists elsewhere) and resisted by Kemal's soldiers, who mutinied against the government that signed it. After a three-year struggle the Turks drove the Greeks out of Anatolia and made Britain's military occupation of the Straits so untenable that all parties agreed to negotiate a new treaty at Lausanne that assured Turkey's independence. All foreign troops would be evacuated. The Allies even recognized Turkey's abrogation of the capitulations, which had granted European residents and visitors virtual immunity from Ottoman laws and taxes. Kemal's revolt was the first instance of a Muslim leader's successfully thwarting the colonial powers of Europe. It left a deep impression on the Muslims of Egypt, India, and other colonies.

MOTIVES FOR COLONIALISM

Having briefly surveyed the history of Western colonialism in the Muslim world, let us now turn to some questions. What did the colonizers want? Since Islam prevails in lands in the center of the Afro-Eurasian landmass, it is natural to answer the question geopolitically. Britain needed to make treaties with Persian Gulf rulers in order to guard its passage to India. Later on, it justified its occupation of Egypt, its condominium over the Sudan, and its mandates in Palestine and Iraq with this imperial reason. France wanted to control most of the lands bordering on the Mediterranean: Algeria, Tunisia, Morocco, Lebanon, and Syria. Russia, longing for assured access to the Mediterranean and also the Indian Ocean, pushed southward against the Ottoman Empire and Iran. Austria wanted to control navigation on the Danube River, hence large areas of the northern Balkans.

Economic motives, too, played a part. The first stage in a colonial tie was usually a commercial relationship, as in the case of Holland with Java, Britain with India, or France with Tunisia. Trade could flourish without political control, but Muslim governments, trying to westernize quickly during the late nineteenth century, often borrowed heavily from European banks and investors. This usually led to outside financial control, sometimes also (in fact if not in form) to foreign rule. Egypt was the classic example, but foreign indebtedness also led to the French protectorate over Tunisia and greatly hampered the freedom of nominally independent states, such as the Ottoman Empire and Iran.

Neo-marxist thinkers maintain that imperialism is the last gasp of a capitalist system choking on its internal contradictions. When capitalists find that they can no longer sell their products to an impoverished working class, they seek colonies to serve as new markets for their surplus goods. Similarly, investment in colonial commerce and agriculture should yield higher profits to capitalists than comparable investments in their home countries.

In fact, though, the value of trade among the rich capitalist countries always exceeded their commerce with the poorer Asian and African lands, even with their own colonies. Some capitalists did invest heavily in their own colonies—for example, the Dutch in Java, Borneo, and Sumatra. But even during the heyday of Western imperialism, most investors found it more profitable to lend money, build factories, or open mines in other independent countries, such as the United States, Brazil, Russia, China, or even the Ottoman Empire.

Some Western imperialism was psychologically motivated. The spread of nationalism in the colonizing countries, a result of increased education and a burgeoning popular press, often led to chauvinism and a competitive spirit like that of a cheering section in a football game. Possessing colonies in Africa and Asia reassured France that it was not really a fading power. Hapsburg Austria took solace, after losing its German leadership role to Prussia, by moving into Balkan lands such as Bosnia. German imperialists talked about winning their "place in the sun," and some Englishmen longed to color whole continents red (the cartographic symbol for British imperial rule). Moral concerns, especially the desire to suppress the slave trade, formed one motive for British imperialism in the Sudan and East Africa.

Considering the heritage of Muslim-Christian antagonism dating from the Middle Ages, did the European powers seek to strengthen Christianity at the expense of Islam? Sometimes they did. Spain and Portugal had tried to do this in the fifteenth century by driving the Muslims from the Iberian peninsula. In the nineteenth century France sent missionary orders into the Kabylia regions of Algeria, hoping to convert the mountain-dwelling Berbers and to drive a wedge between them and the desert Arabs, but both remained steadfastly Muslim. France imposed upon Algerian Muslims the *Code de l'Indigénat*. This effectively barred them from French citizenship, which would require them to renounce the shari'a in favor of the French Civil Code. The Indigénat empowered civilian administrators to use surveillance, internment, individual or collective house arrest, and collective fines to punish disobedience. Algerian Muslims needed administrative permission to move outside the districts in which they lived. These laws did not apply to Algerian Jews or Christians, or to European settlers. The disabilities did not cause many Algerians to renounce Islam.

In the nineteenth century the Dutch in their East Indian empire hindered their Muslim subjects from making the pilgrimage to Mecca, on the ground that returning pilgrims tended to stir up resistance to Dutch rule. The policy was bitterly resented, and by the beginning of the twentieth century the Dutch, advised by the orientalist scholar C. Snouck Hurgronje, had adopted a more liberal policy to encourage the rise of a Muslim reform movement. The Russians persecuted the Crimean Tatars, whom they had conquered in the late eighteenth century, and tried to convert them. Later on, though, they allowed their Central Asian subjects to practice Islam and to enforce the shari'a. The British in the Malay States, India, Egypt, and the Sudan adopted a strict hands-off policy toward Muslim religious observance, often restraining overly zealous Christian missionaries.

As a general rule, the later a land was subjected to Western colonialism, the less religious persecution or pressure its Muslim inhabitants had to bear. According to the shari'a, apostasy from Islam is a crime punishable by death. Few Muslims, therefore, converted to Christianity. Protestant, Catholic, and Orthodox missionaries sometimes served the imperial aims of their home governments (though at other times they did not) and did much to spread education and public health in Muslim lands. Their purely religious work tended, however, to affect extant Christian groups, not Muslims.

If European colonialism was less and less motivated by religion, it certainly did have cultural aims. Every colonial power formulated a policy for schooling an indigenous elite to play a subordinate role in the colonial administration or to join the growing corps of westernized businessmen and professionals. In relation to Islam, these policies varied among the powers, but usually fit somewhere along a spectrum between two attitudes. One, especially prevalent in French thought, was that Islamic culture was decadent and would soon be replaced by the more dynamic and technically advanced Western civilization. France's mission, therefore, was to set up schools in as many cities and towns as possible, and then to invite the best youths to complete their education or professional training in France. This cultural imperialism extended even to Muslim lands outside France's colonial orbit, such as Egypt, the Ottoman Empire, and Iran.

The opposite attitude was that Muslim culture was so different from the Western way of life, and that attempts to bridge the gap would prove so disruptive, that the wisest colonial policy would be to interfere as little as possible with whatever religious and educational institutions Muslims wanted to have. Although no colonial power fully adopted this policy, the British came closest to it in Egypt, where their rule was expected to be temporary. Even there, they gradually anglicized those government schools that had used French as their language of instruction.

EUROPEAN COLONIZATION

To what extent did colonialism mean the actual colonization of European settlers in Muslim lands? Settlement was most apt to occur if the climate was one to which Europeans could adapt, if the opportunities to make a better living outweighed the disadvantages of separation from the mother country, and if the home government's policies encouraged it. Algeria attracted many European settlers, including Spaniards and Italians as well as Frenchmen. These settlers had representatives in France's parliamentary institutions and enjoyed virtually all the rights and privileges of French citizens.

Even before the British occupied Egypt in 1882, Cairo, Alexandria, and the new cities that grew up along the Suez Canal teemed with Greeks, Italians, Maltese, Jews, Syrians, and Frenchmen. Under the British many Europeans flocked to Egypt to engage in business, to work for the Egyptian government or foreign companies, or to practice various professions. They enjoyed the protection of the capitulations until 1937, long after they had been abolished in Turkey. British rule in the Malay states attracted few colonists from Europe but many traders and artisans from China.

As mentioned earlier, the Dutch settled in large numbers in their East Indian empire. Many Russians settled in Muslim cities, such as Bukhara and Tashkent, in the late nineteenth century, just as many French citizens settled in Moroccan cities between 1912 and 1956. In both cases the Europeans established their own suburbs, leaving the existing Muslim cities unmolested but also underdeveloped.

The most thorough case of colonization took place in Palestine, where Jewish immigrants came from Central and Eastern Europe, founded cities such as Tel Aviv, and developed agricultural settlements, like the famous kibbutzim. Inspired by the ideals of Zionism, these settlers wanted to build a Jewish state in what was, up to 1948, a predominantly Arab and Muslim land. At first the Zionists were strictly on their own, but in 1917 they won Britain's support when its government issued the Balfour Declaration, pledging its best endeavors to achieve the creation in Palestine of a national home for the Jewish people.

During the following 30 years, Britain found itself increasingly unable to fulfill its pledge to the Zionists, who, as they grew in numbers, clashed with Palestine's Arabs. The Jewish settlers were hardly agents of British imperialism, even if the Arabs thought they were. The Arab-Israeli conflict originated in the colonial era and was nurtured by the inept policies of the British mandate, but its roots go deep into the historic experience of both Arabs and Jews.

EFFECTS OF COLONIALISM

How well did the colonial powers rule their Muslim subjects? This is not an easy question to answer. The rulers often viewed themselves as correcting past abuses by native Muslim rulers. The emerging nationalists resented colonial tutelage because it barred them from ruling themselves. Some colonizing states were more benevolent or beneficient than others, and conditions often depended on who formulated or administered colonial policies.

When Snouck Hurgronje came to Java in 1889, he alleviated a harsh Dutch colonial policy and fostered a close relationship between the administration and the Muslim reform movement. The British financial expert Sir Evelyn Baring (Lord Cromer) saved Egypt from bankruptcy, promoted irrigation, and raised the living standards of its peasants during his quarter-century (1883-1907) as the British proconsul. The British in the Sudan abolished the slave trade and promoted the spread of agriculture. Marshal Lyautey, who governed Morocco during the first 12 years of the French protectorate, subdued rebellious tribes, promoted trade and agriculture, and established an administration that combined the existing Moroccan government with a cadre of French officials. Other European colonial governors, though often able and high-minded, tended to be more responsive to their home governments or the demands of their traders and settlers than to the needs of the indigenous Muslims.

How did colonial rulers view Islam? By the twentieth century they would usually give lip service to Islamic beliefs and institutions, but rarely did they encourage Muslims to build up their own country on a truly Islamic base. Their prevalent attitude was that Islam had become retrograde, fanatical, and opposed to reform. They tended to bypass Muslim courts, schools, and welfare institutions in favor of imported Western ones. As Lord Cromer said, "Islam reformed is Islam no longer."

Not surprisingly, the soldiers who enforced colonial power and the officials who administered it shared this outlook. The settlers were especially condescending. European Christians tended not to fraternize with Muslims, let alone intermarry or assimilate with them, in contrast with the Turks and Mongols of earlier times. During the heyday of European imperialism, the West regarded Muslims as inferior politically, economically, morally, intellectually, and in every other way. Traumatized by successive military defeats, the corruption of their governments, and the impoverishment of their indigenous institutions, many Muslims, too, saw themselves as inferior to the Westerners. Even men who would later lead their countries' independence movements, such as Egypt's Sa'd Zaghlul, Algeria's Ferhat Abbas, and Pakistan's Ali

Jinnah, began their careers wanting to assimilate their rulers' cultures at the expense of their inherited values.

MUSLIM ATTITUDES TOWARD COLONIALISM

European colonial rule was almost inescapable. Even the Ottoman Empire, which staved off foreign control by carefully balancing its predators against one another, still lost territory, became hamstrung by treaties that limited its ability to govern European settlers, and went heavily into debt to pay for the reforms that were intended to secure its independence. Westernizing reforms tended to centralize power in the hands of the sultan and his ministers. Counteracting this trend toward autocracy, the government did issue some liberal proclamations: the 1839 noble rescript that ended the system of tax farming, the 1856 imperial decree that offered equal rights to all Ottoman subjects regardless of religion, and the 1876 constitution that promised parliamentary government to the whole empire. But each proclamation came in response to a diplomatic crisis and was motivated, at least partly, by the need for European support against a territorial threat. In the political sense, then, the Ottoman Empire was not wholly free from colonialism.

Furthermore, one cannot separate the economic from the political factors in Western colonialism. Independent Muslim states could not even protect their own commerce. Tariffs on goods imported into the Ottoman Empire were limited to 9 percent ad valorem in the 1838 Anglo-Ottoman commercial treaty. Applied also to Egypt after 1841, the treaty had the practical effect of opening the region to a flood of mass-produced manufactures, killing the local industries and hastening the trend toward cash crop agriculture. Artisan and merchant guilds vanished. Iran's Qajar shahs were slower to westernize than their Ottoman counterparts, but their attempt to pay for their reform expenditures by selling concessions to European businessmen hastened Iran's slide into economic, then political, dependence on Britain and Russia.

All the independent Muslim states turned gradually into economic colonies of Europe: producers of food, fibers, and raw materials; purchasers of mass-produced industrial goods; and importers of European investment capital, expertise, and entrepreneurial talent. With the spread of education, whether under foreign missionaries or their own governments, these lands also became cultural colonies. The subjects taught, their content, the language of their instruction, even their teachers and textbooks, had become largely French or English by 1900. Social classes that might have stemmed the tide of dependency were weakened: the nomadic tribes, the military fief holders, the ulama, the guild leaders, and the Sufi brotherhoods. Wealth and power were flowing to foreign residents and merchants, native and foreign government officials, and the professional men and technicians trained by the new (Western) schools. Even socially these nominally independent Muslims experienced European colonialism.

Muslims resented European domination. They disliked its economic, social, intellectual, and cultural emanations, even at times when they invited and often benefited from foreign advisers, customs, and ideas. By the middle of the twentieth century, all Asian and African peoples would seek to strengthen themselves, resist foreign imperialism, and strive for independence. But Muslims, because of their legacy of political supremacy and rivalry with the Christian West, generally marched in the vanguard of Third World reform and nationalist movements.

The tide of outside political dominance has now receded, except for the Muslims of the Soviet Union, Afghanistan, and Palestine. But many Muslims continue to watch anxiously the economic power and the corrosive influence of the West (its consumer goods and its consumption ethic) on their culture and society. Many still feel that colonialism lingers subtly within people's minds and hearts. Echoes of bygone European colonial rule and of Muslim dependency still ring in the ears of many people in many countries.

Predominantly Muslim States

Current Name of Country	Former Name	Population (000s)	Muslim (Percent of Population)	Colonial Rulers
Afghanistan		16,750	99	Invaded by British troops in 1842, 1878-79, 1919; occupied by USSR in 1979
Albania		2,875	70	Ottoman territory from 14th century to 1912

Algeria		20,000	97	Ottoman territory from 16th century to 1830; French territory from 1830 to 1962
Bahrain		375	95	Bound by treaties with Britain in 1820, 1880, 1892; independent in 1971
Bangladesh	E. Pakistan	92,600	85	Part of British India from 18th century to 1947; part of Pakistan from 1947 to 1971
Chad	French W. Africa	4,650	50	French protectorate from ca. 1900 to 1960
Comoros	Comoro Islands	375	80	French colony from 1886 to 1975
Djibouti	French Somaliland; Territory of the Afars and the Issas	335	94	French colony from 1881 to 1977
Egypt	United Arab Republic	44,750	90	Part of Ottoman Empire from 1517 to 1798; French occupation from 1798 to 1801; restored in 1802 to Ottoman rule after brief British occupation; hereditary khedivate from 1841; British occupation from 1882 and protectorate from 1914 to 1936
Gambia		640	90	Portuguese and British trade outposts in the 15th and 16th centuries; British charter in 1618; parts disputed with France from 1677 to 1783;

				treated as part of Britain's Sierra Leone colony to 1888; British protectorate from 1935 to 1965; federated with Senegal since 1982
Indonesia	Dutch East Indies	153,000	89	Dutch colony from 17th century to 1949; occupied by Japan from 1942 to 1945
Iran	Persia	41,000	98	Russian and British spheres of influence from 1907 to 1919
Iraq	Mesopotamia	14,000	95	Part of Ottoman Empire from 1534 to 1916; British military occupation from 1914, protectorate from 1918, and mandate from 1922 to 1932
Jordan	Transjordan	3,475	95	Part of Ottoman Empire from 1516 to 1918; occupied by Britain from 1918 to 1920; part of Britain's Palestine Mandate from 1920 to 1946
Lebanon		2,700	50	Part of Ottoman Empire from 1516 to 1918 (portions autonomous from 1861 to 1914); Allied occupation from 1918 to 1920; French mandate from 1920 to 1941
Libya	Tripolitania, Cyrenaica, and the Fezzan	3,250	99	Part of Ottoman Empire from 16th century; Italy occupied Tripolitania from 1911 and other parts from 1918; German occupation from

				1941; British trusteeship from 1943 to 1951
Maldives	Maldive Islands	160	100	Part of Ceylon from 1645 to 1887; Dutch colony from 1645 to 1798; British protectorate from 1887 to 1965
Mali	French West Africa	7,350	65	French control from 1890s to 1960
Mauritania	French West Africa	1,725	96	Portuguese outposts from 15th century; French control from 1904 to 1960
Morocco		21,275	95	French and Spanish protectorates from 1912 to 1956
Niger	French West Africa	5,650	85	French control from 1890s to 1960
Oman	Muscat and Oman	950	100	Portuguese colony at Muscat from 1508 to 1650; British treaty in 1891 (but no formal protectorate)
Pakistan	West Pakistan	85,500	97	Part of British India from late 18th century to 1947
Qatar		260	99	British treaty from 1916 to 1971
Saudi Arabia	Hijaz, Najd, Asir, al-Hasa, and other regions in Arabia	9,700	100	Some regions part part of Ottoman Empire from 1517 to 1918
Senegal	French West Africa	5,950	86	Portuguese colony from 1444; French colony from 1633 to 1960; federated with Gambia since December 1982
Somalia	Italian and British Somaliland	5,150	99	British part under protectorate from 1888 to 1960;

				Italian part under protectorate from 1889, joined to Ethiopia in 1935, occupied by Britain in 1941, and under British trusteeship to 1960
Sudan	Anglo-Egyptian Sudan	19,150	72	Ottoman (Egyptian) colony from 1820 to 1885; British and Egyptian condominium from 1899 to 1956
Tunisia		6,650	92	French protectorate from 1881 to 1956
Turkey	Ottoman Empire	47,500	98	Part of Ottoman Empire from 14th century to 1923; portions occupied by Britain, France, and Greece between 1918 and 1923
United Arab Emirates	Trucial Oman	800	96	Separate emirates under British protectorate from 1892 to 1971
Yemen Arab Republic	Yemen	8,575	100	Part of Ottoman Empire from 1517 to 1918
Yemen, Peoples' Democratic Republic of	Aden, South Yemen	2,100	98	British colony in Aden from 1839 to 1967 and British treaties with various Arabia shaykhs; Aden Protectorate from 1937 to 1959; South Arabian Federation from 1959 to 1967

Note: Table prepared by Arthur Goldschmidt, Jr., assisted by Kenneth S. Mayers.
 Sources: Information Please Almanac, 1983 (New York: A & W Publishers, 1982), pp. 126f.; Richard V. Weeks, ed., *Muslim Peoples: A World Ethnographic Survey* (Westport, Conn.: Greenwood Press, 1978), pp. 499-527.

8

Muslim Responses
to Colonialism

John O. Voll

Muslims faced dramatically changing conditions during the nineteenth century. The balance of military and political power in the world was tipping clearly in favor of Western states. New intellectual formulations developing in Western societies had great strength and appeal beyond their original homelands. Like other peoples outside of Europe, Muslims faced the challenge of Western military, political, and ideological strength. The rise of the West to apparent global dominance is a major feature of nineteenth-century world history. The Muslim responses to this situation are an important part of modern Islamic history. They were, in many ways, influenced as much by the special character of Islamic traditions as they were by the nature of the Western challenge.

To many participants in nineteenth-century struggles, the interaction between the West and Islamic society appeared to be a life-and-death conflict. Muslim militants, painting the challenge to Islamic existence in dire terms, proclaimed the necessity of defending the faith against the infidels. Similarly, Westerners argued that Islam was an obstacle to progress. They agreed with the militants on at least one point: that westernized and "reformed" Islam would no longer be truly Islamic. However, other Muslims worked to create alternative paths for the further development of Islamic societies. These people proclaimed the compatibility of "true Islam" and modern ideas and provided the basis for "Islamic modernism." In addition to the militants and the modernists, there were Muslims who remained outside the direct control of Europeans for long periods of time. For these, the premodern dynamics of Islamic society remained strong, providing a clearly Islamic basis for later movements of purification and renewal.

Militants and "old-fashioned" revivalists have provided a major basis for Islamic continuity and dynamism in both the nineteenth and the twentieth centuries. In earlier periods such groups were a significant part of the Islamic experience. They were not movements reacting primarily to Western expansion, at least in their origins. It is important to recognize that the "Muslim response to the West" has been part of a broader network of forces at work within Islamic societies in the modern era.

Muslims responded to the changing global role of the West in a variety of ways. In the established states the governmental response was more influenced by the needs of military, economic, and administrative organization than by specifically Islamic factors. The reforms of leaders such as Muhammad Ali in Egypt, Mahmud II in Istanbul, and Ahmad Bey in Tunisia are good examples of this type of response. More explicitly Islamic themes can be seen in the experiences of revivalist Islam and in the development of intellectual responses. These two areas are the two basic types of responses that need to be examined here.

THE REVIVALIST RESPONSE

The basic and natural response of Muslim peoples to European military and political expansion was to fight. Throughout the world of Islam in the nineteenth century there were many wars in which Muslims fought. Many of these have been called "holy wars" because they were explicitly waged by Muslims against unbelievers. One significant feature of many of these militant efforts is that few of the "holy wars" actually began as anti-European movements and even fewer were explicitly "anti-Western" in their approach. They were opposed to "unbelief" in general. The explicit ideological rejection of Western scientific and technological attitudes is, ironically, more a feature of recent movements that oppose being intoxicated by Western ways of doing things than of the early, more traditional Islamic militant groups.

At the beginning of the nineteenth century, there were many activist revivalist movements within the world of Islam. These were movements whose primary goal was a strict adherence to the Qur'an and the sunna of the Prophet. Some were basically quiet reform efforts, while others resulted in major wars. The best-known of these is the Wahhabi movement in the Arabian peninsula. Established by Muhammad ibn Abd al-Wahhab (1703-92) in central Arabia, the movement aimed at creating a state and society in which non-Islamic practices were eliminated. The founding teacher became allied with the Saud family, whose support and military power provided the basis for a fundamentalist state. By 1805 the Wahhabis had conquered the Muslim holy cities of Mecca and Medina and were well-known throughout the Islamic world.

Through its success at the very center of the Islamic world, the Wahhabi movement became the most visible of the militant revivalist groups. Muslim and non-Muslim observers alike see the Wahhabi movement as a prototype for later Islamic fundamentalist groups. Whether or not other revivalists were influenced directly by the Wahhabis, their style of revivalism is seen by many as the archetype of activist revivalism in that era. Consequently, it is worth remembering that this movement developed within the Islamic world as a movement of internal reform. The changing role of the West had little direct impact. Militant Islamic revivalism has maintained this special character. In contrast with modernist and a wide range of other groupings, the motivations of the militant revivalists remain remarkably Islamic. As in medieval times, the existence of revivalism does not depend upon the existence of an external threat. Such a threat may help to define the "enemy," but fundamental motivations continue to be Islamic in many profound ways. This has given Islamic revivalism in the modern era a special sense of continuity and resilience in the rapidly changing conditions of the nineteenth and twentieth centuries.

Other early nineteenth-century militant movements provide examples of the variety of possible responses to Western expansion. At the eastern end of the Islamic world, in the islands of Southeast Asia, there was another activist renewal movement. In Sumatra the effort began as an attempt by local Muslim teachers to purge the life of the local people of non-Islamic practices. Teachers returning from the pilgrimage to Mecca brought a special enthusiasm to this task, and before long there was open fighting. These reformers, usually called the Padris, were, like the Wahhabis, originally a movement of domestic reform rather than of opposition to the Europeans. However, by 1820 the Dutch became involved in the fighting. They hoped to expand the area under their control by aiding local rulers who were challenged by the Padri militants. Eventually the Padris were defeated, and Dutch imperial control was firmly established in the region. This conflict set a tradition of combining Islamic revivalism with opposition to European imperialism.

A different revivalist response can be seen in West Africa, where, at the beginning of the nineteenth century, there was also a militant movement of Islamic renewal. There, Uthman dan Fodio (1754-1817), a religious teacher, began a movement of Islamic renewal that became a holy war against the local political and religious establishments. He believed that the practices of local Muslims were so far removed from the requirements of the Qur'an that they amounted to unbelief. The holy war spirit of West Africa provided the basis for a number of new states. While the dream of a unified and purely Islamic state for the whole area was not realized, a new system of Islamically defined states was created.

The revivalist states of West Africa were the product of local reforming zeal rather than of an anti-European struggle. Even after the expansion of European power in the area, West African revivalists tended to be more concerned with local departures from Qur'anic practice than they were with British and French expansion. The successors to Uthman dan Fodio, in fact, made their peace with the Europeans. A cooperative system of mutual support emerged, especially in Nigeria, where the British system of "indirect rule" provided support for the courts of the old rulers and used the formerly revivalist states as the basis for a system of imperial control. Even a militant movement that emerged after the establishment of substantial European control showed this willingness to come to terms with the Europeans. Al-Hajj Umar Tal (1794-1864), for example, led a revivalist holy war in the middle of the century in the upper Niger River area. He was willing to accept a division of the region between himself and the French, waging his holy war more against local African rulers than against the French.

The response of revivalist Muslims to the West depended upon local conditions. Wahhabis were able for some time to ignore European power. When they clashed with modernized forces, their enemies were themselves Muslims. The end of the first Wahhabi state came in the first half of the nineteenth century, as a result of defeat by the army of Muhammad Ali of Egypt. The West African revivalist tradition found it possible, at least at times, to accept some European presence. Direct opposition to European powers usually occurred when the Europeans allied themselves with local opponents of Muslim revivalists, as happened in Sumatra during the Padri wars. These three experiences illustrate the three possible options at the beginning of the nineteenth century in terms of response to the changing global role of the West: isolation, accommodation, or opposition.

By the beginning of the twentieth century these options had been greatly reduced. The critical factor was the issue of control. The primary goal of the revivalists was the sociomoral reconstruction of society in terms of a strict interpretation of the Qur'an. Because of the comprehensive nature of the Islamic message, this involved political as well as doctrinal activity. Early in the nineteenth century there were still large areas of the Islamic world that remained isolated from European activity. Only in those areas was the option of isolation a viable one. European expansion had reduced those areas significantly by the end of the century. As Europeans moved into previously isolated areas, local Muslims were faced with the alternatives of accommodation or open opposition. Because of the political implications of the Islamic mission, revivalists could not accept the direct rule of unbelievers except as a temporary tactic. Similarly, Europeans tended to mistrust revivalist Muslim leaders, seeing them as potential leaders of anti-European movements.

The end result was that Islamic revivalism came to be identified with local opposition to the expansion of European control. These Muslim groups were clearly anti-European in terms of political and military control, but they remained committed to their original goals of sociomoral reconstruction rather creating ideologies that either opposed or advocated Western ideas.

The major revivalist movements during the nineteenth century provide case studies in this general pattern. These movements were usually active in areas where central governments were not strong. Where relatively effective governments existed, as was the case in Egypt, the central Ottoman Empire, and Iran, governmental policies and reform efforts of a less explicitly Islamic nature dominated the scene. The best-known revivalist movements took place in northern and northeastern Africa and in northern India. An examination of some of them can provide specific examples of the variety of revivalist responses to the West.

The open-holy-war response in the style of the Padris can be seen in the movement of Sayyid Ahmad Brelwi (1786-1831) in India. Sayyid Ahmad's movement was built on clearly Islamic foun-

dations, carrying on eighteenth-century traditions of Muslim reform in India. He believed that the great tradition of Islamic rule in
India was crumbling because Muslims in India were lax in adhering
to their faith. His movement of vigorous preaching soon aroused
opposition and led to open conflict. Sayyid Ahmad was not primarily concerned with opposing the expanding British control. He
stressed eliminating Hindu practices from the daily lives of Muslims. When his movement led to holy war, it was against the non-
Muslim Sikhs. Sayyid Ahmad did not accept the idea of rule by non-
Muslims, and thus was opposed to the British as well as the Sikhs,
but anti-British actions were only a small part of his revivalism.
Sayyid Ahmad was killed in the war against the Sikhs. It was only
with the expansion of direct British rule after his death that his followers became associated with open opposition to the British.
Sayyid Ahmad's followers joined in the great Sepoy Mutiny against
the British in 1857 and were the object of an active British campaign to crush their movement. The movement was reduced in size
and effectiveness, but by the end of the century it represented the
tradition of militant Islamic opposition to British rule.

In North Africa another movement existed that was built on
eighteenth-century revivalist foundations and later assumed the
mission of opposing European expansion. When the French invaded Algeria in 1830, they were opposed by the forces of Amir
Abd al-Qadir (1808-1883), whose father and grandfather had been
active in the work of revivalist reforms. They had established an
educational center and were respected by many people in the
major tribes of Algeria. As a result, the local people looked to this
family for leadership, and Abd al-Qadir organized effective resistance to the French until his final defeat in 1847. This movement
maintained a dual goal of defeating the French and of creating a
truly Islamic community. Abd al-Qadir was not, however, inflexi-
bly and unalterably opposed to the West. He was willing to attempt
an accommodation with the French, but French goals of complete
domination of Algeria made such a compromise impossible. Abd
al-Qadir was opposed to European expansion in political and military terms, but he was willing to adopt new ideas and techniques
whenever they promised to make the operation of his army or his
community more effective. Abd al-Qadir has come to be viewed by
modern Algerians as the first Algerian "nationalist" because of his
opposition to the French. He was, however, a Muslim revivalist having origins and goals similar to those of other nineteenth-century

figures. Building on indigenous inspiration, the militant response to the West was only a part of the basic nature of the movement.

In a variety of circumstances and using different types of organizations, this same general experience was repeated during the nineteenth century. Groups utilizing the revivalist style of the traditional Sufi brotherhood or the inspiration of a messiahlike figure (called "The Mahdi") coming to usher in the new age of divine guidance share many characteristics. The best-known brotherhood of the century, in terms of relations with European powers, was probably the Sanusiyyah, while the most famous "mahdi" was Muhammad Ahmad in the Sudan.

The Sanusiyyah was organized in the middle of the century by Muhammad ibn Ali al-Sanusi (1787-1859). He had been a student of intellectually revivalist scholars in Mecca and Medina after receiving a traditional Islamic education in his homeland in North Africa. As a mature scholar he often clashed with conservative Islamic teachers, but he appears to have had little concern about European ideas. He set out to put his revivalist ideas into practice by establishing a Sufi brotherhood that was dedicated to building a community based on the Qur'an. He carried on his work in the area of modern-day Libya and surrounding territories. The fruit of his labor was a network of centers among the tribes that became the focus of regional intellectual and political life. The heartland of the Sanusiyyah was relatively isolated, but by the end of the century European forces began to limit the areas of the brotherhood's influence. There was a series of clashes with French forces in central Saharan Africa. Then, just before World War I, Italy attacked Libya and the local resistance was primarily organized by the Sanusiyyah. In this way the revivalist organization of Muhammad ibn Ali al-Sanusi became the major instrument of local opposition to European expansion.

The Mahdi in the Sudan, Muhammad Ahmad (1848-85), also began by preaching against the corruptions of the Islamic faith and practice that he saw around him in the Nile valley south of Egypt. He soon was drawn into militant opposition to the government, which at that time was a provincial administration under Egyptian control. For reasons related to global imperial policy, Britain was drawn into the struggle on the side of the Egyptians. As a result, another revivalist, purification effort became a major movement opposed to European military expansion. The Sudanese Mahdi succeeded in establishing a state that lasted for almost a decade and a half after his death before it was finally conquered by an Anglo-Egyptian army. Like Abd al-Qadir in Algeria, the Sudanese Mahdi was later seen as a "first nationalist" because of his struggles against European imperialists. However, in motivation and origin the Mahdi was a Muslim revivalist drawn into conflict with European powers by events rather than simply being an anti-Western "fanatic."

These cases reemphasize that the Muslim revivalist response to the West in the nineteenth century was part of a broader network of forces within Islamic societies. The authentic Islamic tradition, with strong lines of continuity to the past, remained a vital force. These revivalist movements were not simply movements of opposition to European expansion. Many of them had their roots in motivations and developments not directly related to European activities. However, these movements were involved in conflicts with various European powers. Whatever the original situation may have been, the movements became symbols of opposition to Western expansion.

These conflicts were basically political and military in nature. They were contests for control. In most cases of conflict between Muslim revivalists and Western forces, the ideological and intellectual element was limited. Revivalists were quite willing to utilize Western techniques and organizational ideas if it appeared that they would aid the believers in the military and political conflict with unbelievers. Abd al-Qadir, the Sanusiyyah, and the forces of the Sudanese Mahdi made use of Western technology with no real ideological reservation. It is important to remember that the militant revivalist opposition to the West was not opposed to using modern techniques; rather, it was opposed to Western political and military control of Islamic societies. There was also an intellectual and ideological response to the Western challenge, but it came from other Muslims.

THE INTELLECTUAL RESPONSE

The primary issue in the intellectual response to the changing global role of the West was defining the relationship between Western ideas and the Islamic message. In the nineteenth century there were very few Muslims who were willing to question the validity of the basic message of Islam. The debates among Muslims focused, rather, on the definition of what that basic message was and how it was related to Western ideas current at that time, which themselves were not consistent or unchanging.

The development of Muslim intellectual responses took place primarily where there was significant, long-term interaction with the West: Egypt, Istanbul, and India. There were some common factors and assumptions within this variety of intellectual activity. One factor was the older intellectual elite of religious thinkers, the ulama or "learned men" of Islam, who remained remarkably aloof from interacting with Western ideas. Rather than providing a traditional critique of the new ideas, the ulama tended to ignore them. This failure to come to terms intellectually with the West was also the case among the Islamic revivalists, who tended to focus on the political and military aspects of interaction with the West. As a result, those who did deal with the implications of Western thought were less antagonistic toward it than they might otherwise have been, since traditional Muslim thinkers had little to offer as a counterargument.

A second element common to Muslim intellectual response is related to this. The general evaluation of the West was favorable, at least in the sense that the West was recognized as being "successful." Muslims may have had reservations about European life and thought, but there was a common assumption that Europeans were succeeding in many ways. This widely held assumption meant that a basic part of the Muslim intellectual response was the effort to define the basis of European "success" and show how it related to the basic message of Islam. Few Muslims were willing to present a negative evaluation of the West, although finally, by the end of the century, there were some who saw certain aspects of Western life as signs of weakness. The West was, for example, considered too materialistic by some thinkers, but even these people supported the introduction of techniques that would raise the standard of living of Muslims or increase Muslim military power. It was not until the twentieth century that Muslim thinkers began to develop an intellectual response based on the assumption that the West had fundamentally failed or that Western ideas were fundamentally in error.

The withdrawal of the ulama from the arena of intellectual interaction also helped to create a third characteristic of nineteenth-century intellectual responses to the West. While few, if any, Muslims were willing to question the basic message of Islam, most of those who thought about Western ideas were unhappy with the situation of Islamic societies in their own day. The ulama were the people with a reason to defend the ideas and explanations inherited from medieval times. Their withdrawal meant that other Muslim thinkers were free to blame the nineteenth-century weakness of the world of Islam on the inherited ideas and structures of the medieval Muslim communities. These new thinkers, like the revivalists, proclaimed the need to go back to the Qur'an itself rather than simply to accept later medieval interpretations. Thus, the intellectual response to the West was generally highly critical of existing Muslim institutions and intellectual formulations, and set out to respond to European ideas on the basis of a reexamination of the fundamental sources of Islam.

In the first half of the nineteenth century, the ideological implications of contact with the West were not a focus of great concern, even in Egypt, Istanbul, or India. Most attention in those areas was given to the governmental reform effort or, as in India, the more revivalist movements. However, later in the century there was a major scholarly effort in response to the ideological implications of the Western challenge.

In Egypt this effort was primarily the work of individuals. No major organization or institution emerged out of the work of the significant Muslim thinkers. These were people who were active in a context that produced a variety of intellectual trends, ranging from liberal constitutionalism to Egyptian nationalism. Because most of the people involved in all of these trends were Muslims, one might speak of this nationalism or this liberalism as a response of Muslims, but these were not explicitly Islamic responses. At the same time, however, Islamic ideas helped, in some ways at least, to shape emerging nationalist and liberal ideas. A specifically Islamic response also emerged within Egypt that was to have an impact throughout the Islamic world. It was here that the most widely followed form of "Islamic modernism" developed.

By mid-century the effort to provide a basis for integrating Islamic and Western ideas was beginning in Egypt. Rifa'a al-Tahtawi (1801-73) was one of the few ulama who took Western ideas seriously. After working in Paris with a diplomatic mission, he returned to Egypt and was a major figure in communicating an understanding of Western ideas. At the same time he began the process of showing that those ideas were compatible with the Islamic message.

Later in the century another Egyptian thinker created a formal basis for Islamic modernism. This teacher was Muhammad Abduh (1849-1905). As a young man Abduh had been involved in more activist nationalist and Islamic activities, and was a student and associate of another major figure on the late nineteenth-century Islamic ideological scene, Jamal al-Din al-Afghani (of whom more will be said later). Abduh came to accept the political-military realities of British control in Egypt. He set out to provide a full reinterpretation of Islam in modern terms and rejected the medieval formulations and existing Islamic institutions. On the basis of his own direct analysis of the Qur'an, he created a persuasive intellectual integration of modernist rational thought and Islamic ideals.

On the basis of this integration, a new generation of Muslims whose education made them familiar with Western ideas was able to affirm a modernist Islam. Abduh's influence soon spread far beyond Egypt. He called for a return to the basic principles of Islam as exemplified by the lives of the pious ancestors who were companions of the Prophet. The Arabic term for those ancestors is *salaf,* and the intellectual traditions of Abduh came to be called the Salafiyyah. Salafiyyah ideas inspired the thinking and faith of new generations of educated Muslims from Morocco to Indonesia. Salafiyyah modernism became a powerful influence in modern Islamic life. Abduh's synthesis was a basic affirmation of the truth of the Islamic message as presented in the Qur'an and interpreted through the canons of rational thought. It presented the conviction that one could be both modern and a faithful Muslim. Involved in these positions is a belief in the "success" of the West as well as a rejection of the medieval Islamic ideas. Through Abduh and the influence of the Salafiyyah, Egypt became one of the major centers of modern Islamic thought.

In Istanbul the Islamically oriented intellectual response to the West was directed more toward governmental issues. This was especially fitting because Istanbul was the capital of the major remaining Islamic empire in the world, the Ottoman Empire. Governmental reform along modern lines had begun in the early years of the century, under the leadership of Sultan Mahmud II (1785-1839). Although specifically Islamic issues only gradually grew in importance, by mid-century Istanbul was becoming a major center of new Islamic thought. The practical problems of legal reform produced a major effort to integrate Islamic legal principles with new concepts inspired by contact with the West. Later in the century a new group of thinkers emerged, called the Young Ottomans. They presented a liberal interpretation of Islam that stressed principles of equality, arguing that a constitutional parliamentary system represented the basic principles of the Islamic message. This type of politically oriented integration was not uncommon in the Islamic world. Like the thought of Abduh, it started from a favorable definition of the Western experience and sought, as well, to go back to basic Islamic principles while rejecting later medieval Muslim formulations.

At the end of the century, two figures emerged in Istanbul who represent a culmination of a number of trends: Abd al-Hamid II and Jamal al-Din al-Afghani. In both of these men two elements were combined: the integrated Western and Islamic ideas visible in the Salafiyyah and the Young Ottomans, and the more militant mood typical of later Islamic revivalists.

Jamal al-Din al-Afghani (1839-97) was an itinerant scholar who provided intellectual content for late nineteenth-century Pan-Islamic ideals. He traveled and taught throughout the Middle East, and was in exile in Europe for a time. He emerged as a significant defender of Islam in various debating forums, arguing that Islam was compatible with modern ideas. He worked for Islamic political unity, believing it necessary to save Muslims from total European conquest, but he never made the transition that his student Abduh did, of accepting the politico-military realities of the time. Near the end of the century he came to Istanbul, where his Pan-Islamic enthusiasm coincided with the politics of Sultan Abd al-Hamid II. However, the sultan's autocratic methods soon limited al-Afghani's freedom of expression.

Abd al-Hamid II (1842-1918) came to the throne of the Ottoman Empire in 1876. As sultan he carried on reform efforts to modernize the administration and army of that empire, which were made more explicitly Islamic under his leadership. Abd al-Hamid II sought to make the Ottoman sultan the leading spokesman for Muslims throughout the world. To this end he emphasized that he held the title of caliph, or successor to the Prophet Muhammad, in leading the global Muslim community. As a vigorous believer in unifying the political and military actions of the world's Muslims under his own leadership, Abd al-Hamid found it useful to patronize al-Afghani while seeking to establish networks of supporters from Morocco to Indonesia. He represented an interesting and significant combination of modernizing reform and militant activism in the name of Islam. He was also an autocratic ruler who roused the opposition of the more liberal modernizers within the ruling establishment, and was overthrown early in the twentieth century. His type of Pan-Islamic vision survived a while longer but died, for all practical purposes, with the Ottoman Empire during World War I.

Abd al-Hamid and al-Afghani illustrate the militant potential of Islamic modernism. However, in both cases it was European military and political power, not Western ideas as such, that were opposed. Theirs was an effort of militant modernizing synthesis.

In India the situation was very different. Effective military and political opposition to British rule seemed impossible to most Muslim thinkers. The defeat of the movement of Ahmad Brelwi, the crushing of the Sepoy Mutiny in 1857, and the end of real political independence in any form made political activism seem hopeless to all but a very small number of Indian Muslims. As a result, after about 1860, while there were some small-scale Islamic revolts, the major effort was to provide a general reorientation of Islam within the context of foreign control. A luxuriant variety of Muslim options developed by the end of the nineteenth century.

Sayyid Ahmad Khan (1817-98) was the leading intellectual figure in the reorientation of Islamic thought in India. He believed that Muslims had to adapt to the new intellectual conditions of the modern world. In his thinking, nature and natural law, as studied by Western science, represented the work of God, which was explained and interpreted by the Word of God, the Qur'an. He rejected "unscientific" medieval Islamic intellectual formulations, and sought to build a new and comprehensive intellectual basis for Islamic thought. As a result, his major arena of activity was education, and he helped to establish the major center of Islamic modernist thought in India, the Muhammadan Anglo-Oriental College at Aligarh.

A distinctive feature of the Indian situation was that educational institutions emerged as a major focus of the Islamic response. The major intellectual options came to be represented in a number of distinctive and active schools. Ahmad Khan's school at Aligarh became the center of the intellectual life of those who worked for a friendly integration of Western and Muslim ideas. Other educational institutions emerged as the focal points for other perspectives. It was through such institutions that the conservative ulama in India provided an active rather than the normally passive conservative response to the new intellectual challenges.

Conservative Islamic thought accepted the basic lines of medieval scholarship. The idea of utilizing independent personal judgment in interpreting the basic sources of Islam was rejected in favor of basing contemporary analysis on the accepted conclusions of the major medieval Muslim thinkers. In the early part of the nineteenth century, the key institution in maintaining this viewpoint was a school at Lucknow, the Faranji Mahal. The ulama of this school maintained the curriculum based on a syllabus of instruction that had been successfully established in the eighteenth century. Intellectually, these scholars tended to ignore the new elements faced by their society but were more actively involved in presenting the conservative interpretation as an intelligent option. This appears to have been possible because the political dimension of Islamic life in India was reduced by the apparently unavoidable British rule. Conservative ulama in India thus had a freedom to remain intellectually conservative but socially involved that was not possible where Muslims were still, at least in theory, ruling themselves.

While Faranji Mahal ulama tended to ignore Islamic modernist trends, active conservative opposition to the ideas of men like Sayyid Ahmad Khan developed during the nineteenth century. The focus for this effort was a school established in the second half of the century at Deoband. This school gained international prestige for the high quality of its instruction in the traditional Islamic disciplines. It also became widely known as an articulate defender of the conservative Islamic intellectual tradition. The Deoband scholars were not aloof from society. They were willing and able to argue in opposition to modernist positions in a way that most ulama in other parts of the Islamic world would not and could not. The rivalry between the Deoband school and the followers of Sayyid Ahmad Khan produced a school that attempted to integrate the two positions. This was the Nadwat al-Ulama, established in 1894. Although some well-known Indian Muslim scholars, such as Shibli Numani, were associated with the school, as a compromise effort it was neither "orthodox" enough for the conservatives nor "modern" enough for the modernists. Its creation does, however, illustrate the extraordinary fertility and diversity of the Islamic intellectual response to the West in India.

In general terms, during the nineteenth century the Muslim intellectual responses to the West were either conservative or modernist. By the end of the century, few thinkers anywhere in the world distingushed between Western and modern. As a result, the concept of a modernized Islam that was not a westernized Islam was not yet an important element in the thinking of Muslims. This would remain the case until the revivalist stream of Islamic history turned its attention to intellectual issues in the twentieth century.

There were thus two broad types of responses in the Islamic world to the changing global role of the West in the nineteenth century: the revivalist response and the intellectual response. In both cases the responses were shaped by the nature of the inherited Islamic tradition as well as by the characteristics of the Western challenges. Revivalist movements frequently concerned themselves with "responding to the West" only after they had been firmly established on clearly indigenous Islamic foundations. It was the revivalists who maintained the sense of autonomy of Islam during the nineteenth century. This response thus laid the groundwork for the twentieth century Islamic fundamentalist movements.

The heritage of the nineteenth-century intellectual response is the conviction that modern and Islamic ideals are not necessarily in opposition to each other. Significant Muslim thinkers of the century, such as Muhammad Abduh and Sayyid Ahmad Khan, created a vocabulary for modernist Islam and a modernist style of thought that was essential for Islamic intellectual responses. Their strength was that they provided a way in which a Muslim could be both effectively modern and a believing Muslim. Their weakness lay in the fact that because they could not distinguish between Western and modern ideas, their Islamic modernism inevitably tried to adopt Western modes of thought and action. As a result, Islamic modernism appeared to be a borrowed ideology or a derivative way of thinking rather than an authentically Islamic and, at the same time, modern world view.

The Muslim responses to the West in the nineteenth century were diverse and dynamic. They were, in many significant ways, continuations of existing lines of development within Islamic societies. They were also important foundations for the special types of Islamic experiences that were to emerge in the twentieth century. At the time the overwhelming miltary power of European states made it seem that the interaction between Islam and the West in the nineteenth century was a life-and-death struggle. From the perspective of the late twentieth century, one might see that earlier era as a time of transition and transformation, with the Muslim response to the West being part of the long-term evolution of Islamic experiences in history.

9

Muslim Nation-States

Marjorie Kelly

World War I and its aftermath, with the division of Muslim territory into the Western system of international political organization, nation-states, resulted in the final breakup of any semblance of a politically unified umma. The Arabs who formerly lived within the confines of the Ottoman Empire experienced this change forcefully when Britain and France, League of Nations mandates in hand, occupied the Fertile Crescent. They did so ostensibly to develop the region into independent states based on the principles of self-determination and liberal democracy. But European imperialism was hardly a role model for demonstrating the practice of participatory government, for it not only deprived local inhabitants of sovereignty but also made it difficult, if not impossible, for all but a few to develop a sense of allegiance to a state whose boundaries and priorities were determined by European Christians. A sense of nationhood, civic responsibility, and accountable government were stunted. What developed instead was resentment of the West, disillusionment with Western ideals, and regimes that were increasingly susceptible to religious pressures as the masses became more politicized.

While the focus of this chapter will be the Arab heartland (Egypt through Iraq), similar trends and circumstances can be found not only in other Muslim societies—Arab and non-Arab—but in many other Third World nations as well. Here, however, particular attention is paid to the various ideological responses to change—liberalism, nationalism, socialism, and what is called Islamic revivalism—that sprang from the continuing Western challenge to the Muslim world view. It makes little difference whether the Western challenge is identified as secular, Christian, or Jewish; the point is that it is not Islamic. The Muslim intention is to avoid

Western domination while accepting Western technology and still retaining a sense of self based on traditional values and institutions that have been severely called into question, if not discarded or permanently altered.

How should Muslim societies that claim as their basis the eternally valid Qur'an and sunna of the Prophet, deal with technologically advanced societies that value change and export it without regard to its impact on others? Should Muslims trust, as the revivalists did, that by following religious traditions they will inevitably triumph in the end? Or should they opt for adaptation, as the modernists urged, and eventually be forced to determine where to draw the line? The "shoulds" must be left to Muslim thinkers; the experiments in "how" are the subject of this chapter.

THE POLITICAL NATURE OF THE UMMA

Islamic doctrine does not draw a line between state and religion; indeed, it does not recognize the validity of a secular approach to life. Muhammad was simultaneously religious leader, military commander, and head of state. Military success and political power were inextricably linked with the initial Islamic conquests. Islam's expansion and triumph were guaranteed with God as sovereign of a universal Muslim state. In its purest form Islamic government could only be government for the people; it could not be by the people, since legislative power belongs solely to God; nor is it government of the people, since legitimacy rests not with the consent of the governed but in surrender to God's law. Initially, then, power and authority were one and the same.

However, as has been discussed in previous chapters, there arose the problem of the Prophet's successor and who was to hold temporal power. Without a clearly stated principle of succession, division eventually occurred between those holding power and those commanding authority. The Umayyads are regarded as a dynasty of secular monarchs, and the Abbasid caliphs came to be dependent on their military commanders for power. Rulers thus had to be responsive to both the men of the pen—the ulama—and the men of the sword—the military—for the ulama provided legitimacy and authority, and the military provided the means to power.

Theoretically the ruler was responsible only to God; therefore, it was his duty to apply the shari'a, maintain public order, and protect Muslim subjects and territory against non-Muslims. In return, Muslims owed the ruler obedience. Rebellions sometimes occurred against rulers who were regarded as failing to live up to their duties, but far more often even tyrants were given obedience in the belief that civil unrest was to be avoided at all costs. Opposition became tantamount to treason, if not heresy. In a society organized on God's law there could be no concept of or room for a "loyal opposition."

And what of the relationship between ruler and ulama? The ulama studied, preserved, and interpreted the sacred law, thus fulfilling the judicial function of government. While they rarely wielded power, the ulama could manipulate it by legitimating political rule and molding social conduct. In effect, they held a veto power that was flexible in interpretation as long as the political establishment accorded primacy of place to the shari'a. In short, God had legislated, the Prophet proclaimed, the ulama interpreted, rulers administered, and people obeyed.

For Muslims, history was a process that verified this order of things. After all, the Islamic community had enjoyed phenomenal success in a very brief time, and remained hale and hearty for centuries. Then things began to change, and change could only be for the worse. The hadith reported the Prophet as saying that his generation was the finest in Islam, and therefore each succeeding generation would be further from the Truth. Consequently, change was not something to be valued, but something to be overcome by reviving what had once existed. There was a belief that periodically a renewer of the faith would appear in the community; the movements described in Chapter 8 are in this tradition. But another, more secular response was evoked as well by the West, and it involved imitation. Islamic civilization had met and adapted elements of other civilizations before: pre-Islamic Arab customs, Byzantine and Persian administrative procedures, Greek philosophy; but these were all met and mastered in an environment where Muslims were dominant, and on a scale and at a rate of change that made absorption and integration possible. This time the umma were not so favored and the opposition was far more threatening.

Consistently beaten in battle, the Muslims lost territory permanently—and even greater losses loomed. Only competition among

European powers kept the Ottoman Empire alive, if not intact. Muslims were forced to ask themselves two questions: how could this turn of events be reversed, and why had it happened?

THE AGE OF REFORM

Clearly the European way of doing things was very different from that experienced by the inhabitants of the Ottoman Empire. The Ottomans (and their successors) originally believed all they needed to do was determine which element or elements among all those differences accounted for European dominance, and then imitate them. Was it Europe's political ideology and institutions—representative government, constitutions, and parliaments? Was it the educational system—its content, methodology, institutions? Or was it secularism—a world view that put the concerns of this world first? The experiments aimed at answering these questions occurred over time; in the eighteenth and nineteenth centuries the immediate goal was to strengthen that part of Muslim society most directly concerned with meeting the threat from the West, the military.

In 1798 Napoleon was sent by the French to capture Egypt. The French occupation lasted until 1801, when the British destroyed the French fleet. In the course of the occupation, the Ottomans sent an Albanian regiment to Egypt to dislodge the French. One of the regiment's officers was Muhammad Ali, founder of the dynasty that was to rule Egypt until 1952, when King Faruq was exiled. Muhammad Ali rose to power with the support of the traditional twin pillars: the ulama and the army. By 1805 he had secured the support of the ulama and local notables; by 1806 he had replaced the Ottoman appointee as governor with the sultan's consent; in 1811 the members of the previous political establishment who had not already joined forces with him or fled the country were massacred. By eliminating all rivals for power without triggering European intervention, Muhammad Ali was in a position to initiate reforms based on political, social, and economic control to a degree previously unknown in Muslim society.

His goal was not to modernize society, but to modernize the state so it could better defend itself externally and the ruling establishment internally. Reforms thus began with the military, but their impact was felt throughout the society. Soldiers needed training, and foreigners were hired to provide the type that Muhammad Ali desired. New schools were set up, new languages of instruction were learned, new equipment and supplies were produced in new factories run by the state, using materials marketed by the state and produced on land controlled by the state. To pay for the reforms, Muhammad Ali had assumed control of nearly all the country's land and was sole owner of the newly established factories.

Given the systematic demolition of political rivals, his only possible opponents were the ulama. How were they dealt with? Unwilling to offend religious sensitivities, Muhammad Ali made no attempt to reform the religious establishment—which is not to say that he did not come to control it. By making the ulama economically dependent on the state and setting up secular institutions that successfully paralleled the functions performed by the ulama, Muhammad Ali began the process that eventually made the ulama responsive to the secularized government, if not irrelevant. Military schools offered a type of education at great variance with traditional religious training; students read books in European languages rather than the Qur'an and commentaries; commercial and criminal courts were set up outside the scope of the shari'a; religious endowment property was confiscated or taxed by the state; and the state assumed responsibility for appointing the head of al-Azhar University. In short, a policy of benign neglect combined with centralized administration resulted in the decline of religious institutions and the loss of income for the ulama. Left to its own devices, the religious establishment struggled along as best it could.

By 1839 Muhammad Ali's army was a threat to Istanbul, and only British intervention prevented further expansion. Thus curtailed, Muhammad Ali's interest in building up Egypt declined. However, his descendants, especially Isma'il (r. 1863-79), instituted reform programs that expanded Muhammad Ali's efforts. Determined to make Egypt a part of Europe, Isma'il did not stop his building program with roads, bridges, railroads, ports, and canals; he also built an opera house, palaces, an observatory, a museum, a national library—all the cultural trappings of a European capital. Slavery was officially abolished, modern legal codes and banks were introduced, private ownership of land was expanded, and, above all, the Suez Canal was built—to the profit of its European backers and at the great expense of Egyptians. The canal was significant in two respects: it gave Egypt, as part of Britain's lifeline to India, a new prominence in British strategic considerations, and it exemplified the tremendous social and economic toll taken by the wholesale imitation of the West.

Egypt's rulers were not interested in educating Egyptians or in modernizing society. People were trained as needed to staff the new army (officers only), schools, and bureaucracy. (This set the unfortunate precedent of guaranteed government employment for every college graduate that continues to strain the Egyptian economy.) Those who could afford it attended secular institutions on their own initiative—many going abroad to study—with the result that a whole new group of occupations was created (doctor, lawyer, teacher, journalist, engineer) that became the basis of Egypt's intellectual elite. This new elite—in terms of education, occupation, dress, outlook, and life-style—was alien to those elements of society that had not experienced any of the benefits of modernization. The difference between the elite and the masses was now one of substance rather than of degree; and the political, social, and economic disintegration of the country was under way. In the rush to modernize the state, little (if any) attempt was made to integrate the old with the new, and most Egyptians were left behind in the process.

Modernization and secularization, it should be noted, do not, and did not, necessarily mean atheism. Europeanized Muslims did not necessarily become unbelievers. Religion for this group frequently became a private rather than a public matter, and could still be of deep concern on an individual rather than a social basis. The nature of the state changed correspondingly. No longer the means to a religious end, the state became an end in itself, and religion was to become the means of furthering that end by providing legitimacy and social cohesion through a shared value system.

If the Egyptians were divided along social, political, and economic lines, they were united in one respect: their opposition to British rule. Under Isma'il the public debt had grown from £7 million in 1863 to £93 million in 1879. When bankruptcy was declared in 1876, the British and French established a commission to assume control of Egyptian finances and pay off European loans. Eventually the British occupied Egypt, raised government revenue, and paid off the debt. But the British found it easier to enter Egypt than to give it up, and, under one pretext or another, they remained until the 1950s.

Opposition had appeared by 1879 among the army, the intelligentsia, and members of the assembly, aimed at ending foreign control and establishing a constitution. Differences continued to exist between segments of Egyptian society: the elite wanted to create an independent nation-state in imitation of the European model, and the masses longed for an end to Western dominance and foreign ways. In the decades-long struggle for independence that followed, these fundamental differences in world view were glossed over and the socioeconomic factors that caused them went unaddressed or were blamed on the British. The result was an ever-increasing gap between the haves and the have-nots.

THE LIBERAL EXPERIMENT

Despite the British occupation of Egypt in 1882, the country was technically an autonomous province of the Ottoman Empire from 1841 to 1914. When confronted with the Turkish alliance with Germany, the British assumed official control of Egypt and declared it a protectorate. World War I had other effects on Egypt vis-à-vis the British: the quality of British administrators declined as the more able were recalled for military service, and the enlarged British military presence led to inflation and economic hardship for native Egyptians. Two days after the European armistice, the British high commissioner was visited by a delegation (*wafd*), headed by Sa'd Zaghlul (1857-1927), which announced its desire to attend the Paris Peace Conference and argue for Egyptian independence.

The son of a prosperous peasant, Zaghlul was educated at al-Azhar University, studied law in France, and became minister of education. He is best known for founding the Wafd, which was to become the first nationalist party with a mass following, in 1919. In response to his demand for representation at the peace conference, the British exiled Zaghlul, thereby triggering a popular revolt. The British relented, and Zaghlul left Malta to attend the Paris Peace Conference, only to find on his arrival that the United States had recognized the British protectorate. The Wafd was never invited to address the conference. Agitation in Egypt continued until, in 1922, the British unilaterally declared the protectorate at an end and Egypt independent—excepting several areas of concern subject to British interest.

There then began the three-cornered (British, king, and Wafd) political situation that lasted for several decades. The Wafd, now organized as a political party, would win a majority of seats in the parliament and demand complete independence, to which the British would not agree. The king would then dismiss parliament, replace Zaghlul or his successor, Nahas, or suspend the constitution until popular outcry reached the point at which the whole process would begin again. With all the energy focused on political maneuvering, little was left to channel toward eradicating poverty, illiteracy, and disease.

The Wafd was not the only party that existed, however, nor were all of Egypt's elite so involved in politics that they were oblivious to the other problems confronting the country. Intellectuals such as Ahmad Lutfi al-Sayyid (1872-1963), Taha Husayn (1889-1973), and Muhammad Husayn Haykal (1889-1956) grappled with the principles of constitutionalism, liberalism, and secularism, and their application to Egypt. They felt Egypt needed to modernize, and that education was the key.

Other elements of Egyptian society were organized into associations aimed at establishing a different kind of social order. In 1928 Hassan al-Banna founded the Muslim Brotherhood in Isma'ilia. The son of an imam, al-Banna foresaw that even if the nationalists were able to win immediate independence for Egypt, an Islamic social order would not be forthcoming. His Muslim Brotherhood attracted members of the petite and middle bourgeoisie: artisans, clerks, small businessmen, lower-level professionals. It provided them with religious instruction, social services, economic enterprises, and a sense of mission and social cohesion. Fiercely opposed to westernization, it had great influence—not least among nationalist young army officers.

Secular liberalism lost its bright promise during the bitter struggle of the 1930s and 1940s. The reasons were many. First and probably foremost, the liberal democratic institutions developed over centuries in the West did not reflect the values and experiences of the Muslim world. Not only were the political institutions and ideology alien, but there was no educated middle class with a vested interest in maintaining the system. Even if the colonial powers had taken local parliaments seriously and refrained from intervening, it is debatable whether this transplanted form of government would have proved successful.

While the educated surely had a sophisticated understanding of Western political systems and values, they had no experience of it. Parliaments were controlled by the wealthy and powerful, who were not inclined to jeopardize their vested interests by sharing decision making with others. Deeply disillusioned and bitterly frustrated, the younger generations of the educated turned from liberal patriotism to a more urgently felt nationalism. The European powers were no longer the prestigious victors of World War I but the exhausted allies of World War II, and for those who had struggled against them for decades in the hope of obtaining independence, their idealistic talk of self-determination and representative democracy was now viewed with cynicism.

Finally, the entire liberal experiment meant very little to the masses. Their needs continued to go unaddressed and their plight only worsened. The fact that the elite's experiment with European-style government had been tried and had failed meant nothing to them. Their belief system and world view remained largely unchanged. An appeal had yet to be made to them in a language and by a means they could understand.

THE GROWTH OF NATIONALISM

Throughout the nineteenth century the Ottoman Turks and the Arabs of the Fertile Crescent were more closely connected than were the Ottomans and Egyptians. As the Ottoman government centralized its rule, Arab local control diminished. The situation was exacerbated when policy in Istanbul shifted from the Pan-Islam of Sultan Abd al-Hamid II to the Turkish domination of the Committee of Union and Progress. What the Arabs of the Fertile Crescent wanted at that point was greater local autonomy, not separation—much less the colonial rule with which they eventually wound up.

The issue was more than differences in ethnicity or Islam versus secularism—although the Turks were blamed by some Arabs for the backwardness of their society and for "corrupting" Islam. Greater Syria (the region that today is Lebanon, Syria, Jordan, Israel, and a part of southern Turkey) had a large Arab Christian population, many of whom enjoyed the protection of European powers. The French had established a special relationship with the

Maronites, and the Russians did likewise with the Greek Orthodox Syrians. An additional Western influence existed in the form of mission schools. Arabs, and especially Christian Arabs, attended these schools and acquired Western ideas that they were anxious to implement in their own societies. Thus the impact of increased Turkish domination plus a heightened awareness of Arabness through increased literacy and expanded outlook combined to lay the basis for an Arab nationalism to which Arab Christians contributed in a significant fashion.

The political manifestation of a separate identity for Arabs and Turks (as opposed to a united Muslim umma) sprang from a more traditional source: Sharif Husayn of Mecca. A descendant of the Prophet, the sharif had struggled against Ottoman domination and subsequently corresponded with Sir Henry McMahon, Britain's high commissioner in Egypt, with regard to possible British military and financial aid in support of an Arab rebellion against the German-allied Turks. The Arab revolt was proclaimed at Mecca in 1916, in the name of preserving Islam and for the purpose of establishing an independent Arab state. Any understanding Husayn may have thought he had with the British was disregarded in favor of the Sykes-Picot Treaty.

Secretly signed in 1916, the treaty was an agreement among the signatories (Britain, France, and Russia) to divide up the Ottoman Empire, including the Fertile Crescent, after the war. The Communist revolution removed the Russians from the field, but Britain and France proceeded according to plan under the auspices of the League of Nations, with mandates for Syria and Lebanon going to France and those for Iraq and Palestine going to Britain. Additionally, the Balfour Declaration (named after British Foreign Secretary Lord Balfour) of November 2, 1917, spoke of setting up in Palestine a national home for Jews without prejudice to non-Jewish communities already residing there.

After the war Husayn's sons Faysal and Abdullah were given thrones in Iraq and Jordan, respectively, by the British. The French carved Syria into five separately administered sections in a divide-and-rule policy. Using minorities to help administer colonial rule, the European powers proceeded to establish control. There were outbreaks of violence and rebellion, particularly in Syria, that had to be quelled; but equally dangerous to colonial rule were the ideas of Western-trained Arabs who had learned to fight with the pen in seeking to establish a new, Arab-based sense of identity that was antithetical to foreign rule. Interestingly, it was Christian Arabs who led the way against their coreligionists.

Even before the turn of the century, a literary revival had begun in Cairo and Beirut with the appearance of newspapers and journals written in modernized Arabic by Syrian Christians educated in French or American schools. Attracted by the model of Western secularism, Christian intellectuals also saw that, in adopting secular Arab nationalism as the basis for communal solidarity, they could participate as full citizens in nation building as they never could in a reform of the umma. It was proposed that shared language, history, and culture, rather than religion, be the basis of a single Arab nation-state. This is not to say that Islam was not an important component of Arab nationalism, even among Christian Arabs, for it was too deeply woven into Arab tradition to be ignored or discarded. It became, however, an arabized Islam, regarded more as a cultural tradition than as the basis of a society. This integration of nationalism and Islam is in contrast with the post-World War I secularized states of Turkey and Iran. Having maintained their independence, these states may have felt less need to establish a point of reference in contradistinction to an occupying power. For Arabs, however, the Arabic-language Qur'an was an essential part of their identity.

By the 1920s and especially by the 1930s, a new feeling of nationalism had arisen that was impatient with local notables' political alliances and ineffectual dealings with the colonial powers. When, as in 1930 under the Anglo-Iraqi Treaty, an Arab country was given its independence, it was in return for a political alliance with the former colonial power and a military base. Shortly after the end of World War II, all Arab states except those of the Maghrib had gained independence, at least in name, the departing Europeans having turned over power to the local westernized segment of society that was organized in secular political parties.

The opportunity was finally at hand to reestablish Arab unity within a single state, but it never happened: local interests were best served by maintaining the status quo. The concept of secular nation-states based on the European model was too well established. When Iraq's Prime Minister Nuri al-Sa'id proposed a union of Iraq, Transjordan, Syria, Palestine, and Lebanon in 1942, he did not do so for religious reasons and his actions triggered geopolitical rivalry with Egypt—by far the leader of any unlinked configuration of Arab states because of its size and sophistication. The alternative to unification, the Arab League with headquarters in Cairo, was born in 1945. The only thing on which members seemed able to concur was that there should be no Jewish state in Palestine. So much for unifying the Arabic-speaking portion of the umma. In fact, Britain had encouraged the formation of the Arab League, on the assumption that it would make the area easier to control.

In the immediate post-World War II period, nominally independent Arab states were run largely by those who had been active politically prior to independence. Having gotten rid of the colonial powers, many felt little remained to be done but enjoy the fruits of victory. In fact, in the absence of a nationalist ideology, much less a program, they were unable to establish social cohesion or develop a sense of purpose. The social bonds of the umma had been broken. The cultural dualism between the Western-educated elite and the masses continued to persist, only now there was no occupying power to blame for social injustice, economic deprivation, or alien cultural influences. For the masses the political legitimacy that their Western-style governments derived from achieving independence—especially pseudo independence—was not nearly so compelling as the political legitimacy derived by more traditional governments based on divine, rather than Western, law. The Arab defeat in the 1948 war that gave birth to the state of Israel triggered events that graphically demonstrated that difference in legitimacy and political loyalty, as well as the bankruptcy of the secular system. The field was left open for a new form of nationalism to develop that we shall term Nasirism after its chief proponent, Gamal Abd al-Nasir (1918-70).

NASIRISM: NONALIGNMENT, ARAB UNITY, AND ARAB SOCIALISM

Gamal Abd al-Nasir represented a new type of leadership in the Arab world. While he came to power in the traditional way— with military support—it was the first time in centuries that an independent Egypt had a leader who was an Egyptian—and an Egyptian who was not one of the elite. The son of a postal clerk and the grandson of a peasant, Nasir entered the military academy in 1937, a year after it was opened to members of the middle and lower

classes, who could study there free of charge. The rise to power of
Nasir and his associates meant that the concerns of the common
man were reflected at the highest levels of government. The link
between power and authority was reestablished, and thus provided
the new regime with legitimacy. The link was not immediately apparent, however, nor did it last forever.

When the military coup of 1952 deposed King Faruq and terminated the dynasty that had begun with Muhammad Ali, the Free
Officers who led it were seeking to rid Egypt of the corrupt political
system they held responsible for the defeat in Palestine and for the
state of Egyptian society. Not unlike the earlier nationalists, the officers had no preconceived plan or agenda for what to do once the
opposition was routed. Unlike the nationalists, their views more
closely reflected those of the people and an adherence to Islam was
made clear. If, as they willingly admitted, they lacked a ready-made
political program that could immediately benefit the masses, they
were genuine in their desire to free Egypt of imperialism, corruption, and oppression. The question was how to do it, given their dis-
trust of the political parties and institutions that had served the
former oligarchy so well. One attempt was the establishment in
early 1953 of a single legal political organization, the Liberation
Rally, formed to organize popular support for the new rulers.

Members of the former oligarchy were not the only threat to
the new regime. The Muslim Brotherhood had long had relations
with members of the Free Officers, and felt this was their opportunity to come to power. But the Brotherhood made the mistake of
backing General Nagib, the figurehead leader of the Revolutionary
Command Council, rather than Nasir, its real leader. The rivalry
came to a head when a member of the Brotherhood shot at Nasir in
October 1954, triggering a wave of arrests and the execution of six
Brothers. The scenario was replayed in 1965 when, after a general
amnesty, the Brotherhood was again accused of plotting a coup
and arrests were made, including that of Sayyid Qutb, the leading
writer and theorist of the Brotherhood after the death of al-Banna,
its founder. Qutb was executed in 1966.

Nasir was not motivated by an antireligious bias in these con-
frontations, but by a firm intention to retain control of all political
life in Egypt. He was secular enough to reject a theocratic concept
of statehood, but he still valued Islam, completely apart from whatever his own personal beliefs may have been. In 1961 al-Azhar University was brought under government control and its structure

reorganized so that modern subjects, such as medicine, agriculture, and engineering, were taught as well as the traditional religious ones. The ulama became more than ever functionaries of the state. Nasir's efforts may also be seen as an attempt to unify Egypt by bringing its most traditional elements into the fold, so as to lead an unfragmented society toward modernization. Like Muhammad Ali, Nasir realized that a unified political base in Egypt was necessary to accomplish major reform; unlike Muhammad Ali, Nasir was concerned about social as well as economic and political reform. Unfortunately for Egypt, Nasir's energies were diverted from internal problems when he became the hero of the Arab world in 1956 and offered his leadership to a much larger following.

In the mid-1950s the Cold War was on in full force, and Secretary of State John Foster Dulles was anxious to link the newly independent Third World countries to the West in order to contain Communism. The 1955 Baghdad Pact was a regional defense agreement of this nature whose signatories were Britain, Iraq, Iran, Turkey, and Pakistan. It was hoped that Jordan and Syria could also be persuaded to join, so Iraq would not be the sole Arab member and labeled a stooge of imperialism. The pact's denunciation by Nasir in exactly these terms dashed those hopes. The lines of battle were drawn. The rivalry between Iraq and Egypt was renewed, and leadership of the Arab world was the prize.

Nasir's largest confrontation with the West—and the one that made him a hero in Arab eyes—was triggered in 1955 by a large-scale Israeli retaliatory raid against Palestinian commandos living in the Egyptian-administered Gaza Strip. It convinced Nasir that his military arms were inadequate, and later in the year, after trying unsuccessfully to buy arms from the West, he purchased them from Czechoslovakia—the first such purchase of arms from a Communist country. Amazed that Nasir had dared to obtain arms from somewhere else after rejecting its impossible terms, the West reacted with alarm and relations rapidly deteriorated: the United States refused to finance the High Dam at Aswan, Egypt nationalized the Suez Canal, and Britain, France, and Israel invaded Egypt. The pullback of the three countries' troops under pressure from the United States was viewed as an astonishing success for Nasir and a victory for the Arab people. Nasir's brand of nationalism and the evident and long-awaited success it apparently engendered captured the imagination of the Arabic-speaking world.

Nasirism and Communism were two very different ideologies, regardless of the view of cold warriors of the period. Egypt, along with much of the Third World, regarded the Soviet Union as a counterweight to Western imperialism, a source of arms, and, for Nasir, a source of financial and technical aid for the High Dam at Aswan. Nasir viewed local Communists with suspicion, however, since they espoused a foreign ideology and competed for political control. His attitude was at times a source of embarrassment to his Soviet allies. He had used the Soviets—and American support—to come out of the Suez crisis victorious, ready to lead the Arab people in an attack on imperialism under the banner of nonalignment.

The most realized effort toward that end occurred in 1958, when Syria initiated a union with Egypt to form the United Arab Republic. Syria was a country in need of leadership, and the founders of the Ba'th (Renaissance) Party, Syrians Michel Aflaq and Salah al-Din Bitar, believed they had an ideology that was just what Nasir was looking for. Reality struck when Nasir treated Syria as he had treated Egypt, which is to say he sought complete control over its political life and began by dissolving all parties, including the Ba'th. A new mass organization was to function in their place, and in the 1959 elections for National Union representation the Ba'th did poorly. Later that year the Ba'thist leaders resigned in despair.

There were more than political differences, however, between the two countries. Syria is not Egypt. Nasir's increasing intervention in Egypt's economic system took place in response to foreign or native elite ownership of large businesses and land, plus the unwillingness of the private sector to assume responsibility for development. His attitude was pragmatic and based solely on the Egyptian experience. Consequently, the large number of Syrian entrepreneurs were unhappy with the UAR nationalization laws of 1961 that also limited landholdings to 100 acres and put a ceiling on salaries. In addition, given Egypt's much larger population and political clout, Egyptians predominated in important posts. The union fell apart when Syria withdrew in 1961.

Even at the height of his prestige Nasir was not without rivals. The 1958 coup in Iraq brought to power Abd al-Karim Qasim, who renounced imperialism but, far from following Nasir's lead in a policy of nonalignment, came to be labeled a stooge of Communism by Nasir. On the other side was Saudi Arabia's King Faysal, who, according to Nasir, served Western imperialist interests. The

Islamic conferences convened by Saudi Arabia were a threat to the hegemony Nasir sought to establish in the Arab world.

With the end of the United Arab Republic, Nasir's government took a more socialist turn. Arab unity, Nasir reasoned, required careful groundwork based on a revolutionary transformation of society that did away with the last remnants of imperialism and successfully developed the country. Once that was achieved, he assumed, unity would follow of its own accord.

Nasir's Arab socialism was less an ideology than a pragmatic attempt to develop Egypt in keeping with its history and circumstances. Arab socialism was an extension of the fight against Western imperialism, now cast in an economic guise rather than the military occupation of former times. Parallels were drawn between Muhammad's struggle against the corrupt Meccan oligarchy and the fight of contemporary Egyptians against economic exploitation and social injustice. Given the connection between capitalism and the West, Nasir rejected that economic system for Egypt's development; nor, given his policy of nonalignment, did he seek a Marxist solution. He appealed instead to Islamic social morality and nationalist pride; the state was once again to be entrusted with carrying out its obligations toward a more secularly defined umma. In keeping with tradition, opposition was not to be tolerated; only now the centralized state had the means of being far more effective in dealing with any opposition. It was not a matter of workers or peasants assuming responsibility for the means of production, but of the bureaucracy's working on the people's behalf.

Albert Hourani has written that Nasirism was less an ideology than an attitude. Truly, Nasir was not a popular leader because of a well-conceived (much less well-executed) policy for dealing with Egypt's enemies and developing the country. His words and deeds got attention because they addressed the issues of concern to the common man in terms that the common man could identify with and appreciate, and because, on occasion, Nasir could translate those feelings of rage and impotence into dramatically successful action. In the end—and a disillusioning end it was, given the results of the 1967 war—his legitimacy and his power rested on the incontrovertible fact that he was one of them.

BA'THIST SOCIALISM

The history of Syria during the twentieth century parallels Egypt's quite closely. Colonial efforts to moderate local rule met with nationalists' demands for total independence. Syria (and Lebanon) were recognized as independent in 1941, but it was not until 1946, after the French bombing of Damascus in 1945, that French forces were withdrawn. The National Party took over the reins of government and, as in Egypt, party politicians were held responsible for the debacle of 1948. Again as in Egypt, the military was manned with members of the lower middle class (the landed Muslim families disdained the army as a profession) who were out-raged at the government's ineptness and determined to set the country in order. Three military coups took place in 1949, with Colonel Adib Shishakli emerging as the victor. In contrast with Egypt, politicized officers were not members of the Muslim Brotherhood and political parties were not done away with. In fact, one of them—the Ba'th—eventually came to dominate, if not in its original form.

Ba'thist founders Michel Aflaq (b. 1910) and Salah al-Din Bitar (1911-80) were both from Damascus; Aflaq was a Greek Orthodox and Bitar, a Sunni Muslim. While students in France, the two disco-vered socialism. After returning home to teach, they organized the Ba'th Party in 1943. Its objectives were Arab unity, in order to re-generate Arab society; freedom for the individual and from col-onialism; and socialism—that is, economic and social justice. Aflaq, though a Christian secularist, included Islam in Ba'thist ideology by portraying it as an Arab movement and an expression of Arab nationalism. He insisted it was a vital part of Arabism and should be recognized as such.

Akram Hawrani was from a Sunni landowning family in Hama, where he had organized peasants in 1950 to form the Arab Socialist Party. He joined forces with Aflaq and Bitar in 1953 to form the Arab Socialist Resurrection Party, which combined ideological appeal with grass roots political strength. When Syria returned to civilian rule in 1954, the party won a solid bloc of seats and was on its way. Having played a decisive role in the union of Syria and Egypt in 1958, the Ba'th soon found itself dismissed along with the other political parties. Nasir was not Hawrani, and did not feel he needed Aflaq and Bitar's ideological contribution. The union dissolved in 1961, and by the spring of 1963 the Ba'th had bounced back via coups in Iraq and Syria. After one unsatisfactory union of Arab states, a second one was not seriously contemplated. This time Pan-Arabism took second place to local interests, with men from minorities—particularly the Alawis and Druze—in power. Ideology had proved no substitute for institutions or traditional communal solidarity.

The 1963 coup broke the political power of the merchant-landowner class, while the agricultural reforms of 1964 and the nationalizations of 1965 broke their economic power. A 1966 coup drove the Ba'th's founders into exile and split the party into Iraqi and Syrian segments. The 1970 coup brought Hafez al-Assad to power, demonstrating that the military members of the Ba'th, and not the party functionaries, literally call the shots. Assad, a pragmatist rather than an ideologue, dominates as the party's secretary-general, the government's president, and, most important, the military's commander in chief.

What of the role of Islam in all these changes of government? Because of the mixed nature of Syria's population, secular ideologies such as regional Syrian nationalism and Ba'thist Arab nationalism find a more ready audience than might be the case in other states. While Islam has never been recognized as the official state religion, the 1973 Constitution requires the head of state to be a Muslim and cites the shari'a as a principal source of legislation. Assad, an Alawi, stresses that sect's full membership in Islam while arguing that religion should be excluded from politics. Since Alawis are not numerous enough to make up a majority in party, government, or the military, members of other communities are included or co-opted. For its part, the ulama regards socialism as an alien import and contrary to Islam. The Muslim Brotherhood, in Syria since the 1940s, has been particularly active in opposing the Assad government and has been brutally dealt with as a result.

The material presented above on Egypt and Syria traces the secular ideologies used by two representative Muslim nation-states in their quest for at least parity with the West as well as internal development and stability. To summarize, many elements of society were left untouched by the reforms of the nineteenth and twentieth centuries. A negative nationalism arose that more or less recognized Islam as a cultural achievement even as it focused almost exclusively on ousting the foreigner and replacing him in the secular seat of power. Discredited by the 1948 war, the old parliamentarian elites were removed from office by idealistic military officers from the lower and middle classes. With no clear ideology, they sought to rid their countries of corruption and establish socioeconomic justice. Various alliances—among themselves and with the Communist bloc—were experimented with in the name of Arab nationalism and nonalignment. They found that state planning was not a function of socialist ideology so much as a necessity if development was to take place. Political participation was channeled into mass organizations that functioned from the top down. In short, the goal, though greatly expanded in scope, has not changed all that much from the days of Muhammad Ali, when the necessarily pragmatic military—Islam's first line of defense and the traditional source of power—sought to protect society from outside threats while keeping internal rivalry to a minimum. But the military was never the source of political legitimacy in and of itself, and the ideologies that were used—whether foreign or domestic—were never entirely convincing. How well have these regimes succeeded in reaching their stated goals and, consequently, how much support have they managed to acquire?

THE QUEST FOR LEGITIMACY

The first obligation of a Muslim government is to defend the umma. Hence the Arab loss to Israel in 1967 was even more devastating than the one of 1948, for no longer could one blame colonial masters or imperialist stooges. Arab rulers now came from the native ranks—the native military ranks, at that. The old ideological rivalries were at once made irrelevant, since Israel had defeated Nasirist Egypt, Ba'thist Syria, and Hashemite Jordan. Arab unity—under anybody's leadership—was no longer an issue, since more fundamental questions, such as survival, were at stake and it did not seem that uniting would help provide a solution. Perhaps Sa'd Zaghlul's reply of decades before had been right: when asked his opinion of Arab unity, he reportedly answered, "What is the sum of zero plus zero and yet another zero?"

And yet that response was not entirely accurate in 1967, for there were Arab states that had not been defeated militarily, and a few in particular that were doing very well financially and were willing to come to the rescue. The irony was that such states as Saudi Arabia had been among Arab socialism's most consistent critics. With the 1973 war Saudi Arabia's impact became all the more pronounced through its use of the oil embargo and postwar payments to states facing Israel. The religious dimension of this situation will be referred to below; for the present we only note that the immediate impact was a more moderate, conciliatory tone among Arab states. (It was also helped by a new cast of characters: in 1970 Nasir was succeeded by Sadat, King Husayn of Jordan defeated the PLO, and Assad came to power in Syria to end its chronic series of coups.) The region gained a new stability and, ironically, became far more interdependent than it had ever been in the days of Arab nationalism, when establishing hegemony was a major ideological goal.

In the continuing effort to achieve development, Sadat shifted to an open-door economic policy that encouraged the investment of foreign capital in Egypt. Meanwhile thousands of Egyptians were migrating to jobs in the oil-rich states of the Gulf, as were large numbers of Muslims from other countries. This was a two-edged sword, however. While huge amounts of money flow to the labor-exporting countries in the form of workers' remittances, the money is spent largely on consumer goods by the workers' families, triggering an inflation that is particularly burdensome to government, agricultural, and underemployed public sector workers. Governments are then under pressure to spend money they do not have on subsidies and public services. In addition, the labor-exporting states have lost the services of some of their most productive people to the Gulf states while the unemployable remain at home.

Meanwhile, Egypt's investment capital is spent largely on commercial, rather than agricultural or industrial, development. It goes for luxury housing, consumer luxuries, and tourist facilities. Development is thus not just having the necessary capital but putting it in the hands of the right people for the right projects in the right sector. Unfortunately, with a swollen civil service that functions to provide jobs for the educated, innovative and efficient management is not the norm and development has been stymied.

To round out the labor picture, cities grow and public services are overworked as people continue to stream in from the countryside. These new migrants, without education, jobs, or housing, retain many of their rural values and behavior patterns. One now

speaks of the ruralization of the cities rather than their modernizing effect on the rural migrants. The birth rate continues to be
problematic for many countries; governments cannot provide
enough housing, education, health, and transportation facilities
for their citizens.

Thus we see that the socioeconomic equality that has so often
been cited as the goal of Muslim governments appears to be as unrealized now as in the past. In terms of absolute numbers of the
educated and employed, the results are impressive, but the task remains herculean and there are signs that people are becoming increasingly impatient with their governments. The educated in particular are anxious for greater political participation. The bureaucrats, managers, and military have emerged as a new kind of elite—
no longer combatants in the nation's struggle for survival and development, but beneficiaries of new regimes of greed and corruption. What, then, are the options?

Some blame the defeat in 1967 on too small a dose of socialism:
it was never implemented enough to make a difference. Others feel
there was too much. Now that the West is not perceived in so
threatening a light, some feel it should be encouraged to assist in
the modernization effort—especially economically. But a third
voice has been heard with increasing frequency, and that is the Islamic response. It points to the West's immorality, violence,
materialism, racism, and corruption, and sees no reason to follow
that alien path when God has provided the Qur'an as guidance. For
those espousing the Islamic response, the loss in 1967 and the de-
teriorating social situation indicate how far from the truth Muslims
have strayed. Saudi Arabia's increase in prestige and its economic
progress are seen as proof of the correctness of the traditional Islamic approach. Even Israel, viewed as an intruder in the Dar al-
Islam and an outpost of imperialism, is pointed to as proof that a
state based on religion (in this case, of course, Judaism) is more formidable than governments that follow alien, imported ideologies.

It is rather misleading to label this perspective Islamic revivalism, since it has been present all along. Western observers and
westernized elites, speaking almost exclusively to each other in secular language, have become sensitized to it only in recent years.
Their explanations are numerous: with the failure of all competing
ideologies, only Islam is left untarnished and untainted. It provides
comfort and a sense of direction to an uprooted, alienated
populace that finds solace in its familiar concepts. It guarantees vic-

tory to those who follow its teachings. Political analysts see Islam as being used by power seekers as a rallying point and a means of challenging the government, and by power holders in their efforts to establish legitimacy and/or mobilize the masses. Certainly as nationalism has become more of a mass and less of an elitist means of political participation, the religious tone has increased. This interaction between segments of society and their appeals to Islam will be detailed in Chapter 10.

It is interesting to note where support for an Islamic order comes from. Having been diminished and co-opted by secular governments, the religious establishment—with the major exception of Iran—is of little note, either in legitimating a regime or in challenging the established order. Rather, populist movements like the Muslim Brotherhood, organized by lay Muslims, are the means of expressing discontent with current policy. The order they seek to establish is not unlike the goals set by others: socioeconomic justice, dignity, a renaissance of the spirit and society. Their shortcomings are also familiar: holistic prescriptions rather than detailed programs, statements of condemnation rather than practical plans for positive action.

Only time will tell whether the Islamic alternative will be implemented, much less proved successful. But the issue to be addressed it obvious: effective institutions, not elitist ideologies, need to be set up that reflect the needs of the peole, in order to gain their support and bring about the social cohesion and stability that are so necessary for development.

Socioeconomic Indices

Country	Population (millions)[a]	Percent Natural Growth Rate[b]	Percent Literacy Rate[c]	% Urban Population[d]	Per Capita GNP ($U.S.)[e]
Egypt	47.0	2.7	43.5	44	690
Iraq	15.0	3.4	24.2	68	—
Jordan	3.5	3.6	67.6	60	1,690
Kuwait	1.6	3.2	59.6	90	19,870
Lebanon	2.6	2.2	—	78	—
Saudi Arabia	10.8	3.0	24.6	70	16,000
United Arab Emirates	1.5	2.2	53.5	81	23,770

[a]Population estimate, mid-1984. Based on data from a recent census or by incorporating estimates made by the UN, the U.S. Bureau of the Census, and official country publications.

[b]Annual Natural Increase—birth rate minus the death rate.

[c]Literacy rate of population 15 years of age and over (10 years and over in Egypt), derived by subtracting total population illiterate from 100. Dates of Survey: Egypt (1976), Iraq (1965), Jordan (1976), Kuwait (1975 figures include non-Kuwaiti residents), Saudi Arabia (1980), U.A.E. (1978).

[d]Percentage of total population living in areas termed urban by that country. Estimates refer to some point in the 1970s or early 1980s.

[e]Per Capita Gross National Product, 1982. Estimates provided by the World Bank.

Sources: Population Reference Bureau, Inc., *1984 World Population Data Sheet* (Washington, D.C.: Population Reference Bureau, 1984); Literacy figures from UNESCO, *1982 and 1983 Statistical Yearbook* (Paris: UNESCO, 1982 and 1983).

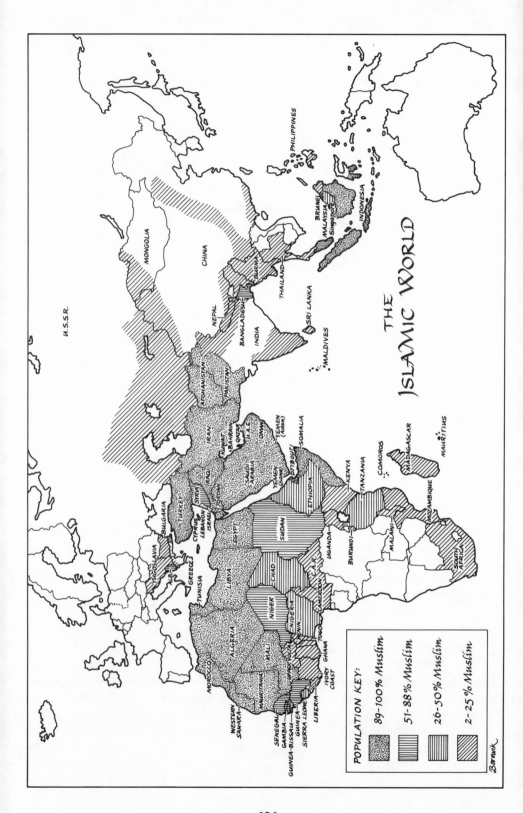

THE ISLAMIC WORLD

POPULATION KEY:

89-100% Muslim

51-88% Muslim

26-50% Muslim

2-25% Muslim

Borowik

196

10

Muslim Societies Today

John L. Esposito

At the heart of contemporary Islamic revivalism is a search for identity in the modern world. Despite differences in their local experiences, agendas, degree of militancy, and Islamic orientation, a general criticism made by Islamic activists focuses on the westernization of their societies and the consequent loss of their own history and values. The process of modernization, which applied alien models to the political and sociocultural development of Muslim countries, has failed to produce its desired goals and has resulted in a serious identity crisis. Nationalism, capitalism, and a variety of socialist experiments have not met the needs of Muslim societies. Problems of political legitimacy and authoritarianism continue to exist. The gap between rich and poor widens. Traditional patterns of social and religious life have been disrupted. This concern for identity or authenticity has motivated a broad spectrum of Muslims to look to their Islamic heritage in order to establish more firmly some continuity between their past history and values and their future direction.

Recognition of the need to reaffirm one's heritage has contributed to calls for the renewal of Muslim society to bring about a renaissance. An increase in religious observances (prayers, mosque attendance, religious dress, fasting during Ramadan) has been quite evident in many parts of the Muslim world. This revival has seen the reemergence of Islam not only in personal but also in political life. Muslims have reasserted the traditional Islamic belief that the true Islamic state is based upon the unity of God and actualized through governance by Islamic law, a society in which religion is an integral part of public life: politics, law, and society. This reaffirmation has meant increased calls for a more authentic, indigenously based society.

While the contemporary quest for identity is generally characterized as an Islamic resurgence, the unity implied by this term can be quite deceptive. Indeed, far from being a monolithic phenomenon, the "Islamization" process, upon closer examination of individual Muslim countries, is revealed to be complex, with differing and, at times, contradictory results. This chapter will analyze six countries that provide sharp and vivid examples of the search for identity in the Muslim world today: Turkey, Saudi Arabia, Libya, Pakistan, Egypt, and Iran. Our focus will be on their attempts to forge a national identity and ideology and to assess what this has meant in terms of the politics, structures, and institutions of these societies.

The pattern of postindependence political development in Muslim countries reveals three general orientations in their governments: secular, Islamic, and Muslim. At the secular end of the spectrum is Turkey, where from 1924 to 1938, under Ataturk, a series of reforms was implemented that progressively created a secular state—that is, the institutional separation of religion from politics. At the other end of the religiopolitical spectrum are the self-styled Islamic states of Saudi Arabia, Libya, and Pakistan, whose rulers have affirmed the Islamic character of their state and the primacy of Islamic law. They use this Islamic commitment not only to legitimate their home rule but also to enhance their use of Islam as a tool in their foreign policy toward other Muslim countries.

The vast majority of Muslim countries emerged as Muslim states—while Western in their political, legal, and social development, they have incorporated certain Islamic trappings or constitutional provisions. In some Islam is declared the state religion, and the shari'a is stated to be "a" source of law, whether or not this is true in reality. Most require that the head of state be a Muslim and provide some state support/control over religious affairs. Tunisia, Algeria, Egypt, Syria, Iran, Jordan, and Malaysia reflect this approach. Events since the latter half of the 1970s have challenged and altered this picture somewhat, so it is important to take a careful look at several countries that exemplify the struggle to establish a modern national identity and ideology within a Muslim context.

TURKEY

Once the heart of the Ottoman Empire, Turkey provides the sole example of an attempt to establish a totally secular state in the Muslim world. It was created as a modern national republic in which Islamic religion and culture were not denied, but the foundation of the new state of the "People of Turkey" was to be the "national will," "national sovereignty." The dismemberment of Ottoman territory and the flight of its minorities had left a culturally and ethnically homogeneous culture of 97.3 percent Muslim Turks. Therefore, common language, culture, and territory could provide the ingredients for Turkish nationalism.

As Mustafa Kemal defined and autocratically implemented his blueprint for modern Turkey (a role that would later win him the appellation Ataturk, Father of the Turks), the model adopted in nation building was that of the modern, secular Western state. From 1924 to his death in 1938, Mustafa Kemal implemented a series of reforms that progressively created a modern secular state characterized by the institutional separation of religion from politics. In 1922 the sultanate was abolished; in 1924 the Turkish National Assembly abolished the caliphate. At the same time the chief religious office of the state, Shaykh al-Islam, and the Ministry of Religious Affairs and Pious Endowments (waqf) were terminated. Passage of the Law on the Unification of Education made all education secular, thus eliminating the traditional Islamic educational system. The ultimate purpose and orientation of Mustafa Kemal's program was formalized in 1928, when a constitutional amendment deleted the phrase, "The religion of the Turkish state is Islam," as wll as other references to Islam. Moreover, the Constitution declared that the Turkish Republic was a secular state.

The movement from Islamic state to secular state may have been symbolized by the abolition of the sultanate and the caliphate. However, in terms of classical political thought, it was effected with the displacement of the shari'a by civil or man-made law. In April 1924 the shari'a court system was abolished, its judges retired, and its jurisdiction absorbed by the secular court system. In February 1926 Islamic law was totally replaced by a Swiss-based legal system. Thus, the centuries-long practical criterion for the existence of an Islamic state—governance according to the shari'a—had been definitively removed.

The attempt to establish a Turkish nation-state extended to the Turkification of Islam. The purpose was to replace Arab Islam, which was viewed as conservative and backward, and more interested in a romanticized past than in the present, with a modern, scientific, Turkish Islam. Reforms were introduced to have Turkish replace Arabic as the language of religion. Having rejected Ottomanism and Pan-Islam, Islam in Turkey was to be a national religion. Ataturk encouraged the translation of the Qur'an into Turkish. Turkish replaced Arabic in the muezzin's five daily calls to prayer as well as in the Friday congregational prayer and sermon in the mosque.

Kemal's ambitious program of political and social transformation owed much of its success to his total political control of the parliament and government. This enabled him to single-mindedly implement and impose his program. Only one political party was permitted, the Republican Peoples Party (RPP), which he created in 1924. After his death the RPP continued the Kemalist legacy. However, the situation changed with the introduction of a multiparty system in 1946. The newly created Democratic Party (DP) won the general elections of 1950.

Under the DP, during the post-World War II period, the rigorous secularist position of Kemalism was progressively modified. The introduction of a multiparty system, and consequent greater competition for votes, strengthened the sensitivity of politicians to the power of Islam in the lives of most Turks; or, as Howard A. Reed has said, "a kind of rediscovery of the continuing attachment of the peasant majority to traditional Islamic values and rituals." Many middle-class Muslims had remained religiously observant as well. Although committed to the ideals of the Turkish state, many were concerned that the pendulum had swung too far, inhibiting Islam from playing its role in personal life and from providing the basis for social morality. While modern nationalism and secularism were the cornerstones of public political life, Islam had remained, in the words of Kemal Karpat, the "practical criterion for Turkishness," commanding loyalty and providing internal unity. Thus, the continued strength of Islam in the majority of Turkish Muslims' lives made politicians and political parties more open to concessions that eased restrictions on religious practice. For the political opposition, religion offered an effective appeal to a strong, widespread popular sentiment.

As a result, during the post-World War II period the restrictive secularist policies of the state were somewhat loosened. Religious education was reintroduced in Turkish schools. The Faculty of Divinity was restored at the University of Ankara to train religious leaders. New mosques were built and old ones repaired. By 1960 some 15,000 new mosques had been erected. Mosque attendance and participation in the pilgrimage to Mecca increased to the extent that today Turkey ranks among the leaders (third in 1982) in the size of its delegation to the hajj. The *imam-hatep* (prayer leader-preacher) training schools, which had ceased to exist in 1932, were revived. They grew rapidly from 7 in 1951 to 506 by 1980. Voluntary associations that support such activities as Qur'an courses and mosque building grew from 237 in 1951 to 2,510 in 1967.

The easing of religious restrictions during the post-World War II period was accompanied by the increased involvement of religious groups in politics. The DP, having found religious appeals useful in its defeat of the Kemalist RPP in 1950, forged an alliance with an Islamic group, the Followers of Light, led by Sa'id Nursi (1867-1960), which favored the reestablishment of an Islamic state based on the shari'a and guided by the ulama.

At the same time a number of religiously oriented parties began to appear. In 1948 the Nation Party, which advocated private enterprise, economic planning, and a greater role of Islam in the states, was created. Outlawed in July 1953 for using religion to attempt to subvert the republic, it was later restored as the Republican Nation Party. A Sunni political party, the National Order Party, was established in 1970 by Professor Necmeddin Erbakan. Outlawed for its antisecular religiopolitical activities, it was replaced in 1972 by the National Salvation Party (NSP), which won 12 percent of the vote in 1973. The NSP argues that the failure of Turkey's modern, secular identity to provide a sense of history, pride, and values for society can be rectified only by a reappropriation of Turkey's Islamic heritage. Its ultimate goal is an Islamic state, and it advocates the Islamization of Turkish life politically, economically, and socially.

By 1980 Turkey's stability was seriously threatened by a variety of problems, including widespread terrorism conducted by militant leftist and rightist groups. The "right" is composed of conservative and Islamic fundamentalist parties such as Erbakan's NSP and

Alparslan Turkes' National Action Party. The Turkish military stepped in and took control of the government, arresting Erbakan and Turkes and reaffirming the state's commitment to Kemalism. Thus, while the excessively secularist spirit of early Kemalism has been tempered, the Turkish government remains committed to its secular path.

SAUDI ARABIA

Saudi Arabia has long provided an example of a self-styled Islamic state. The Saudis proudly proclaim, and their history and practice seem to confirm, their Islamic character. Modern Saudi Arabia is the product of an alliance struck in eighteenth-century Arabia between an Islamic revivalist, Muhammad ibn Abd al-Wahhab, and a local ruler, Muhammad ibn Saud. Abd al-Wahhab denounced the moral laxity and spiritual malaise of his society, which he attributed to the compromising of Islam's radical monotheism. He preached a message that called for a return to the central doctrine of Islam—God's Oneness (*tawhid*)—and a rejection of popular superstitions and idolatrous innovations. A return to a "purified" Islam, cleansed of those historical accretions that had compromised the original message of the Qur'an and the Prophet Muhammad, would unite and revitalize the Muslim community. In 1744 reformer and prince wedded spiritual vision and temporal ambition in this holy war, and produced a successful religiopolitical movement that by 1818 had united the tribes of Arabia in what seemed a re-creation of Islam's seventh-century beginnings under the Prophet Muhammad.

Although these early gains were reversed in the nineteenth century, Abd al-Aziz ibn Saud (1880-1953) regained and realized the family mission at the turn of the twentieth century. Once more he combined military leadership with religious fervor and commitment. The Ikhwan, groups of bedouin fiercely committed to Islam and the *muwahhidun* (unitarian) goals, and attracted by the lure of conquest and booty, provided his militia. Through force, statesmanship, and ideological mobilization, the tribes of the Arabian peninsula were once more united, and by 1932 the kingdom of Saudi Arabia was proclaimed. The union of the twin forces of Islam and the Saud family is vividly symbolized in the Saudi flag, which combines the confession of faith with the crossed swords of the house of Saud.

Islam has provided the ideological basis for Saudi rule and its legitimacy. Of equal significance, it has been effectively utilized by Saudi rulers to validate programs and policies. From its beginning the kingdom has appealed directly to Islam as its raison d'être. Although monarchy is not an Islamic institution, it has been rationalized by the claim that all, even the king, are subservient to the shari'a. By declaring the Qur'an to be the state's constitution and the shari'a its law, the Saud family has sought Islamic justification and legitimation. The Qur'an and the shari'a provide the basis and fundamental structure of the state, its law, and its judiciary.

Islam has also been used to validate government actions. For example, the ulama serve as advisers in the drafting of royal decrees. Their legal opinions are sought to justify, through Islamic principles, important political actions, ranging from the 1964 deposing of King Saud and transfer of power to his brother, King Faysal, to the 1979 religious sanctioning of the government's military actions in regaining control of the Grand Mosque in Mecca and executing the rebel leaders.

Even when religious opposition to aspects of modernization has occurred, appeals to Islam have been utilized to win over the religious establishment and the masses. For example, Prophetic history and traditions concerning the employment of non-Muslims in early Islam were cited by King Abd al-Aziz to justify the importing of oil technicians. Furthermore, King Abd al-Aziz and King Faysal advanced Islamic rationales to win religious support for such innovations as radio, telephone, automobiles, television, and women's education.

Islam has also proved useful in Saudi foreign policy. The Saudi emphasis on its role as protector of the sacred sites (Mecca and Medina) and, by extension, as leader of the cause to liberate Jerusalem has enhanced its prestige and leadership in the Muslim world. King Faysal's appeal for a Pan-Islamic scheme to counter the Pan-Arabism of Egypt's Nasir, the founding and funding of international organizations such as the Muslim World League and the Organization of the Islamic Conference, and the Saudi role as protector and patron of Islamic fundamentalist movements such as Egypt's Muslim Brotherhood and Pakistan's Jamaat-i-Islami have further enhanced their influence.

Perhaps the most important lesson to learn from the Saudi experience is that even in a state that is ostensibly fundamentalist rather than reformist, Islam is flexible enough to permit, and even legitimate, the development of a modern state. The use of the Qur'an in the place of a formal constitution has allowed the royal family great leeway in most areas that are not covered by Scripture. Although the Hanbali school of law followed in Saudi Arabia is the strictest, most rigid of the four Sunni law schools, where the written law is silent, change is possible. Moreover, though clearly circumscribed, interpretation has remained open to its jurists in principle. Finally, the history of Islamic jurisprudence provides vast resources that a shrewd leadership has used in rendering change. A judicious use of independent reasoning or interpretation, selection (the right to choose from varying teachings of accepted law schools), and appeals to public interest or social welfare provide the means for substantive legal modernization where the Qur'an and sunna are silent.

Furthermore, while the shari'a is the law, and thus human legislation is technically proscribed, Muslim governments have long had the power to enact rules and regulations in areas not covered by Islamic law. Islamic jurisprudence accepts the ability of rulers to enact administrative decrees in order to better assure shari'a governance. Thus, the Saudi government has been able to promulgate various codes, such as The Regulation on Commerce (1954), The Mining Code (1963), The Labor and Workman Law (1970), The Social Insurance Law (1970), and The Civil Service Law (1971).

As can be seen, Islam has been used effectively by the Saudis to unite the Arabian peninsula, legitimate their rule, provide a state structure and institutions, validate policies, and justify change. However, although Islam has been sufficiently flexible to legitimate and validate Saudi rule and governance, it may prove in the long run to be a two-edged sword. A society forced to adjust in the course of a few decades to the influx of vast wealth, rapid development, the presence of large numbers of expatriate workers, the rise of technocrats or a modernizing middle class, and the strains and problems that issue from this process of rapid change renders the Saudi rulers increasingly vulnerable to the very Islamic character and standards they have so carefully cultivated. While the group that seized the Grand Mosque in 1979 may itself be insignificant, some of its concerns (corruption and bribery, consumption of alcohol, and other "un-Islamic" practices) are noteworthy. The well-known and publicized examples of moral corruption and bribery among members of the royal family, other officials, and influential businessmen is a matter of concern for many Saudis.

Despite great strides in improving housing, education, and medical resources for the poor, the gap between rich and poor, haves and have-nots, continues to widen. A growing elite of Western-educated technocrats and military officers contrasts with a majority of the population that is traditionally, Islamically educated. Moreover, this new middle class has a new sense of political values and expectations. The substantial salary increases given to civil servants and the military, as well as promises to establish a more constitutional government, show a concern to head off potential political problems.

For a county in which tribal affiliation and loyalty remain strong, in which one-third of the population of 6 million are foreign workers, national identity and political stability remain important concerns. The situation has been exacerbated by a series of disturbances in the Eastern Province, which has a substantial Shi'i population and is the location of Saudi Arabia's oil reserves. The Shi'is, who make up 35 percent of the ARAMCO work force, have been subjected to constant anti-Saudi propaganda from Iran. Moreover, since the seizure of the Grand Mosque there has been a renewed emphasis on the Saudi commitment to modernize in a manner that is sensitive to—indeed, rooted in—traditional Islamic values—demonstrating a recognition of the need to assuage those who fear the spiritual and cultural ravages of rapid development.

In particular the house of Saud will need to continue to work with the ulama and thus receive legitimation from the religious establishment. Thus far this has occurred through the Sauds' intermarriage with leading ulama families because they have institutionalized and bureaucratized religion: education, the pilgrimage, and religious endowments. Thus, the ulama have become part of the elite, supported to a great degree by the state. Yet, in general, they remain somewhat independent and are respected by the people for their integrity. Leading ulama like Shaykh ibn Baz have felt free to warn against rapid modernization and the un-Islamic character of imported "alien" practices. Recently the Saudi government has taken a number of steps to reaffirm its commitment to the rule of Islam. New regulations restricting mixed housing for unmarried workers of foreign companies have been issued. The Gulf

Cooperation Council, of which Saudi Arabia is a leader, has announced tht the Gulf states will coordinate an effort to unify and completely Islamize their penal and commercial laws.

The debate over the extent and pace of modernization continues as the government emphasizes that it will modernize but not westernize its society—that Saudi Arabia will preserve its Islamic identity and values. Ideological mobilization was responsible for the establishment of Saudi Arabia. The continuing challenge to the house of Saud is maintenance of its Islamic identity and ideology in such a way as to facilitate change while credibly demonstrating the compatibility of its modernization efforts with Islam.

LIBYA

On September 1, 1969, the government of King Idris (1890-1982) was overthrown by a clique of military officers headed by Muammar Qaddafi. Libya had been a monarchy ruled by the grandson of Muhammad ibn Ali al-Sanusi (1787-1859), founder of the Sanusiyyah Sufi order. Like other eighteenth- and nineteenth-century Islamic reform movements, such as the Wahhabi in Saudi Arabia and that of the Mahdi in the Sudan, the Sanusiyyah had united many of the tribes (in what are today Libya, Chad, and western Egypt) into a movement that sought to purify Islam and establish an Islamic state. After Italian colonial rule in the twentieth century, Libya gained its independence in 1951 as a monarchy under King Idris, a descendant of the Grand Sanusi and head of the order.

The legitimacy of the monarchy and its Islamic character rested upon King Idris' position as both ruler and hereditary religious head of the Sanusiyyah. The royal family was assisted in governing Libya by a small group of prominent families and Sanusi religious leaders. The non-Sanusi religious establishment (ulama) was incorporated within the state's bureaucracy. With the exception of Muslim family law, Libya's legal system was based upon French and Italian legal codes, reflecting Libya's colonial past. Libya had followed the general pattern of most Muslim countries, which had, from the nineteenth century, under colonial influence, westernized their legal system.

With Colonel Qaddafi's announcement shortly after the 1969 coup that Islamic law would be reinstated, Libya experienced an apparent shift to a more formal, Islamically based and Islamically oriented state. Combined with Qaddafi's strong admiration for Egypt's Gamal Abd al-Nasir and his brand of Arab nationalism, Qaddafi and his Revolutionary Command Council seemed to be placing Libya on a path of arabization and Islamization. Both within Libya and abroad, Libya was seen as an Arab Islamic state. The early statements of the new government set Libya on an Islamically based socialist path. The Revolutionary Command Council committed itself to "the spiritual precepts emanating from the heart of our Sacred Book, the Noble Qur'an . . . ." Its social policy was to be the socialism of Islam, "a socialism emanating from the true religion of Islam and its Noble Book."

A series of reforms underscored Libya's Arab Islamic identity and orientation. Vestiges of a Christian European colonial past were suppressed; churches and cathedrals were closed. Arabic was required in all government transactions, and Arabic names and street signs replaced their Western counterparts. Islamic measures prohibiting gambling, nightclubs, and alcohol were introduced. In October 1971 a commission was established to review all Libyan law in order to bring it into conformity with Islam. In 1972 Qur'anically mandated criminal penalties were reinstated: amputation of a hand for theft, stoning for fornication and adultery. In addition, several other Islamic regulations were announced that affected the collecting of zakat (alms tax) and banking interest. However, these were limited measures; there was no widespread introduction of Islamic law. Moreover, by 1979, with the publication of Qaddafi's *The Green Book,* it became clear that while Islam was tied to Libya's Arab nationalism and socialism, ultimately Qaddafi would define and determine Libya's identity and ideology as well as its Islamic character.

The Green Book consists of three volumes that present Muammar Qaddafi's "Third Way" or "Third International Theory," an alternative to capitalism and Communism. Taught in the schools and required reading for all Libyan citizens, the three small volumes—*The Solution to the Problem of Democracy, Solution to the Economic Problem: Socialism,* and *Social Basis of the Third International Theory*—delineate Qaddafi's blueprint for Libyan society. As he has stated, "*The Green Book* is the guide to the emancipation of man . . . the new gospel. The gospel of the new era, the era of the masses."

Although using Islam, as other regimes do, to provide religious legitimacy, Libya's new path is certainly different from that of other Islamic states. The shari'a has not been implemented except for a handful of laws and regulations. Moreover, Qaddafi increasingly has imposed his own distinctive brand of Islam. Traditional Islamic law is based upon, but not limited in its sources to, the Qur'an and sunna of the Prophet; it provides the comprehensive ideal blueprint for state and society. Although Qaddafi appeals to the Qur'an as the source of his revolutionary theory ("in it are solutions to the problems of man . . . from personal status . . . to international problems . . .") and maintains that Libya's socialist program emanates "from the true religion of Islam and its Noble Book," specific references to Islam are conspicuously absent from *The Green Book*. Qaddafi has also shunted aside the traditions of the Prophet, claiming, along with many Muslims, that many are not authentic. Instead, he maintains that the Qur'an and *The Green Book* are the basis of Libyan society. The Qur'an is restricted to religious observances (prayer, fasting, almsgiving), while *The Green Book* guides society. Thus, *The Green Book* has replaced the traditional role of the shari'a.

Mixing populist ideological statements with a broad range of political, social, and economic experimentation, Qaddafi has undertaken nothing less than his own cultural revolution. Libya's new identity and ideology were symbolized in 1977 when the General People's Congress, which had replaced the Revolutionary Command Council, changed Libya's name from the Libyan Arab Republic to the Socialist People's Libyan Arab Jamahiriya. *Al-Jamahiriya* (the masses) is to be a decentralized, populist, participatory government of people's committees that control government offices, schools, the media, and many corporations. Qaddafi encouraged such committees to take over Libya's embassies and seize control of its mosques. This new socialist experiment has expressed itself in the abolition of private land ownership, wages, and rent in favor of worker control and participation in the means of production.

Qaddafi's experiment in redefining Libyan identity with his "Third Way" has alienated not only many of the landed and business classes but also the religious establishment. The ulama have condemned Qaddafi's "innovative" interpretations of Islam—his rejection of the binding force of Prophetic traditions, his substitution of *The Green Book* for shari'a governance, and his abolition of private property—as deviations from the Islamic tradition. While the outside world views Qaddafi as an "Islamic" leader governing an Islamic state, for many, including Libya's religious establishment, Qaddafi's experiment in redefining Libyan identity is far from Islamic.

PAKISTAN

Although Pakistan was established as an Islamic state in 1947, the implementation of its Islamic identity and commitment has remained an unrealized ideal. In 1977, when General Zia ul-Haq came to power through a coup d'etat, he pledged his government to the rectification of Pakistan's failure to live up to its Islamic commitment and to the establishment of an Islamic system of government (*Nizam-i-Islam*). As a result, Pakistan provides the most complete case study of many of the questions and issues that accompany attempts to Islamize state and society.

In 1947 the Indian subcontinent was carved into two independent nations, a secular India and Pakistan. The new state of Pakistan consisted of two major provinces: East Pakistan and West Pakistan, separated by 1,000 miles of Indian territory. Though juridically a nation, Pakistan was in fact a composite of people who had shared neither common territory, ethnic background, nor language but, rather, a socioreligious heritage—Islam. Culturally, despite a common Islamic background, there were distinctive differences between the Urdu West and the Bengali East. Moreover, strong regional sentiments were reinforced by linguistic divisions resulting from 5 major linguistic families with 35 distinct spoken languages.

During the early post-independence period, questions of national identity and ideology were overshadowed by issues of national survival: settlement of vast numbers of Muslim refugees from India; Muslim-Hindu communal rioting, which resulted in the mass migration of Hindus from West Pakistan to India; the untimely death in 1948 of Muhammad Ali Jinnah, Pakistan's founder-architect; and the assassination of his successor, Liaqat Ali Khan, in 1951. As the new state struggled to establish a system of government and maintain law and order, major ideological questions remained in the background. In what sense was Pakistan an Islamic state? How was its Islamic character to be reflected in the ideology and institutions of the state? Addressing these "Islamic" questions was further complicated by religious divisions and orientations, especially those of a Western-oriented political and bureaucratic elite versus those of the more traditional religious leadership. The drafting of the Constitution of 1956 exemplified the difficulties in articulating an Islamic identity.

The process of framing Pakistan's first constitution lasted almost nine years. The ideological debates underscored the sharp differences between political elites concerned with what they perceived to be the pragmatic and technical issues of political, social, and economic development and religious leaders who desired a state based upon the shari'a, a society governed by Islamic law. The final form of the constitution reflected the sharp differences in perspective, the lack of any real agreement regarding Pakistan's Islamic identity, and the manner in which Islamic ideology was to form the institutions, programs, and policies of the state.

The resultant compromise was a constitution similar to that of most Western, secular states that, in addition, contained several limited Islamic provisions, which were added to appease religious factions. Among the principal provisions were the title of the state—the Islamic Republic of Pakistan; the stipulation that the head of state must be a Muslim; the establishment of a research center to assist in the "reconstruction of Muslim society on a truly Islamic basis"; and the "repugnancy clause," which stipulated that no law contrary to the Qur'an and sunna of the Prophet could be enacted. There was no systematic statement or implementation of an Islamic ideology.

Thus, Pakistan's Islamic nature was not significantly reflected in its law or in its constitution. Despite its designation as an Islamic republic, it was not distinctively different from the majority of Muslim states, which had chosen a more secular path. Indeed, the tendency to separate religion from the state was evident when, in 1962, the new constitution omitted "Islamic" from the official name of the republic; under public pressure, it was restored by an amendment in 1963.

Despite more than two decades of nation building, when Zulfikar Ali Bhutto came to power in 1971, Pakistan's Islamic identity and raison d'être remained unclear and ill-defined. While religious concerns had to be respected, Islamic ideology was not a major issue in political or social development. Bhutto was a modern secular politician with an ideological bent toward socialism. However, a series of unforeseen events caused a sharp change in Pakistan's political climate as Islam reemerged as a central political issue. Pressure from a religious opposition, composed of the majority of the ulama and led by Maulana Mawdudi (d. 1979) and his Jamaat-i-Islami (Islamic Society), had motivated Bhutto and his Pakistan Peoples Party (PPP) to align their socialist policies with Islam. Increasingly, governmental legitimation was sought by speaking of an "Islamic socialism," rooted in Islamic solidarity and expressed in slogans like Islamic Equality (*Islami Musawat*) and Equality of Muhammad (*Musawat-i-Muhammadi*).

The Pakistan-Bangladesh civil war of 1971 proved to be a pivotal event; Pakistan's loss of its eastern wing (East Pakistan became an independent Bangladesh) brought Pakistanis face to face once more with questions of national identity and ideology. Once again they asked: What was the common purpose or factor that united the disparate peoples of Pakistan into a nation? and Why Pakistan? The result was a reexamination of the meaning of Pakistan's founding as a Muslim homeland. At the same time, Bhutto turned to the Middle East as he sought to align Pakistan more closely with the oil-rich Arab Gulf states by emphasizing their common Islamic heritage and bond.

Bhutto's appeals to Islam did not assuage his critics, who in 1977 united under the banner of Islam and formed a coalition of political parties, the Pakistan National Alliance (PNA). Though spanning the political spectrum, an opposition movement was formed under the umbrella of Islam with a commitment to establish a more Islamic system of government. Bhutto's last-minute introduction of Islamic measures, such as the banning of gambling, nightclubs, and alcohol, and the promise of more Islamic law did little to stem the tide.

In July 1977, amid charges of voting irregularities in Pakistan's national elections and widespread political agitation, General Zia ul-Haq seized power in a bloodless coup d'etat, declaring, "Pakistan, which was created in the name of Islam, will continue to survive only if it sticks to Islam. That is why I consider the introduction of an Islamic system as an essential prerequisite for the country." Maintaining that little had been done to realize Pakistan's Islamic identity and ideology, Zia ul-Haq committed his martial-law regime

to the restoration of an Islamic System, Nizam-i-Islam, "to trans-
form the country's socio-economic and political structure in accordance with the principles of Islam." A presidential address in De-
cember 1978, "Measures to Enforce Nizam-i-Islam," was followed
in February 1979 by the decree "Introduction of Islamic Laws."
Since that time a series of regulations affecting Pakistan's political,
legal, social, and economic life has been introduced.

Politically, Islam has functioned to legitimate General Zia ul-
Haq's coup and continued rule. Elections have been canceled or
postponed twice, and all political parties declared defunct, while
the government and its appointed body, the Islamic Ideology
Council, studied the questions of whether Pakistan's Western-
based political system was Islamic and what kind of Islamic government would be suitable for Pakistan.

Islamic regulations that enforce the public observance of the
Ramadan fast, require that workers be excused during prayer
periods, and reintroduce the imposition of Islamic criminal
punishments for such crimes as drinking, theft, and adultery have
been enacted. Thus, Pakistan's penal code has been amended to
permit such penalties as amputation, flogging, and the stoning of
an adultress. Only the punishment of flogging has actually been enforced.

The Islamization of Pakistan's society has affected not only its
law but also its judicial system. Shari'a courts have been established
to review petitions that challenge the Islamic acceptability of Pakistan's law—that is, to determine whether a law or provision is repug-
nant to Islam, contrary to the Qur'an and sunna of the Prophet.
The shari'a court has reviewed a broad range of issues, from judging whether Islam permits cinema to the stoning of an adultress
and land reform.

The reassertion of Islamic identity and ideology has affected
Pakistan's economic system with respect to the state collection of Islamic taxes and limited implementation of interest-free banking.
With substantial assistance from Saudi Arabia and the United Arab
Emirates, a zakat fund was created in June 1979. The zakat, an alms
tax of 2.5 percent, is levied on all wealth (income and assets) and de-
ducted directly from bank accounts, annuities, and insurance.
Ushr, an agricultural tax of 5 percent on productive land, although
originally announced in 1979, was not implemented until 1983.

The potentially most far-reaching Islamic change is the abolition of interest or usury. In January 1981 interest-free bank ac-

counts were introduced on a voluntary basis on all savings and fixed-deposit (time-deposit) accounts. The system, called Profit/ Loss Sharing (PLS), is based upon the traditional banking institution of *mudaraba,* under which a depositor and the bank enter into a partnership, and thus share in profits or losses. In addition, government housing and financial institutions have been placed on an interest-free basis.

The reassertion of Islamic identity and ideology in Pakistan has often seemed to create more conflict and questions than unity and harmony. The use of Islam to cancel elections, outlaw political parties, impose taxes and punishments, and ban alcohol and certain forms of entertainment has caused many to ask, Whose Islam is this? and Why have we emphasized a negative Islam? General Zia's interpretations of Islam have often alienated secularists and religious leaders, both of whom resent the restriction of their political rights in the name of Islam.

Conservative religious leaders are critical of the government's slow, piecemeal approach to the Islamization of Pakistan's state and society. They are especially critical of General Zia's usurpation of their traditional role as the interpreters of Islam and the conscience of the community. In particular, many note that General Zia's martial-law decrees are not subject to review by the shari'a court, and that all decisions of the shari'a court must be endorsed by Zia before implementation. Thus, while many Pakistanis initially welcomed Zia ul-Haq's interim government and its commitment to realize Pakistan's Islamic purpose and identity, the practice of Zia's Islamic ideology has raised as many questions as it has answered.

EGYPT

Egypt, unlike Saudi Arabia, Libya, and Pakistan, has never proclaimed itself to be an Islamic state. From the nineteenth century, Egypt progressively pursued a Western, secular path in its political, military, and socioeconomic development. While Islam was acknowledged as "a source" of law, Egyptian law was Western in its origins and outlook, as were the constitution and system of government in general. When Gamal Abd al-Nasir came to power after the 1952 Free Officers' revolt, Egypt continued on its secular path, respecting Islam but generally separating religion as far as possible from the state. However, since the late 1950s, under Nasir and later under Sadat, Islam has reemerged as an important factor in Egyptian politics and nationalism.

Nasir sought to proclaim an ideology that would unify the Egyptian people behind him and establish his leadership in the Arab world. He broadened Egyptian nationalism into Arab nationalism, rooted in a common Arab/Islamic heritage. He appealed to a common history, language, religion, and sense of solidarity as the basis for Arab unity and identity. This turning away from a total reliance on the West and search for a more indigenously rooted identity and ideology were reflected in the Egyptian Charter of 1962. Moreover, Nasir increasingly used religious symbols, language, and appeals to Islamic principles and values to legitimate and win mass support for his ideological formulations, programs, and policies. A state-sponsored Supreme Council of Islamic Affairs was established.

In the Council's journal, *Minbar al-Islam* ("The Pulpit of Islam"), Islamic beliefs and values—such as the unity and equality of the Muslim community and social justice in Islam—were reinterpreted to demonstrate the Islamic character of Nasir's Arab nationalism and socialism, respectively. Legal opinions or decrees were obtained from Muslim legal experts, who utilized Islam to support government programs in birth control, land reform, and nationalization. The effectiveness of Nasir's appeal to an Arab/Islamic identity was evident in his long-term popularity at home and throughout much of the Muslim world.

However, for many Egyptian Muslims, Nasir's use of Islam was increasingly seen as simply political and manipulative. Thus, while Nasir's government appealed to Islam, he was challenged by an Islamic movement that was to play a significant role in Egypt and to influence other Muslim countries. The Muslim Brotherhood had been founded in 1928 by Hassan al-Banna (1906-49), an Egyptian schoolteacher who had both a traditional Islamic and a modern education. Although it accepted modern science and technology, the Brotherhood sprang from al-Banna's conviction about the deleterious effects of westernization and secularization on Egypt and the need to revitalize Islamic life and society.

In common with earlier Islamic revivalist movement such as the Wahhabi of Saudi Arabia, al-Banna attributed the ills of society to its departure from the Islamic ideals embodied in the Qur'an and sunna of the Prophet. This loss of identity could be reclaimed only by turning away from the West and returning to Islam. Al-Banna reaffirmed the need to reestablish a proper Islamic state and society based upon the ideology and law of Islam:

> Until recently writers, intellectuals, scholars and governments glorified the principles of European civilization, gave themselves a Western tint, and adopted a European style and manner; today, on the contrary, the wind has changed. . . . Voices are raised proclaiming the necessity for a return to the principles, teachings, and ways of Islam . . . for initiating the reconciliation of modern life with these principles, as a prelude to a final "Islamization."

Although the Muslim Brotherhood supported the revolution of 1952, initial cooperation between the Brotherhood and Gamal Abd al-Nasir turned to disaffection and political opposition when Nasir did not establish Egypt as an Islamic state. In 1954 and 1965 the Brotherhood was accused of attempting to assassinate Nasir. A number of its leaders were executed; many were imprisoned. Although the Brotherhood was suppressed, it continued to exist underground and reemerged under Nasir's successor, Anwar Sadat.

Anwar Sadat came to power in Egypt at a low period in its history. The pride that Nasir had fostered and the hopes of his Arab socialism collapsed with the total and catastrophic defeat of Egypt in the 1967 Arab-Israeli war, which had profound psychological as well as military, political, and economic consequences. The swiftness and magnitude of the Israeli victory challenged Arab/Islamic identity and pride. Colonial rule had originally raised the question, What had gone wrong in Islam? The 1967 war seemed to be the nadir in Arab and Muslim history.

For religious traditionalists the answer was simple. Success and power were signs of God's guidance, and his reward to a faithful community. Loss of power was God's punishment for Muslims' departure from the straight path of Islam through its blind following of the West. Therefore, as Hassan al-Banna and other Islamic revivalists had maintained, there must be a return to Islam.

The intense self-criticism of this period encompassed modern elites as well as religious traditionalists. They had cast their lot with a Western-oriented future even while they continued to see themselves as alienated victims of Western neocolonialism. American support for the establishment of Israel and continued massive military and economic assistance in every Arab-Israeli war seemed to be a testimony to American colonialism in the Middle East. Post-World War II nationalism, whether liberal nationalism or Nasir's Arab nationalism/socialism, failed to significantly improve the masses' political, social, and economic lot. For modernists as well as traditionalists, self-criticism and condemnation were accompanied by an attempt to anchor national identity and pride more firmly in their Arab/Islamic past.

Anwar Sadat reflected both Nasir's use of religion in politics and the search for a more indigenous (Islamic) alternative in political development—that is, he sought to establish greater continuity between modernization and traditional values. Sadat declared that his 1971 rectification program was based upon faith and knowledge, both terms with strong Islamic connotations. Sadat used this title "The Believer Muhammad Anwar Sadat, Father of the Believing Nation." He referred to himself as President of the Believers"— a title reminiscent of the early caliphs, who were called "Commander of the Believers." Moreover, unlike Nasir, Sadat permitted Islamic groups like the Muslim Brotherhood to return to public life and publish its magazine, al-Da'wa ("The Call"). He supported Islamic educational and cultural societies as well as Sufi orders. Sadat used Islam both to enhance his political legitimacy and to counter the influence of Nasirites and leftists who opposed his new pro-Western policies.

Sadat's use of Islamization was especially evident in the 1973 Arab-Israeli war. Unlike the 1967 war, the 1973 war was heavy with religious significance, Islamic symbolism, and slogans. This was the Ramadan war (named for the holy month of fasting, during which it occurred); its code name was Badr, a famous early Islamic victory led by Muhammad; its battle cry was "God is most Great," the traditional Islamic battle cry for the defense of Islam; those who died were not only patriots but also martyrs in a holy war.

Like his predecessor, Sadat exercised a great deal of control over the religious establishment. Thus, he marshaled the support of Shaykh Abd al-Rahman Bissar, rector of al-Azhar University, and leading ulama to support his policies. For example, Bissar declared that the Egyptian-Israeli peace treaty was "in consonance with Islamic law, because it was based on a position of strength after holy war and victory," a reference to the 1973 war.

However, Sadat was not able to control Islam entirely. His government and his increasingly authoritarian style came under attack from many quarters of Egyptian society. Among his most vocal critics were Egypt's burgeoning Islamic organizations, which attacked his peace treaty with Israel and continued to view his policies as too pro-Western and insufficiently Islamic. Sadat's support of the shah and condemnation of Ayatollah Khomeini were seen as further proof of his hypocritical manipulation of Islam. This seemed confirmed in February 1979, when he warned, "Those who wish to practice Islam can go to the mosques, and those who wish to engage in politics may do so through the legal institutions." Under pressure, Sadat had opted for the separation of religion and state, a position seen as un-Islamic by Muslim organizations, which called for an Islamic state and the reestablishment of Islamic law.

Increasingly, more militant Muslim groups like the Takfir wal Hijra (Ex-communication and Emigration), Jund Allah (God's Army), and Jamaat al-Jihad (Holy War Society) resorted to acts of violence. These groups reflected a general resurgence of Islam in the Muslim world. While varying in their acceptance and use of force, they share a general commitment to the revitalization of Islamic identity and ideology. They are committed both to personal religious reawakening and to political change, believing that it is only through a return to Islam and the implementation of an Islamic government that the political, socioeconomic, and moral disease that has enfeebled Muslim societies can be eradicated. Their leadership is pious, bright, and well-educated, with degrees in science, engineering, and medicine. It was one such group—al-Jihad, an offshoot of Takfir wal Hijra—that was responsible for the assassination of Anwar Sadat. Since that time Egypt's new president, Hosni Mubarak, has suppressed Islamic groups, closed down their publishing houses and centers, and generally avoided any mixing of religion with Egyptian politics.

IRAN

From his accession to the throne in 1941, Shah Muhammad Reza Pahlavi continued the process of modernization begun by his father. He emphasized intensive military and economic development and selective social change. Though educational reform had produced a modern middle class, political development was restricted. In principle the shah was a constitutional monarch; in fact he controlled and dominated the political institutions of the state. Cabinet, parliament, senate, political parties, individual government officials—all served at the pleasure of the shah.

While Iran's modernization programs made some real improvements, these were offset by the fact that reforms were imposed from above, often autocratically; fruits of modernization tended to be concentrated primarily among elite urbanites; and its negative side effects progressively alienated large segments of the population, especially the traditional religious and commercial establishments. As criticism of the shah's policies increased, so did the activities of his secret police: politicians, religious leaders, intellectuals, and students were imprisoned and tortured; meetings were disrupted; and presses were closed, publications suppressed, the media controlled.

Opposition to the direction and pace of Iran's modernization had existed for some time, and had included secularists as well as religious leaders. A central theme of critics was the blind, uncritical westernization of Iranian society. In 1962 Jalal Al-e Ahmad, a leading secularist intellectual, published his "Westoxification" (or "Weststruckness"), in which he warned of the loss of Iranian identity and the negative economic and cultural effects of a modernization program that mindlessly imitated Western patterns of development. Instead, he recommended learning from the examples of Japan and India, which seemed to blend modernization with their own cultural traditions. Religiously oriented Iranians, whether the more conservative ulama or the Western-educated Islamic modernists like Dr. Ali Shariati and Mehdi Bazargan, voiced similar criticisms and calls for a return to Iran's Islamic roots. America's strong support for an increasingly autocratic and repressive government, as well as the presence of Western military and multinational companies, simply reinforced the sense of Western dominance—politically, economically, militarily, and culturally.

As opposition mounted within Iran, Shi'i Islam emerged as the most viable vehicle for an effective mass movement. It provided a common set of symbols, a historic identity, and a value system that were non-Western, indigenous, and broadly appealing. It also offered an ideological framework within which a variety of factions could function. Moreover, the religious leadership had remained untainted by not having cooperated with the government while also providing a hierarchical organization and leadership through its charismatic ayatollahs. A number of them (the ayatollahs Khomeini, Talequani, and Shariatmadari) had suffered under the shah for their opposition to the government. Moreover, Islamic lay reformers like Shariati and Bazargan enjoyed the respect of many, especially of an alienated and increasingly militant younger generation. The *mullah* (religious leader)-mosque system provided a natural, informal, nationwide communications network. The thousands of mosques scattered throughout every city and village became the foci for dissent, centers for political organization and agitation. Mosques offered a sanctuary, the Friday sermon became a political platform, and the clergy represented a vast reservoir of grass roots leadership.

Most important, Shi'i Islam offered an ideological view of history that gave meaning and legitimation to an opposition movement, for in a very real sense Shi'i Islam is a religion of protest. Unlike Sunni Islam, with its sense that early success and power were signs of God's favor, for Shi'i Islam, history documents the persistent denial or frustration of God's will regarding leadership of the Islamic community. The martyrdom of Ali's son Husayn in 680 and its annual ritual reenactment during the month of Muharram provide Shi'i communal belief with the character of a protest or opposition movement in which a small, righteous party struggles against overwhelming forces of evil. This battle against corruption and social injustice is to continue until, with God's guidance, a messianic guide (Mahdi) returns as leader to usher in God's rule and a socially just society.

Thus Shi'i Islam, the religion of most Iranians, provided the ideology and symbols for a popular revolutionary struggle. For many Shi'is the shah and his overwhelming army, like the army that martyred Husayn, represented the evils of corruption and social injustice. The righteous must revolt against this Satan in a holy war to restore the reign of goodness, equity, and social justice required to make Iran Dar al-Islam. Toward that ends, self-sacrifice and even death are to be freely accepted, for to die in God's struggle is to become a martyr and win eternal reward.

Under the umbrella of Islam heterogeneous groups in the Iranian political spectrum, from secularists to conservatives and Islamic modernists, and from liberal democrats to Marxists, joined together. They marched behind three banners that symbolically declared their options: the stars and stripes, the hammer and sickle, and Allah. Crossing out the first two options on their banners, they rejected the West and the Soviet Union and chose the third, more authentic, Iranian/Islamic alternative. It should be emphasized here that while there was a common purpose—opposition to the shah and a desire for a more indigenously rooted modernity—the religious and political outlooks and agendas of the various groups were quite diverse. For many, the Islamic alternative symbolized by the name Allah meant a return to Islam, the establishment of an Islamic state and society. Others wished to reclaim their identity or selfhood through a more conscious incorporation of their cultural heritage, its history, and its values within Iran's modernization.

Even among the religiously committed, there were sharp and distinctive differences in their interpretations of Islamic identity and ideology. Nowhere was this clearer than in the juxtaposition of banners depicting the Ayatollah Khomeini and Dr. Ali Shariati in street protests and homes. The former emerged as the leader of the revolution, and the latter served as its ideologue. For Khomeini and many of the religious leadership, Islam is, by and large, the tradition as developed and preserved in classical Islamic law. In this sense they are conservatives, traditionalists. Shariati and other Islamic modernists represent a far more innovative, reformist approach. If Khomeini follows his religious education and looks to tradition for answers, Shariati, the product of a traditional education and holder of a Sorbonne Ph.D., viewed Shi'i Islam in a more creative, evolutionary manner.

For Shariati, Shi'i Islam provided the symbols for a much-needed cultural revolution. He rejected both the blind imitation of the West and the uncritical, static acceptance of classical medieval formulations of Islam, many of whose regulations were no longer relevant or appropriate. Thus, Shariati advocated a reinterpretation of Shi'i Islam to formulate a more indigenous ideology—Iranian/Islamic rather than Western/imperialist. He offered this new ideological approach to all, religious and nonreligious:

> . . . we must distinguish between the Islam that generates consciousness, that is progressive and in revolt, the ideology . . . from its traditional aspect which has caused decline. The return to the self . . . is the starting point. . . . The image of Islam must, therefore, be changed: the socially traditional transformed into an ideology; the collection of mystical studies, currently being taught must be replaced by self-conscious faith, the centuries' long decline into a resurgence. . . . With this shape, the en-

lightened thinker, religious and non-religious would return to the self. He would confront the cultural imperialism of the West and through the force of religion, awaken his own society stupefied with religion.

It was Shariati's blending of traditional terminology with fresh interpretations incorporating the ideas of modern social science, socialism, and Third World liberation themes that captured the attention and imagination of a wide following.

While the shah provided a common cause and Islam a unifying symbol, the sharp differences among revolutionary factions came to the surface shortly after the downfall of the shah. The rupture occurred as Iran's new leaders turned to the task of articulating and implementing Iran's Islamic identity and ideology—the establishment of the Islamic Republic of Iran and the drafting of its first constitution. Given the role of religion, the religious establishment, and popular religious support, the influence of Khomeini and the mullahs was to be expected. However, there was a sharp division over the role of the mullahs and the implementation of Islamic law.

There were two major schools of thought regarding the place of Islam in politics. The liberal constitutionalists were willing to give the clergy an indirect role in government through the creation of a committee of religious scholars who could veto any law judged contrary to Islam. This group included Islamic modernists, secularists, and some religious leaders like the Ayatollah Shariat-madari. However, the second camp, led by Ayatollah Khomeini and supported by a majority of the mullahs, advocated direct rule by the religious leaders and the full implementation of traditional Islamic law. The latter position has won.

Thus, while the new constitution of the Islamic Republic of Iran has many of the provisions for a modern parliamentary system of government, the Ayatollah Khomeini and his Council of Guardians oversee the conduct of the state. Moreover, the clergy-dominated Islamic Republic Party controls the Parliament. Under Khomeini's doctrine of *velayat-i-faqih* (governance of the jurist), Islamic government is the rule of Islamic law, as interpreted by the supreme leader or Islamic jurist. Utilizing this doctrine, Khomeini oversees affairs of state: selecting half of the 12 members of the Council of Guardians, approving the credentials of the president and prime minister, serving as supreme commander of the army and so on. Thus, the determination of Iran's Islamic identity and ideology has been concentrated in Khomeini and a group of religious leaders.

While continuing to enjoy general support, the interpretation, use, and enforcement of Islam have caused division and dissent, involving some of the leading Islamic figures in the revolution. Ayatollahs like Shariatmadari have been isolated and silenced, Mehdi Bazargan (Iran's first prime minister after the shah's departure) resigned, President Abol Hasan Banisadr fled the country, and Sadeq Qotbzadeh, a former aide to Khomeini and government minister, was executed for plotting the assassination of Khomeini.

Islamic government and law have often appeared to be restrictive rather than a direct path to be freely followed. Press and book censorship; measures to assure the ideological purity of university professors and curricula; prohibitions on alcohol, gambling, nightclubs, drug use, and sexual offenses—all have been enforced in the name of Islam. Islamic judges and courts have been used to justify punishment by execution for a range of offenses ranging from drug smuggling and homosexuality to political dissent. The abuses of the court system were so blatant that Ayatollah Khomeini himself issued a warning to Islamic judges.

Finally, the activities of the Islamic Republic of Iran have drawn attention to an issue that has surfaced in other Muslim areas—the status of non-Muslims in a Muslim or Islamic state. If a state becomes more Islamic, what are the implications regarding the rights of its non-Muslim citizens? Traditionally, non-Muslims were viewed as "protected" people. In exchange for payment of a poll tax, non-Muslim citizens of the Islamic state were free to follow their own religion and observe their own personal status or family laws (marriage, divorce, inheritance). In contrast, many modern Muslim states have granted full political rights to all citizens, regardless of religious affiliation.

However, the contemporary resurgence of Islam has been accompanied by greater communal tension and conflicts, such as those between Muslims and Coptic Christians in Egypt, Muslims and Bahais in Iran, and Malay Muslims and Chinese in Malaysia. Some Islamic activists insist that non-Muslims should not be permitted to hold major government positions, arguing that their religious commitment would preclude an ability to be fully committed to the Islamic ideology of the state. Thus, in addition to the offices of president and prime minister, they would argue, non-Muslims should not serve in such posts as attorney general or chief of the armed forces.

While Islam functioned effectively as a battle cry and standard for an anti-shah movement, the attempt to delineate Iran's more authentically rooted Islamic identity has proved far more difficult. Some would argue that Iran's Islamic government still has the support of the majority of the population and that the regime has created an infrastructure in the midst of the chaos that follows such revolutions. However, others would ask: At what price? Although the experiences of Pakistan and Iran are in many ways dissimilar, their respective attempts at Islamization raise similar questions: Whose Islam is this? and Why emphasize a negative Islam?

THE SEARCH FOR IDENTITY

The contemporary Muslim quest for identity has taken many turns. As Muslims seek to reclaim, and then to integrate their Islamic heritage into their development, Islam has reemerged in personal religious life as well as in Muslim politics. As our case studies demonstrate, throughout the 1970s and early 1980s, not only in established Islamic states like Saudi Arabia, but also progressively in many other contemporary Muslim countries, Islam has reasserted itself in the politics, ideology, and institutions of the state. Politically, it has been used by incumbent governments to legitimate their rule and policies, and by opposition movements to organize and mobilize mass support to overthrow corrupt "un-Islamic" regimes. Islam has proved to be effective as a rallying cry and a unifying symbol for resistance.

However, the formulation and implementation of Islamic ideologies for state and society have raised many questions. Whose Islam is this? Who should determine and oversee the Islamization of state and society: the ruler, the traditional religious establishment, or Islamic organizations with predominantly lay leadership? What Islam is to be implemented: that of conservative traditionalists, who turn to early Islamic history and seek to apply traditional beliefs and practices as embodied in classical law, or that of Muslim reformers, who wish to utilize Islamic principles and values to formulate appropriate responses to modernity?

While conservatives seek to restore a classical world view in specific detail, reformers advocate a fresh interpretation of Islam. While they would agree with conservatives on the need to look to the Qur'an and the example of the Prophet and the early Muslim community, reformers would also insist that these sources offer inspiration and guidance in the form of general norms that must be reapplied in each age. They wish to provide a new synthesis that will support and sustain an Islamically oriented modernization, free of excessive westernization and secularization. Thus, they would selectively choose from their tradition and from the West, and they would also incorporate their own interpretations of Islam.

How the Islamization of politics and society will be realized also remains an unanswered question. Shall it be imposed from above, or must it come from below? Thus far, leadership in development within the Muslim world has come from a relatively small number of modern elites. Their Western-oriented education and world view have equipped them as technocrats and bureaucrats who can apply, rather than plan, create, or adapt, development models that are sensitive to cultural concerns. Religious leaders, on the other hand, are among the traditional elites who have been displaced by modernization. Given their more traditional religious training and education, they are generally unable to provide the creative reinterpretation of Islam required in modern society. Contemporary Muslim reformers tend to combine excellent modern educations with an Islamic orientation. However, they are few in number. Realizing that they must prepare the way for a new generation, they emphasize education and the formation of associations like the Islamic Student Association and the World Assembly of Muslim Youth to train and form Muslim youth. They believe that if Muslims are to rediscover and incorporate their past into their present and future, then models for political, legal, and social development must be adapted, not blindly adopted. Where necessary, new forms must be created. This process will require social architects equipped to bridge both worlds—traditional and modern.

Finally, for reforms to be effective, they must be accepted by religious leaders and by the majority of the population. Thus, educational reform is a key prerequisite. The bifurcation of education in Muslim societies, introduced during the colonial period by the establishment of a modern educational system alongside the traditional religious schools, has produced two different mind-sets or outlooks: modern, Western versus traditional, religious. If Muslims are to formulate and implement Islamic reforms effectively, the participation of the traditional religious establishment is required. The acceptance of reforms by the ulama and by the general population will be dependent upon the development of an intellectual reform that facilitates recognition of the creative, dynamic, adaptive nature of Islam.

While the West had several centuries to absorb the impact of modernization and to make the transition from traditional to modern societies, the Muslim world has had only several decades. The process of forging a new synthesis will take generations. The diverse experience of Muslim countries like Turkey, Saudi Arabia, Libya, Pakistan, Egypt, and Iran demonstrate the variety and complexity of this effort.

11

Islamic Law

Ann Elizabeth Mayer

The role that the shari'a should play in the legal systems of contemporary Muslim countries is one of the main political and intellectual problems preoccupying the Muslim world today. Few Muslims would question the continued relevance of the shari'a as a source of religious and ethical guidance, but they are in sharp disagreement about the extent to which it should be applied as the law of the land. If they want to see the shari'a reinstated as the official legal norm, they may still dispute whether it must be applied in accordance with the standards developed by medieval jurists, or whether it is permissible to construct a reformed version of the shari'a that reflects modern attitudes and changed needs. Advocates of modernization and reform of the shari'a find many ideas of the medieval jurists unsuited for application in present circumstances.

One of the modern criticisms of the classical shari'a is that simply finding an answer to a legal problem in the medieval law books is usually difficult and time-consuming. The classical treatises of shari'a law were written by and for highly trained specialists in Islamic religious sciences, the ulama—and, more particularly, the group of scholars specializing in Islamic jurisprudence, the *fuqaha*. Such learned scholars were often little concerned with making their ideas intelligible to outsiders or with practical application of the legal principles they elaborated. As a result their books have an organization and style that make them cumbersome, if not impossible, for specialists to use in administering justice.

Another problem in applying the classical shari'a today is that the rules developed by the medieval jurists reflect the legal concerns and social background of their day; hence many problems of twentieth-century life are simply not addressed. For example, juristic entities like the modern corporation were not envisaged, so one looks in vain in the classical treatises for guidance on how to organize and operate a modern business in corporate form. In other instances, where the medieval fuqaha did elaborate shari'a rules, the rules may seem archaic—for instance, punishment by physical mutilation for certain criminal offenses, tribal responsibility in the scheme of penalties, notions of compensation for death or personal injury (which may be stated in terms of numbers of camels), or rules of evidence that preclude or devalue testimony by women and rely heavily on the ritual swearing of oaths.

Would-be reformers of the shari'a take the position that the medieval and archaic features are not actually mandated by the sources of Islamic law and that products of mere human reason, like the writings of the fuqaha, cannot bind Muslims. Their attempts to introduce enlightened, progressive interpretations of the shari'a are often met with skepticism or even hostility by conservatives, who oppose what they perceive as attempts to undermine respect for Islamic tradition and to dilute true Islamic legal doctrines by incorporating alien concepts borrowed from the secular West. To eliminate the possibility of deviating from the true path, many conservatives invoke *taqlid,* the doctrine of obedience to established authority, which entails deference to the shari'a as it was developed by about 900 C.E. According to the doctrine of taqlid, independent reasoning on issues resolved by the early fuqaha is precluded. The rationale is that the early Islamic community was closest to the authentic tradition. In the eyes of such conservatives, any tampering with the early doctrines involves blameworthy innovation.

Yet another feature of the classical shari'a that many Muslims find unworkable in today's circumstances is that it precludes the possibility of legislation by the state to make and to change the law. The fuqaha as a class monopolized the shari'a in accordance with their conviction that law could not be made, only found. Therefore, no state could undertake legislation without incurring their condemnation.

THE NATURE OF ISLAMIC LAW

A striking characteristic of the shari'a is that it does not make the distinction between religious and mundane matters that one finds in many other religious and legal systems. Many Muslims consider this a particular strength and virtue. Within the shari'a one finds the expected elaborate regulations covering the details of the pilgrimage to Mecca, how to select a prayer leader, and ritual ablutions necessary to attain the state of purity required for prayer. But one also finds that Islamic law covers personal grooming and dress, the choice of utensils for eating and drinking, and the conduct of horse races—as well as encompassing areas that are usually covered by secular law in other legal systems, such as real estate transactions, the organization of business partnerships, the ownership of sub-surface minerals, and courtroom procedures. The result is that all acts are evaluated in a system in which law and ethics are interrelated. Thus, in following the shari'a, the believer conforms his or her conduct to the will of Allah down to the last detail.

Because it is meant to function as a legal system, the shari'a sets criteria for determining when an act is legally valid or invalid, and also provides penalties for violations of its precepts. At the same time the shari'a also sets moral guidelines so that believers can know the ethical character of their acts. Acts are categorized according to whether they are commanded, recommended, morally neutral, reprehended, or prohibited. While many violations of Islamic law are meant to be penalized by legal sanctions in this life, whether the penalty is, in fact, carried out is in a sense irrelevant, because the ultimate Judge of a believer's conduct is Allah. On the Day of Judgment He will assign all persons to eternity in paradise or hellfire on the basis of their degree of obedience to His law. Believing that divine sanctions and rewards are the underlying principles of lawful behavior, it is difficult for Muslims to imagine that a legal system with only the enforcement power of a temporal government behind it can effectively deter humans from wrongdoing or inspire them to aim for the highest standards of ethical conduct.

SOURCES OF ISLAMIC LAW

Qur'an

The least controversial element in Islamic law, and the one most closely associated with divine inspiration, is the Qur'an, the revelation delivered to the Prophet Muhammad. Muslims believe that the text of the Qur'an was accurately recorded soon after the death of the Prophet in 632 C.E., and that the text in circulation today is a totally authentic representation of the actual speech of Allah. The legal rules set forth in the Qur'an are generally regarded as absolutely binding.

It should be noted, however, that the traditional view has been that one cannot accurately understand what the Qur'anic rules mean unless one has advanced training in the religious and legal sciences. Certainly, reading Qur'anic passages without knowledge of how they have been traditionally interpreted by shari'a scholars could lead one to erroneous conclusions as to what the shari'a is understood to require of believers. In particular, as Fazlur Rahman explains in Chapter 2, it is very important to know which verses are abrogating and which are abrogated.

A common but erroneous assumption is that a major part of the shari'a comes directly from the Qur'an. In fact, the Qur'an states few definite rules. One could say that just as the American Constitution has shown itself capable of generating many specific principles out of a small number of broadly written guidelines, so the Qur'an has served as a source of wide-ranging legal guidance based on a limited number of explicit laws. Although the exact number of lines in the Qur'an that are of legal nature is disputed, one might put the number at about 600.

The subject matter covered in these verses is limited; the bulk have to do with inheritance and family law. The remaining legal provisions of the Qur'an deal with such topics as certain criminal offenses, aspects of contract and commercial law, and some rules of evidence. Except in matters of family law and inheritance, most of what is known as shari'a law is therefore not based directly on the Qur'an.

Sunna

A much more extensive source is the sunna or, roughly, custom of the Prophet Muhammad. Although the collections of hadith, or reports of what the Prophet said and did, vary in size and content, in many one would find about 4,000 reports covering many more topics than do the verses of the Qur'an. It is important to note that the sunna of the Prophet is followed because he is considered by Muslims to have been divinely inspired, not because Muhammad himself is regarded as divine. In the traditional view the sunna is treated as a legal source on a par with the Qur'an.

However, the place of the sunna in the hierarchy of sources of Islamic law has never been as rock-solid as that of the Qur'an. One reason is that the hadith collections were not recorded until the second century after the death of the Prophet. There are different collections of hadith with different and even sharply conflicting, or at least inconsistent, content. For example, the Sunnis and the Shi'is, who have radically different understandings of who were the rightful successors to the Prophet's leadership of the Muslim community, each have in their hadith collections reports that confirm their respective positions. Even at the very early stages of the development of Islamic legal science, there were scholars who opposed the adoption of the sunna as a source of shari'a law, but the overwhelming majority of Muslims have tended to accept the sunna as legally binding.

For many decades the prevailing thesis among Western scholars of Islamic law has been that a major part, if not the majority, of the hadith literature consists of what might be called pious forgeries. It is believed that early Muslim scholars concocted the hadith to provide an Islamic rationale for many in-place, non-Islamic practices that were adapted by the burgeoning Islamic empire for administering its newly conquered territories. Many modern Muslims are also inclined to undertake critical reexamination of the hadith literature and to challenge at least part of it as being the product of forgers.

The extent to which one accepts the hadith as authentic has a tremendous impact on how much of the traditional shari'a one accepts as binding; and while there are many Muslims who continue to believe that the hadith are a reliable source of Islamic law, there are others who deny the validity of all the classical shari'a rules save those that can be shown to derive from the Qur'an. Between these extremes are Muslims who regard the hadith literature as a potential source of Islamic law but advocate that it be used with varying degrees of selectivity.

Qiyas

The task of Muslim jurists has been to expand the legal principles based on the Qur'an and sunna so as to regulate all aspects of human activity, using criteria that are identifiably Islamic. Sunni Muslim scholars used analogical reasoning, known as *qiyas*, to achieve this end. An example of how this has been achieved may be seen in the shari'a rules regarding the consumption of alcohol. The Qur'an prohibits by name a wine consumed in western Arabia at the time of revelation in the seventh century. This might be taken literally. In fact, the Zahiri school of shari'a law, which became extinct in the Middle Ages, advocated literal readings of the Qur'an and sunna, since any human "interpretations" would run the risk of obscuring their pure meaning. Following the Zahiri position on this question, the prohibition would apply to only that particular type of wine. However, using analogical reasoning, jurists have expanded the shari'a rules to extend the coverage to other intoxicants, although they have not been in total agreement as to which substances should be covered by the prohibition.

The use of analogy as a basic tool of legal science has meant that classical Islamic law does not state broad, general principles but, rather, focuses on a series of very specific questions. That is, one does not find in the classical law books a statement like "All substances containing more than 2 percent alcohol in relation to total volume are prohibited." Instead, one finds rulings on the licitness of individual substances, such as whether beer, wine consumed for medical purposes, tobacco, and hashish are covered by the prohibition. Many Muslim scholars believed that if general legal principles were extrapolated from the Qur'an and sunna, the original meaning would become distorted. In contrast, it was felt that analogical reasoning that limits jurists to rulings on specific and concrete questions is essential to keep subjective, personal judgments from entering the shari'a.

Even in the medieval period, not all Muslims accepted this point of view, some arguing that a freer use of human reasoning was necessary for developing an understanding of the ultimate principles and purposes of the shari'a. Today the strict use of analogical reasoning is becoming less favored in many circles, as

Muslims struggle to find answers to broad social, economic, and political questions for which more innovative and flexible interpretative techniques seem to be required.

Ijma

Consensus is typically classified with analogical reasoning as a fundamental principle of Islamic legal science, although, again, there are differences of opinion among Muslims as to its validity and its requirements. It is widely accepted among Sunni Muslims that if all the jurists of a given generation reach a consensus on a point of law, this view becomes final and can never be challenged. Historically consensus counteracted the centrifugal tendencies inherent in legal development in the works of law schools dispersed over far-flung regions. Today ijma is also a subject of critical reexamination, as many Muslims question whether they should be bound by the juristic interpretations of medieval predecessors—or even whether ijma should be democratized or popularized, so that a fresh consensus can emerge, more accurately reflecting contemporary standards for communal and individual conduct.

Other Legal Sources

Different sects and schools of law have their own criteria for developing and expanding the sources of Islamic law, often in addition to the ones so far mentioned. One of the most important of these is the principle of public welfare, which many jurists have insisted must guide the interpretation of the requirements of the shari'a. A small minority even argues that public welfare should supersede rules set forth in the Qur'an and sunna. Modern Muslims who favor the liberalization and reform of the traditional version of the shari'a have tended to focus on the principle of public welfare as a rationale for adapting shari'a rules to the needs of modern society. Thus, for example, they would argue that insurance contracts (which conservative scholars tend to find in violation of the shari'a rules against wagering) should be tolerated because of their social benefits.

SUNNI AND SHI'I LAW SCHOOLS

One of the striking features of traditional Islamic law is its general tolerance of diversity. The Prophet Muhammad is reported to have said, "Diversity of opinion in my community is a blessing." Historically Muslim scholars have tended to exhibit a generous respect for different interpretations of Islamic law. In the Sunni world the once numerous legal schools have coalesced into four, all of which are regarded as equally orthodox. Thus, a student at Cairo's prestigious al-Azhar University, the world's oldest university and the traditional center of Islamic religious and legal education, can choose to study law as taught by the Hanafi, Maliki, Shafi'i, or Hanbali schools. Although congruent in broad outline, the schools are different enough in their specifics that a variety of legal outcomes may result, depending on which school is followed.

Law schools have predominated in various geographical areas over time. Today the Hanafi school claims the allegiance of perhaps 60 percent of all Muslims and is dominant in the eastern Mediterranean and the Indian subcontinent. The Maliki school dominates in North Africa, but has scattered adherents in other areas as well. The concentration of Shafi'i school tends to reflect ancient trade routes, so Shafi'is are found in eastern Africa and other coastal areas, as well as in the Muslim countries of Southeast Asia, such as Indonesia. The Hanbali school has few adherents outside the Arabian peninsula.

Shi'i law schools and Sunni law schools vary most on the question of government, a difference that stems from their opinions on who should succeed the Prophet, as discussed in Chapter 3. The Shi'i community is divided into subsects, each of which has its own school of law. Thus, the Shi'i schools are more isolated from each other than are Sunni schools. The most numerous subsect is that of the Twelvers, who dominate in Iran and parts of Iraq and Pakistan. The Zaidis are concentrated in the Yemen. And the Isma'ilis, who follow the Aga Khan, are geographically the most wide-spread, with large numbers in the Indian subcontinent and East Africa.

Just as the schools expanded geographically, so their doctrines expanded over the centuries as new jurists added their comments on previous treatises and their solutions to new legal problems. The literature of Islamic legal scholarship became voluminous. To reduce the material to manageable proportions, one particular scholar would typically be treated as the standard reference by members of a given school within a specific geographical area at one period of history.

TRADITIONAL COURTS AND
LEGAL FUNCTIONARIES

The details of how the shari'a should be administered by judges and the structure and operations of courts had to be worked out in the course of historical experience, since there was very little explicit guidance on these points in the sources.

The judge in the traditional shari'a court was called a *qadi.* The first qadis were persons deputized by political leaders after the Muslim community grew too large for the ruler to resolve all disputes—as had been the case under the Prophet Muhammad and his immediate successors. The qadis were subordinate to the ruler, at whose pleasure they served. The ruler chose the law school whose doctrines the qadi was to apply, and he could limit the qadi's authority to certain types of cases. The jurisdiction of qadis' courts was often limited to cases involving family law, inheritance, pious endowments, and some contracts.

Ideally, qadis were meant to be experts in shari'a law, but in practice this was not always the case. Many of the great fuqaha refused appointments as qadis, feeling that working for the government could compromise their reputations for independence and integrity. There were no lawyers in the traditional shari'a system, although there were clerks and other legal functionaries who could help parties with the technicalities of preparing their cases. The parties to a dispute presented their cases to a qadi, who ruled in favor of one or the other on the basis of very rigid rules of procedure and evidence. In a traditional shari'a system a qadi's judgment was final and not subject to appeal, since there was no hierarchy of courts.

Occasionally legal problems would arise that presented issues that had not been resolved in previous shari'a scholarship. Such issues were referred to a *mufti,* whose ruling on the issue was known as a *fatwa.* Fuqaha could act as private muftis, rendering fatwas on problems that people brought to them, but there were also public muftis who were appointed by rulers to render official fatwas that were intended to have more far-reaching effect. While decisions made by judges had no precedential value, the fuqaha incorporated fatwas they respected in their treatises, adding them to the ever expanding corpus of Islamic law.

Today, when other features of the traditional system of shari'a justice have long since been abolished as a result of westernization, the institution of the official mufti has generally been maintained. Leaders of Muslim countries fear criticisms that they are not following Islamic law, and rulings by muftis can serve an important legitimating function. For example, when Nasir undertook his extensive land reform measures in Egypt, he not only justified them in terms of Arab socialism but also succeeded in obtaining a fatwa from a prominent Egyptian mufti that held that land reform did not, as many were charging, violate the shari'a. While other fuqaha were insisting that the land reform program was incompatible with the protection that the shari'a afford private property, the mufti in this case ruled that land reform was covered by the shari'a principle that vital resources are to be owned in common by the members of the community.

Another important official in the shari'a system was the market inspector, or *muhtasib,* whose responsibility it was to ensure that good order was observed in public. The muhtasib and his deputies would make rounds throughout a city, on the lookout for any conditions or behavior that violated shari'a standards or that could endanger public health, safety, welfare, and morality. They were entitled to mete out summary punishments to offenders. The muhtasibs' major function was inspection of the public markets. Typical objects of their sanctions would be merchants who sold adulterated goods or used false weights, people who built structures that obstructed the public way, or women who went out in immodest dress. Their mandate accorded with the general shari'a injunction to all Muslims to command what is good and forbid what is evil.

The qadis' courts had no enforcement powers, so they were dependent on other parts of government for the execution of their judgments. Their rigid procedures have already been mentioned. In practice the qadis' courts were often superseded by other tribunals that were better able to ensure that their decisions would be executed and were not bound by the strict shari'a rules of procedure. One such court was the *mazalim* (court of complaints), where people could bring claims of miscarriage of justice and abuse of authority against government officials. The police had their own tribunals, where summary justice was meted out to those deemed guilty of criminal misconduct. Over the centuries the administration of criminal justice tended to be assumed by the police, at the expense of the qadis' courts. In other areas disputes that did not reach the qadis' courts were resolved by such mechanisms as intervention by the political authorities, arbitration, social pressure, or customary law.

STATE LEGISLATION

As previously noted, the shari'a developed as a jurists' law, and in classical theory there was no role for the state as lawmaker. There was, however, a legitimate role for the state in the legal arena: that of exercising *siyasa shar'iyya,* administrative measures needed for the implementation of the shari'a. Despite the jurists' unwillingness to accord the state a greater role, the state could not indefinitely be precluded from all legislative activity. In the guise of administration, states found indirect ways to shape legal systems. In the Ottoman Empire the government began openly issuing secular laws, known as qanuns—the word "qanun" being borrowed from the Greek word for rule and corresponding to the word used to designate the canon law of the Roman Catholic Church. Perhaps the most important of the Ottoman sultans in this regard was Suleiman the Magnificent (1520-60), who in the Muslim world is known as Suleiman Qanuni, or Suleiman of the Qanuns. The early initiatives in this regard were taken with caution and concern to avoid any overt challenge to the theoretical supremacy of the shari'a. They were presented as manifestations of siyasa shar'iyya, as measures intended to supplement but not supplant the shari'a. Although the qanuns covered various topics, many were enacted in the area of criminal law, where the shari'a was deemed to be seriously inadequate.

This was the germ of what was to be an important development in the legal history of Muslim countries. The concept of qanun was extended to cover the kind of codified law that was developed in Europe. Beginning in the nineteenth century, Muslim states enacted codes of secular law in areas formerly covered by the shari'a. These codes eventually superseded the shari'a in most areas of law, so that what was originally an exceptional category became the norm.

In the nineteenth century, when several experimental codifications of shari'a law were drawn up, there seemed to be possibilities for compromise between the governments' wishes to enact modern codified legislation and loyalty to the shari'a. The most notable and successful of these experiments was the Ottoman Majalla, a codification of Hanafi law on obligations that was promulgated in 1877. However, most governments eventually decided to adopt new codes derived from French models, though the Indian subcontinent, as part of the British Empire, was obliged to follow the less efficient common-law model. Thus it was that codified European law, rather than codified versions of the shari'a, came to replace the classical treatises of the fuqaha as the law in Muslim countries.

Although men continued to be trained in classical Islamic law in institutions like al-Azhar, their learning was of ever less practical importance as the jurisdiction of the shari'a courts was reduced, and then finally eliminated, in most countries. Their former prestige and influence were eclipsed by the emerging profession of Western-trained lawyer. Those with traditional training represented the great majority of the population, who still possessed traditional attitudes and were offended by the notion that they needed to imitate the culture of the alien, Christian West. They were receptive audiences for Muslim intellectuals who argued that the answer to the backwardness of Muslim society lay in either a reaffirmation of commitment to the classical shari'a or its renewal and reform. Advocates of what has come to be known as Islamization have typically placed a high priority on reinstating shari'a law—most often without acknowledging that there are significant differences of opinion as to what shari'a law requires of Muslims.

ISLAMIC LAW AS IDEOLOGY

In addition to the variety of the classical interpretations of shari'a law, there are a number of contemporary theories that view Islamic law more as ideology than as a legal system. That is, many Muslims no longer look to the shari'a for guidance on the legality of a particular transactions or the ethical evaluation of a particular act.

Rather, they seek in it a comprehensive scheme for ordering all social, economic, and political relations. The assumption they make is that once the divinely ordained scheme is identified and implemented, Muslim societies will be able to achieve unequaled harmony, prosperity, and justice. Those who claim to have found such a perfect societal blueprint in the shari'a believe that their interpretation in this ideological sense is not just correct, but also the only one that is correct. Unlike classical jurists, contemporary proponents of ideologized versions of Islamic law are not willing to treat each other's interpretations as deserving of equal respect.

An example of the modern, ideologized version of Islamic law may be seen in the new theories of Islamic economies that have been developed from the shari'a. Classical jurists viewed the charging of interest as unethical and illegal, but they did not deal with the macroeconomic implications of interest charges. Instead, they concentrated on giving specific advice for the individual believer on which transactions violated or complied with the rule prohibiting interest. Many classical jurists believed that interest charges were legal under the shari'a as long as the formalities of the transaction disguised the interest charges so that they looked like licit profit. For example, a borrower "sold" his creditor something immediately, agreeing to "buy" the item back at a later date for a higher "purchase price." The lender's profit on the sale was actually the interest on the loan. Many books were compiled by classical jurists on such subterfuges for evading inconvenient features of shari'a commercial law, indicating that there was widespread acceptance of the idea that interest charges were not bad in themselves, as long as one stayed within the letter of the law.

In contrast, theorists of Islamic economics believe that the shari'a prohibition of interest involves a macroeconomic principle, and that Muslim countries must reinstate the shari'a prohibition of interest in order to cure the economic ills of their societies and make them prosperous and productive. Tolerating interest in a disguised form, they claim, is an obstacle to economic development. According to this perspective, the Qur'anic prohibition is not a mere ethical guideline for the behavior of believers seeking to stay within the boundaries of Islamic morality; it is a general principle of sound economics. Thus, the reasoning goes, it is not permissible under Islamic law for a bank to charge another bank interest on a letter of credit. Most serious proponents of Islamic economics would also say that interest charges in disguise—say, as "service charges"—are equally prohibited.

Islamic economists believe that they have identified a way of doing business that reconciles the need for incentive in the form of profit with the Islamic prohibition of interest. Taking as their model a form of partnership outlined in the medieval shari'a, Islamic economists have determined that the critical aspect of licit credit arrangements is a willingness to share in profit making and/or risk of loss. Thus, they conceive of Islamic banking as an institutional framework for lending on a profit-sharing basis. Depositors in an Islamic bank participate in the profits—and potentially also the losses—of the enterprises in which their deposits are invested, while the bank's borrowers agree to share a fixed percentage of the profits from their enterprises with the lending bank. Since not all loans can be made on a profit-sharing basis, some loans have to be made on a charitable basis.

A large number of Islamic banks have been fostered by private initiatives in the Muslim world. Pakistan in 1979 committed itself, as part of its Islamization campaign, to eliminate interest from the economy on a nationwide basis, a commitment that, if realized, would mean the institution of Islamic banking on a much broader scale than has heretofore been accomplished. Because of the difficulties inherent in carrying out such an ambitious economic transformation, Pakistan's changeover has proceeded slowly.

The treatment of the zakat, the Islamic alms tax, in new Pakistani legislation also reflects the ideological influences that are transforming shari'a institutions. Rather than an act of personal piety and charity, the zakat in Pakistani law is now a compulsory tax for all Sunni Muslims, the proceeds from which are used for some of the purposes described in the Qur'an but primarily for a national social welfare scheme and job-training program.

Not all modern Muslims accept such ideologized versions of Islamic law as authentic. For example, on the question of the meaning of the Qur'anic prohibition of interest, many would argue that the prohibition was directed against certain exploitive practices prevailing in pre-Islamic Arabia, and is really aimed at stopping one person's exploiting the needs of another to gain an unfair and unearned profit. They would therefore argue that practices that do not involve such exploitation of the weak by the strong—such as one bank charging another bank interest in a commercial transaction—were never meant to be outlawed by the shari'a.

An example of the ideologization of the shari'a in the political sphere can be seen in the use that Muslim politicians today make of the concept of *shura* (consultation), which is briefly mentioned in the Qur'an. By interpreting consultation as an essential legal requirement of Islamic government and making provision for consultation in their governments, President Zia ul-Haq of Pakistan and Muammar Qaddafi of Libya have attempted to present their respective military dictatorships as consonant with Islamic law. In Pakistan there is an appointed national consultative assembly, the Majlis-i-Shura, which is allowed to debate selected political issues.

In Libya, Qaddafi has apparently decided that if consultation has a Qur'anic stamp of approval, the more consultation a government fosters, the closer it must be to the Islamic ideal. Having selected popular committees as the appropriate vehicle for consultation, Qaddafi has required them in all institutions and has appointed a committee on the national level to consult and deliberate on those issues he chooses to submit for the members' consideration. Muslim political thinkers outside government circles who do not need to rationalize military dictatorships in Islamic terms tend to interpret the Qur'anic call for Muslims to consult among themselves as a mandate for more democratic governments with broader and more effective citizen participation. That is, they invoke the requirement of shura against the regimes in power.

EXPERIMENTS WITH THE REVIVAL OF QUR'ANIC LAWS

Despite the lack of present-day unanimity as to what Islamic law actually requires on many questions, many Muslim societies are currently engaged in experiments to revive various provisions of Islamic law, and others feel political pressure to follow suit. For the most part, such campaigns have placed the highest priority on reinstating those principles set forth in the verses of the Qur'an that concentrate on family law and inheritance. (Family law is considered in Chapter 12.)

Muslim conservatives have demanded that the traditional Qur'anic criminal penalties be retained or revived as the law of the land. Dismayed by what they view as the high crime rates and moral laxity in the West, these conservatives argue that only the threat of punishment, such as the amputation of a hand for theft, can prevent similar immorality in the Muslim world. Only a few crimes are mentioned in the Qur'an: fornication, slanderous accusations of unchastity, theft, brigandage, and the drinking of alcohol, plus, in some opinions, apostasy from Islam and rebellion against a duly constituted Muslim government. Because these particular offenses were singled out for explicit condemnation in the Qur'an, and because the harshness of the penalties involved is so squarely at odds with modern, Western values, a willingness to reenact these penalties as the law of the land may be treated as the litmus test for a regime's commitment to the shari'a.

Libya's Muammar Qaddafi was one of the first leaders in the Muslim world to assess accurately the propaganda value of sponsoring the reenactment of some of the Qur'anic punishments into law. When he did so in the 1970s, he was regarded overnight as a champion of the shari'a. In fact, with the exception of occasional floggings for alcohol consumption, these Qur'anically inspired criminal laws seem to have remained largely a dead letter. Their lack of real impact is hardly surprising, since Qaddafi left their implementation to the judges and courts of the westernized portion of Libya's legal system, who had little enthusiasm for overseeing the execution of what to them seemed the laws of a bygone era. (It is noteworthy that at the same time that Qaddafi was officially reviving these shari'a punishments, he was also abolishing the remnants of the shari'a court system, which had until then survived the westernization process.) The nonenforcement of the penalties called for by these laws—already watered down from what was required by the sources—is probably traceable in part to Qaddafi's own squeamishness, which he publicly admitted, about their severity. Qaddafi confessed that he would have preferred an interpretation of the Qur'anic verses on theft that could have obviated the need to amputate the hands of the convicted offenders. As it is, the Libyan law, while keeping the amputation penalty, provides that the procedure should be carried out in a hospital as a regular surgical procedure.

The ambivalence conveyed in this Libyan law suggests how hard it is for modern, secular governments to accept turning the clock back without some adjustment for modern attitudes and sensibilities. In Pakistan, after the 1970 reenactment of several Qur'anic criminal laws, the military tribunals, which have great power under Pakistan's regime of martial law, have reached convictions and ordered some punishments that seem to be loosely modeled on Qur'anic law, but the regular courts seem reluctant to impose the most severe Qur'anic penalties.

In contrast, fuqaha who are still immersed in the medieval tradition are less troubled by the incongruities of medieval criminal laws in a modern setting, as shown by the support of the fuqaha of Iran and Saudi Arabia for carrying out flogging, physical mutilation, and executions in the traditional manner. According to the perspective of such guardians of tradition, the great merit of the Qur'anic penalties is their supposed deterrent value. To act as deterrents, criminal penalties must be brutal and they must be carried out as a public spectacle, the bloodier the better, to instill a proper degree of horror in the onlookers. The great differential in willingness to implement Qur'anic criminal law in these different countries is thus attributable to the distinctly modern and antimodern mentalities of the ruling groups involved. In Iran, where the fuqaha recently regained political power, and in Saudi Arabi, where they never lost it, there is no effective pressure—as there apparently is elsewhere—for mitigating the Qur'anic criminal penalties.

It is not surprising that Muslims today are reinterpreting the doctrines of Islamic law. Throughout Islamic history Muslims have sought to define their relationship with, and base their behavior on, the shari'a. In the first centuries of Islamic civilization, before legal doctrines had assumed their classical form, there was a great variety of views on what the principles of Islamic law were. Today the challenges of adjusting to industrialization and the economic and social transformations that industrialization brings in its wake confront all Muslims with the problem of how to remain faithful to their own traditions.

The aim of modern redefinitions of Islamic law is to maintain the viability of the shari'a in today's changed circumstances without sacrificing the historical continuity that serves as the basis for the authoritative character of the law. Which of the currently competing interpretations of Islamic law succeeds in winning the greatest allegiance among Muslims will have a critical impact not only on how legal tradition is perceived but also on the organization of political, social, and economic life in the future. While the precise meanings to which the shari'a is susceptible are in dispute, the continued relevance of the shari'a for modern Muslims is indisputable.

12

The Changing
Arab Muslim Family

Afaf Lutfi al-Sayyid Marsot

Understanding the ethos of any family requires an examination of the relationships that create the unit we call a family: male-female relationships, parent-child relationships, and the economic nexus of the unit. Each of these clearly involves more than a religious relationship, and it encompasses social and economic linkages as well. To talk, therefore, of a "Muslim family" is to talk in the abstract or in ideal terms. Every Muslim family differs from the others, depending on its respective standing in society, its economic condition, the period of time under discussion, and the customs and mores of the country in which the family lives, to say nothing of the level of education and the quality of personal relationships within the family unit. We shall take as a model, derived from the teachings of the Qur'an and the sunna, an ideal Arab Sunni Muslim family, bearing in mind that such a family does not necessarily represent reality past, present, or future. We can describe some Muslim families in specific Arab countries that have a Muslim majority, and show some of the differences that have developed over time and from country to country. The discussion will not touch upon non-Arab Muslim countries such as Indonesia, Malaysia, or Senegal, whose historical experience makes them differ from Arab Muslim countries.

MALE-FEMALE STATUS

According to the teachings of the Qur'an, men and women are created mates, a pair, to treat each other with affection and compassion within the bonds of matrimony. Yet Sura 4:34 includes a

passage that has aroused controversy over male-female relationships, and continues to do so. The passage reads (in the Rashad
Khalifa translation):

> The men are placed in charge of the women, since God has en-
> dowed them with the necessary qualities and made them bread-
> earners. The righteous women will accept this arrangement obe-
> diently, and will honor their husbands in their absence, in accor-
> dance with God's commands. As for the women who show rebell-
> ion, you shall first enlighten them, then desert them in bed, and
> you may beat them as a last resort. Once they obey you, you have
> no excuse to transgress against them. God is high and most pow-
> erful.

Some scholars interpret the passage to mean that men are
given preeminence over women and are their guardians in all matters. Others see the obligation as one in which men, because of their
greater wealth, are enjoined to support women materially, and that
it does not imply any other form of superiority, especially when
that passage is allied to the one in which males and females are described as a pair. There is no Qur'anic passage that implies any
other disparate relationship. The scholars who believe the verse to
mean a male superiority relationship adduce further proof from
the sentence that allows the male to chastise his wife. Other scholars
believe the second passage is not related to wives who do not respect
or "honor" their husbands when they are away from home. There
is no single interpretation, and scholars continue to argue the
point. The issue of equality, therefore, is one that constantly sur-
faces in male-female relationships, especially in the realm of marriage, divorce, and inheritance.

Marriage

In Sura 4 we learn that a man may marry one wife, or two, or
three, to a maximum of four, if he can treat them with equity. The
passage continues, "But if ye fear that ye cannot, marry only one."
Scholars in past ages have interpreted this passage to mean that a
Muslim man is entitled to marry up to four wives. Others, especially
some modern-day scholars, interpret the passage as a prohibition

of polygamy. They reason that it is impossible to treat four women with equity, so the solution is to marry only one. There is a variety of other interpretations, of which the latter is only one—and not the most popular one.

Marriage is universally enjoined on Muslims, the single state being socially frowned upon as unnatural and potentially leading to sin. Generally women tend to marry men who are slightly older than themselves and are financially capable of supporting a family. In most Muslim Arab countries the legal age of marriage is set at 16 years, although in the states of the Arabian peninsula the legal age is lower. Marriages between very young girls and old men rarely occur except in far-flung areas where the laws of the central government rarely obtrude, somewhat akin to underage marriages in Appalachia, for example.

The prerequisite for any marriage is the consent of the woman. Her consent is either explicit or implicit: silence is interpreted as a sign of consent. Marriage is expected to occur between equals, the element of parity being of importance, so that a wife expects to receive the same material well-being that she had in her father's house.

Since marriage is a contract between individuals, the bridewealth is specified in the contract. It is divided into two unequal parts: one portion is paid prior to the marriage and forms part of the bride's personal capital; the other is paid to the bride only if and when her husband repudiates her. The bridewealth is the woman's own property, to do with as she pleases, and thus is inalienable and imprescriptible. A woman may choose to have her marriage contract include a prohibition against her husband's taking a second wife.

Polygamy was current in earlier ages, although how current is unknown, since there are no figures prior to the nineteenth century. It has diminished in recent years in most societies, with increasing urbanization and the changeover from the extended family residing within a single dwelling to the nuclear family, for polygamy is often tied to economic factors, although not exclusively so. By the mid-twentieth century Egyptian national statistics show that 0.5 percent of marriages are polygamous. Today it is still practiced among the very rich, who can afford to support more than one wife, even though in modern society it is frowned upon and socially unacceptable, rural tribal societies, and the very poor, who may accept it as an alternative to divorce, although economic distress militates against its happening frequently.

In some sects of Islam polygamy has been prohibited. In 1962 the Aga Khan issued a decree forbidding polygamy among the Isma'ili sect of Muslims. In Tunisia and Turkey laws prohibiting polygamy have been passed. In Pakistan, to contract a second marriage a man needs the permission of the court in addition to the permission of his wife or that of an arbitration council. In Egypt, since 1979 a man must notify his wife if he intends to embark on a second marriage, and the wife is allowed to sue for divorce. In Lebanon a wife can insert a clause in the marriage contract that automatically grants her a divorce should the husband contract a second marriage. The extent of polygamy in a society is perhaps not so important as the fact that it is a possibility, and can be used to harass wives or as a threat to extract obedience or concessions from them. But the same can be said of divorce in most societies.

Interfaith marriages between Muslim men and Christian or Jewish women are permissible. In such marriages the wife forfeits her right to inherit her husband's property. Muslim women, however, are forbidden to contract marriages with non-Muslim men. The sole exception to that rule is in Turkey, which has established a civil code. In all cases of interfaith marriages the children are legally Muslim and share in their father's estate.

Divorce

Men can repudiate their wives at will by repeating three times "I divorce thee." Women must sue for divorce, which is granted on the basis of certain specified grounds that differ in each of the four main schools of jurisprudence. The Qur'an states that divorce is hateful in the eyes of God and binding on the conscience of man. Should divorce become necessary, the male is enjoined to treat his wife with kindness and to give her back the remainder of her bridewealth, her property, and personal possessions.

In the early centuries of Islam, grounds for divorce ranged from physical abuse to desertion and impotence. One school of law allowed a woman to sue for divorce if her husband deserted her for five years. Another school specified the period of desertion as 99 years. The Prophet allowed a woman to divorce her husband on the ground that she did not love him; but the schools of jurisprudence, save for the Maliki, were not so lenient. Today the laws of divorce and the grounds for divorce have changed. A man now can divorce his wife only in a court of law; a verbal divorce before witnesses is no longer valid. In Tunisia and Algeria women can obtain a divorce without having to show cause. In Egypt a woman can sue for divorce on all the traditional grounds plus cruelty or treatment in a manner intolerable to someone of her social standing—here again the concept of parity comes in. "Irretrievable difference" is now accepted as a valid cause for divorce in South Yemen, which, along with Turkey, is the only state to institute civil personal status and family laws.

Upon divorce a man must give his former wife the balance of her bridewealth. In the past, when that involved a large sum of money that the male was unwilling to pay, he could resort to polygamy or treat his wife so miserably that she sued for divorce and forfeited her right to the bridewealth, which is paid only if the husband repudiates his wife. More recently laws have mitigated such abuse on the part of the husband. In Egypt, for example, upon divorce the wife is granted alimony for a year and compensation up to two years' maintenance. She is also granted child custody, as prescribed in the Qur'an, and is entitled to retain the conjugal house or apartment. This last clause is a consequence of the shortage of housing in urban areas, especially in Cairo.

There are limitations on what a court can do. The court can issue an injunction to bridewealth and alimony, but the husband may default. The divorced wife must then go back to court, a costly and long procedure. Defaulting on alimony or child support, of course, is not unique to Muslim countries; it is found all over the world.

Child Custody

Child custody, as specified by the shari'a, is automatically awarded to the mother, unless she has been proved guilty of moral turpitude. According to the Hanafi school of jurisprudence, a girl lives with her mother until she reaches the age of puberty. According to the Maliki school, she remains with her mother until she is married. A boy remains with his mother until he reaches the age of seven in the Hanafi school, or puberty in the Maliki school. Since custody is traditionally granted to women, if the mother is not granted custody, the children go to her mother or grandmother, unless the woman consents to grant custody to her former husband. This is feasible only if the paternal grandmother is willing to take charge of the children. In most Arab Muslim countries today girls remain with their mothers until they are married; boys go to the father's custody when they reach the age of puberty, which in Egypt has been successively raised from seven to nine to fifteen years of age. A further complication arises in cases where a mother with custody of her children decides to remarry: her former husband may receive custody of his children unless he waives that right.

Inheritance

The Qur'an specifies that a female inherits half the male share. Inheritance is therefore a basic right granted by God to women. Both historically and today there is a gap between the religious ideal and reality, and denial of inheritance has often been condoned by a male-dominated society. In times of recession or financial crisis the legal injunction to give women their inheritance may be set aside. During the eighteenth century in Egypt and Palestine women did not inherit land—nor did other legal heirs—for land went to the eldest son, a direct contravention of Qur'anic law. This was the case, however, only among the poorer segments of society, where possession of land was only a usufructuary right and did not mean ownership of land, held as crown domains. On the other hand, women of the elite did inherit land, in the sense that they inherited tax farms, so that by the end of the eighteenth century, the main tax farmers were the military ruling oligarchy, the ulama, and women.

The rationale behind a female's inheriting a lesser share than a male lies in the male's responsibility for the material expenditures of the household. A woman's property is her own, to do with as she pleases; she is not expected to support her husband with it. However, nonsupport of a wife is grounds for divorce, no matter how wealthy the woman. A brother is as responsible for his single or widowed sister's support as he is for his mother's—or that of any elderly or unmarried female in the family. In reality a woman's fortune is frequently managed by her husband, a brother, or some other male relative, although many women control their fortunes.

Today most Muslim countries follow the rules laid down in the Qur'an regarding inheritance. A woman can inherit from her father and grandfather, her mother and grandmother, her husband, siblings, children, and grandchildren. They in turn have a share in her estate, although children preclude other potential heirs, save spouses, from inheriting.

With changing economic conditions a woman's fortune is no longer limited to defraying her personal expenses; more often than not it is used to supplement the family income. In working families it is expected that the husband's salary covers the essentials while the wife's salary is used for luxuries. This situation raises a question: why should a woman inherit half the man's share if she contributes the same kind of support that he does? While at present the issue occupies women who work, and therefore covers only a small percentage of families, it can well become a major issue in the future, as the number of working wives and female-head-of-household families increases.

Some modern-day parents have tried to skirt the Qur'anic injunctions by giving their daughters shares of their inheritance during their lifetimes or by selling property to a daughter so that it is removed from the estate. This is especially the case if the daughter has no brother, and cousins would inherit along with her. Some parents provide their daughters with expensive trousseaux and jewelry to supplement their inheritance.

In no case can a Muslim dissipate his or her wealth or cut out legal heirs with a proverbial penny. Legal heirs can sue profligate relatives on grounds of financial incompetence and have the court name a guardian over the possessions of that person to prevent a loss of patrimony. Still less can a person bequeath his or her entire wealth to anyone other than a legal heir; he or she can will only a portion of his or her wealth. Such legal injunctions ensure that legal heirs are not cut out by a later wife or husband or an extramarital relationship.

WOMEN'S ROLES AS WIVES AND MOTHERS

A popular tradition from the Prophet Muhammad asserts that "Heaven lies at the feet of mothers." Consequently the hold of mothers in Muslim societies is particularly strong, especially since they control both sons and daughters through their formative years. After the age of seven the boy is under his father's care; he helps in the fields, learns his father's trade (should he be an artisan), or is apprenticed to another. Among the middle and upper classes he remains under his mother's control until he finishes school and enters the university. However, when children go to school, it is the father who helps them with their homework, unless he is a professional who has no time, for many of the mothers in the poorer classes are illiterate. Children, especially sons, are the most important element of a marriage, if not its prime reason, for it is one's sons who will carry on the family name and, it is hoped, provide for their parents when they are elderly. A son provides social insurance and functions as old-age pension, while a daughter's economic value is controlled by her husband's family. Among the rural inhabitants a son ensures that the land will continue to be serviced and remain in the family.

Female children are less highly prized because they are viewed as a threat to the family honor if their virtue should be impugned. This is particularly the case among rural inhabitants, who fear their daughters may be seduced, and thereby disgrace the family. Girls are therefore closely watched and their freedom of movement is restricted. They are married off at the earliest opportunity, so that the burden of protecting their virtue is passed on to the husband. Older brothers are expected to be the guardians of their sisters' virtue, which is why the birth order within a family is important. It is always hoped that a family's first child will be a boy, so as to ensure protection of the family honor by looking after his sisters.

While these concepts of family honor are anchored in the rural milieu of class groupings, among urban people such concepts are less rigidly held, especially among the more affluent classes. Urban working-class people feel about girls as do rural people; but the more affluent a family becomes, the more it feels that a daughter can protect her own virtue because she leads a more sheltered life and is not subject to the same advances as are females in rural and urban settings who have to work with or around men. Nonetheless, in whatever class of society, girls are believed to need the protection of their families, while men are the ones who do the protecting. Whatever a male child may do, he cannot bring shame on his family because shame is interpreted only in terms of female sexuality, with virginity being the prize a girl offers her husband.

Fertility rates among Arab Muslim women are high compared with those in the West, but they are clearly declining in highly urbanized countries such as Egypt, Lebanon, Turkey, and Tunisia. Rural areas have higher birth rates than urban ones, while working women have fewer children than nonworking ones. The degree of education a woman possesses seems to be the determining factor in the number of children she has, with a direct correlation between small families and higher education.

By and large, children in the Arab world are socialized by their mothers. Within the extended family of the past, which still exists in some communities, the elder women of the household—grandmothers, aunts, widowed family relatives or, more rarely, unmarried female relatives—all shared in bringing up children. In traditional families, where daughters are married early in life, a mother and daughter may bear children simultaneously, suckle each other's offspring, and bring up each other's children. The process of socialization is thus an extended one that involves more than one person and is shared among a number of females. As a result, tensions between individual family members are eased because of the numbers who interpose themselves to reduce that tension. When children feel misunderstood by one family member, there is always another available in whom they can confide, who will calm tempers, soothe, advise, and work out a compromise or cajole both parties to reach an accommodation.

Girls are taught good manners, obedience, and social behavior as well as domestic skills and personal hygiene by their elders. More important, social traditions are passed down through the female members. Tasks within a household are assigned by the women, and up to the age of five or six both boys and girls help around the house. Among educated groups differentiation between male and female roles is marked. Even in schools, which are supposed to have the same curriculum for both sexes, girls will be taught home economics but boys will not. This is frequently the case in schools in the Western world as well. Consciously or unconsciously the pattern is laid for the differentiation of tasks, careers, and professions. Thus social mores and prejudices are the inhibiting factors rather than any religious injunction, for there is nothing in Islam that prohibits a female from pursuing the same educational curriculum as her brother. Parents and educators—in fact, the whole of society—are the ones who decree that women are to cook and sew, while boys are to learn mathematics.

In most households it is customary for the female to serve the male members in matters pertaining to food, cleaning, and sewing, which are viewed as "women's business." Even when both members of the household are professionals, the burden of household tasks invariably falls on the woman. Today that burden is being shared more and more among the younger generation, but there is still the notion that housework and child rearing are female concerns.

Care of the elderly is also part of the woman's domain, for it is seen as an extension of her role as homemaker. Homes for the aged are rare, if not unheard of, and families take it for granted that they will have to look after elderly relatives, whether simply aged or senile and bedridden. In a large extended family that posed less of a problem than it does today. Now space, or the financial means to shoulder such a burden, may be lacking. Nonetheless, though it may present tremendous problems, the elderly will always be taken in, for there is no other option.

Oddly enough, as the financial situation of a country deteriorates, it becomes easier to provide for the elderly: in a country such as Egypt, for example, where overpopulation, lack of housing, and lack of modern household aids abound, the extended family is experiencing a comeback. Young people who wish to get married have little chance of finding an apartment to rent or of being able to afford it once one is found. The alternative is to live with their parents. For young married couples who both work and have children, it is the grandmother, in whose house they live and who probably is not employed, who looks after the children. When the grandmother becomes too old to help around the house, she still has a role to perform in socializing children. She remains a "voice in the house," a souffre douleur, a confidante, a settler of quarrels, a voice of reason.

WOMEN'S ECONOMIC ROLE

Throughout the ages female labor was a necessary element in the household economy, especially in the rural areas. In precapitalist days, when the family unit was self-sufficient at a subsistence level, women fed and clothed the family and produced whatever surplus there was for barter. Differentiation within the family unit was based on the division of labor.

With the advent of a cash economy, the sexual division of labor was transformed. By the end of the eighteenth century, cottage industries in some Muslim countries were displaced by cheap European imports. In some areas—for example, Egypt under Muhammad Ali (ruled 1805-48)—cottage industries were forbidden for a while. In an attempt to encourage industrialization, the ruler prohibited spinning and weaving save in government establishments, which hired women as well as men. The change from subsistence farming to a cash-crop economy involved greater exploitation of the peasant: he had to spend more man-hours growing new crops that could not be eaten, such as cotton, flax, indigo, and sugarcane. This change also meant payment of taxes in cash as well as in kind. Males were forced to direct all their efforts to the land, which supplied the principal means of livelihood, while women continued as ancillary labor. The main source of family income was the man's efforts, and the position of the female in the family unit became marginal. If anything happened to the husband, the males of his family took over his landholdings and the widow became a liability that none wanted to shoulder. We have many cases dating from that period of women suing in the shari'a courts to regain a share in their husband's land or to claim support from male relatives.

Urban working-class women were intimately involved in their men's professions, especially if these trades dealt with the preparation and sale of foodstuffs. While we do not know whether women were allowed to become guild members in their own right, we do know that in some countries—Turkey, for instance—women retailers who sold goods from house to house did form a guild of their own. The same may have been true of Egypt, but not necessarily of Syria. Women butchers frequently worked with their spouses in the shops. Whether they continued to keep the shop when the husband died is unknown. Generally, the more affluent the husband, the less the wife was involved in his business; but there were exceptions. Al-Jabarti, the famous historian of Egypt of the eighteenth century, tells us of the wife of a man who eventually became rector of al-Azhar University. She "bought and sold" and made her husband's fortune. This was no isolated instance, for we are told the same happened in other parts of the Ottoman Empire. At the highest echelons of society we find women making money in their own right, even while in a harem. Women possessed land, traded, and were involved in commercial transactions. The wives of the military oligarchy that ruled Egypt ran their husbands' affairs when the men were absent on campaigns, which was fairly frequently.

Today women manage their private property, as they did in the past. Women are found in all professions, from taxi driver to engineer and cabinet minister in some countries. Some Arab Muslim countries continue to isolate their women in harems; others do not. The liberation of women today seems to be a question of the internal economy of a country. When a country needs women in the work force, they are encouraged to seek jobs; when it does not, they are discouraged from leaving the household. The exception to that is the woman who is from either extreme—from among the very poor or the very wealthy. Women of the more affluent classes were the first to become emancipated, and to seek a role outside the family. This was a relatively easy achievement for them because their higher education qualified them for professions or made it easier for them to think in terms of a profession. On the other hand, working-class women have always worked, either side by wide with their husbands or because they had no one to support them. The middle-class woman has been the last to become emancipated.

WOMEN'S POLITICAL ROLE

The emancipation of women in the Arab Muslim world was a consequence of political revolutions. The 1919 revolution in Egypt for independence from the British occupation was the direct incentive to women's liberation, for when their husbands were arrested by British authorities, the women of the elite shouldered the nationalist cause and demonstrated in place of the men. The veil was removed as a direct consequence; and women, having gone out into public life, could not be shoved back into seclusion when the revolution ended. They simply took charge of social services. The same happened in Turkey. Other Muslim countries slowly followed the Egyptian example, for Egypt was and is the trendsetter, although some Muslim countries have refused to follow that trend and continue to veil their womenfolk.

Women's suffrage came as a consequence of a second revolution in Egypt, that of the Free Officers in 1952. After a hunger strike carried out by a group of feminists, Nasir passed a law permitting women to vote. Once again some Muslim countries have granted women suffrage and others have not. But every Muslim Arab country today has made a point of encouraging female education, so that the role of women in political life will undoubtedly expand with their education and involvement in social life outside the home.

The best example of how revolutionary activities have helped emancipate women is the Palestinian women in the diaspora, for they have become not only emancipated but also activists who share an equal burden with their men in all walks of society. Among all Arab Muslim women they are perhaps the most emancipated today.

We have mentioned veiling of women a number of times. While to Western women the veil is a sign of female subjugation, it is not necessarily so to Muslim Arab women, who view it as a sign of modesty and of virtue. Emancipation of women in Muslim countries does not mean sexual emancipation, for those societies do not have a single standard for males and females. The dress code is therefore addressed to the sexual mores of the country, and has little to do with the degree of education or of economic freedom that a woman has. Just as a Western woman would not bare her breasts in public, save on some beaches, the Arab Muslim woman believes her body—which may include her face—is a private vessel that is not to be revealed to anyone but her male relatives. A number of Muslim Arab societies have opted for the Western style of clothing and have removed the veil, believing it, in Western terms, to be a sign of subjugation. Other societies have seen the veil as a sign of their own national dress, and refuse to give it up. This brings us to the resurgence of Islam.

Most Muslim countries today witness a movement calling for greater attention to the teachings of Islam in all facets of life: political, economic, and social. There have been calls for "Islamic government" and "Islamic banking." The resurgence of Islamic fervor is a manifestation of the social dislocation that societies are undergoing as a result of too rigid modernization and the importation, along with technology, of Western dress, consumer habits, and even mores. In protest against the overwhelming tide of westernization, some members of society have opted for a return to traditional culture and indigenous roots, which seem to be threatened with extinction. Hence the invention of what has been called "Muslim garb," which is a modest form of attire having nothing to do with the clothing of early Islamic periods, as some erroneously assume. Rather, it is a recently invented mode that has modified Western garb and replaced it with a form of dress that owes nothing to changing Western styles that strain the pocketbook as well as the sense of credulity. Included with the more modest garb is a veil that covers the head, or even the entire face. This form of clothing is a political statement, as well as a social and economic one. It states that the wearer, male and female, chooses his or her own traditions over those imported from the West, and opts for the native, Muslim culture, rather than that of the West.

Some Western and Muslim scholars have seen this movement as one of regression; others, including myself, see it as a form of protest against inefficient government, creeping westernization, and a consumer society that Third World countries can ill afford.

WOMEN'S CHANGING ROLE
IN THE FAMILY UNIT

One of the greatest transformations of Arab Muslim society has resulted from temporary labor emigration from poor countries to oil-rich countries. Seeking economic mobility outside one's society was commonplace in the past among citizens from Arab countries such as Lebanon, Syria, and Palestine. Today it has become common among people from the traditionally more settled societies of Egypt and Jordan. Since the 1970s people from all classes of society have moved in search of better wages, especially with the influx of petrodollars and the programs of rapid modernization and construction being carried out in the oil-rich countries. In some cases families went along; in other cases the labor contract was of limited duration and may even have specified that families were not to accompany the worker.

In the latter case, once the man emigrated, the wife was left to shoulder the responsibilities of the household alone. In brief, she became both father and mother to her children, and took on the tasks normally allotted to the husband. When the husband returned to visit the family, he found his role "usurped" by his spouse. The clinging vine was no longer clinging, and the male felt relegated to the role of a visitor. On his permanent return tensions were generated by his loss of status and his wife's reluctance to return to her previous submissive role. This was especially prevalent among middle-class families, where females were traditionally more submissive than females of other classes.

With the changing role of women in modernizing Arab Muslim societies, laws change, and so do religious interpretations. Today three types of Muslims exist in the same society: westernized modernists; traditionalists, who still follow the old ways and are not much affected by westernization; and those who, after exposure to the West and modernization, seek new ways to reaffirm their non-Western Muslim Arab identity. The last group wishes to develop a new society based on religious foundations and injunctions, but one that is not corrupted by Mongol, Persian, or Ottoman practices, as some past Muslim governments have been. How such a society will come about is not clear, but the need for it is clear to all Muslims, whose history abounds in tyrannical rulers, exploitive elites, and a growing gap between the small number of rich and the ever-growing number of poor.

Whatever the outcome of such a search for a new society, the fact remains that the condition of the citizens of such societies will be determined by the social and economic conditions of their age, and the states in which they live. Just as the past has shown that different conditions produce different customs, so the future will show that different conditions will develop different societies, even among those who profess to follow the same religion.

13

Muslims in
the United States

Yvonne Yazbeck Haddad

For the average consumer of popular media in the United States, Islam is clearly a foreign phenomenon and often is associated more or less exclusively with the Middle East. It generally comes as a surprise to most Americans to realize that vast numbers of Muslims are located outside the Middle East, and an even greater surprise to learn that there is a very sizable and growing Islamic community in America. While figures are unreliable and estimates vary widely, probably between 1.5 million to 3 million persons in the United States and Canada identify themselves as Muslims.

In the broadest strokes the Muslims in North America can be divided into two groups: immigrants from other parts of the Islamic world, and persons who are indigenous to this area (the converts). Obviously, if the term is subjected to critical analysis, the children of immigrant Muslims are in one sense indigenous to the American scene while maintaining a marginal identity with the country and customs of their parents. Furthermore, what we refer to as indigenous Muslims in the North American context can be subdivided. A few are white converts (estimated at about 75,000), mainly women who have married Muslim men and adopted the faith of their husbands; some are members of neo-Sufi organizations located in cities throughout the United States, the largest centers being in Philadelphia, San Antonio, and Albuquerque, with members concentrated on the east and west coasts. For the most part, however, the term "indigenous" refers to the sizable community of African-American converts.

While the name Black Muslims has been in vogue since its coining by sociologist Eric Lincoln in the 1960s, it is not a term that has been consciously adopted by the African-American community, and suggests a homogeneity that can be deceptive. In fact, there are today African-Americans who are members of the Hanafi confession, as well as two major groups of those who were originally in Elijah Muhammad's Nation of Islam. These latter are the followers of Elijah's son Warith Deen Muhammad, now calling themselves the American Muslim Mission, and those under the leadership of Louis Farrakhan, who retain the name Nation of Islam.

THE COMING OF MUSLIMS
TO THE UNITED STATES

It is probable that the earliest Muslim immigrants to America were among the slaves brought from the west coast of Africa in the eighteenth and nineteenth centuries. While more of the Muslims exported in the slave trade were sent to South and Central America, a small number seem to have come to the American South. Despite accounts of valiant attempts on the part of some of these African Muslims to retain their faith, it was inevitable that it was suppressed for fear of insurrection fostered as religious revolt, as happened in Brazil. Because these slaves are believed to have been forced to relinquish their religion and become Christians, they cannot remain in the category of immigrant Muslims. It is, rather, to the Middle East that we must look for the beginnings of what have been several major waves of Muslim immigration.

The first significant influx of Muslims to America came between 1875 and 1912. They were from the Levant (what is now Syria, Lebanon, Jordan, and Israel), primarily from lower educational and economic groups who hoped to find the financial success that they heard reported by Lebanese Christian emigrants. The economic situation in the Middle East at the turn of the century had worsened, increasing the numbers of those seeking a better life. While a few of the early immigrants returned home, having made their fortune in America, many remained and began to form Muslim communities. Those who were originally farmers generally found it difficult to continue that profession in the United States. Many suffered from lack of education or lack of facility in English, and were forced to work in factories and mines, or as peddlers or petty merchants. They tended to settle near industrial centers, and because of the difficulty of integrating into American society, socialized almost exclusively with fellow Muslims and compatriots. A second wave of Muslims came in the decade before World War

II, another from 1947 to 1960, and a fourth from 1967 to the present. In addition to the world wars, major changes in immigration laws have accounted for lulls in the flow.

Since the early days the makeup of Muslim immigrants has changed considerably. In addition to the countries of the Middle East, there are substantial numbers of immigrants from India, Pakistan, Eastern Europe, the Soviet Union, and many other parts of the Islamic world. Along with a common religious heritage, they have brought with them a variety of ethnic and cultural identities. Beginning in the middle of the twentieth century, a new kind of Muslim immigrant began to arrive. Political as well as economic factors played a major role in the decision to come to this country, and many educated Palestinians, Egyptians, Syrians, East Europeans, and others oppressed by their respective regimes looked to the West for political freedom. For the most part these persons, unlike the earlier immigrants, have been educated professionals who come not with the intention of making a fortune and returning home, but of staying and enjoying the economic and political advantages of the United States. They have been followed more recently by yet another wave of Muslim immigrants, mainly semiskilled workers from Pakistan, Yemen, and Lebanon. Economically, things are much better for recent Muslim immigrants than they were for the early newcomers. Due in large part to a considerably higher level of education and professional training, they generally have been able to find employment, and often secure positions of importance in a variety of fields.

THE PRACTICE OF ISLAM IN AMERICA

For the earlier immigrants Islam was an important communal identity in the midst of an alien culture into which they did not easily integrate. Because of the rigors of economic survival, however, these Muslims were less likely to be actively involved in organized religious activities. Congregational prayer, if practiced at all, was often held in homes or small mosques, and proselytization was extremely limited. Many of the most recent immigrants (those arriving in the 1970s), with the exception of westernized, highly educated post-World War II professionals, have been more active in their attempts to maintain an Islamic identity and, in fact, to propagate the faith. The quest for an Islamic identity, however, has often seemed to compete with the need to assert other kinds of commonality. In larger cities having a concentration of Muslims, the community has been fostered through ethnic identity—Pakistanis with Pakistanis, Syrians with Syrians, etc.—with the occasional result of tensions between national groupings as well as between older and newer immigrants. In smaller towns and cities recent and older immigrants, Arab and non-Arab, have had to join resources and work together in establishing and maintaining mosques and communities. While this has led to some intracommunal strains, it has also served to contribute to the life and strength of the individual groups. Islamic teachings of equality and the brotherhood of all believers, regardless of race, color, and national origin, have helped to overcome potentially disruptive divisions.

One of the questions faced by any transplanted people is the degree to which the original culture should, or can, be maintained in the new environment. Sociologically Muslims have followed the well-documented pattern of first-generation allegiance to the country of origin and second-generation attempts to reject the old and amalgamate with the new. Along with this there has been a continuing attempt to maintain Islam as a vital and living institution, but one in which certain forms of adaptation to American culture are recognized as both inevitable and necessary. In some instances mosques have taken on the look of churches in both structure and activity. In addition to the Friday service, many mosques have Sunday morning meetings and religious education classes. Weddings and funerals, not generally held at mosques in Muslim countries, normally take place there in America. Because the mosque serves the essential purpose of maintaining cultural contact as well as religious identity, a great many social activities are held there, such as dinners, bazaars, and bake sales.

Professional imams, for those mosques lucky enough to have them, have taken on many duties in addition to the traditional ones of leading the prayer, preaching, and teaching Qur'an and law. They are responsible for the general administration and upkeep of the mosque, perform many of the counseling and advising functions of a clergyman or parish priest, and act as spokesmen for Islam in communities in which, often, little is known about the Muslim faith. They are invited to talk about Islam in schools and neighboring churches and synagogues, and on local television programs.

Muslim immigrant women have played an active role in communal religious life, often finding opportunities for involvement not available to them in their home countries. They have been engaged in planning and canvassing for the building of new mosques, teaching the religious classes, and participating in planning the social events of the community. In many places they have attended prayer services alongside, or at least in the same room with, the males of the community. Increasingly, however, these activities of and for women are being seriously curtailed. Particularly in mosques where leadership is assumed by imams who have been educated at al-Azhar University in Cairo or in Saudi Arabia, women often find their freedoms limited and their opportunities for full participation diminished. In some instances newly arrived imams are working in cooperation with revivalist Muslims in their mosques to have women behind curtains or in separate rooms rather than worshipping with the men. Many of the second- and third-generation immigrants, however, are upset by these reactionary moves, and feel strongly that any attempt to keep women from full participation in the religious and social life of the community is un-Islamic.

This attempt to return to and preserve traditional Islamic ways is, of course, a response to what many immigrant Muslims see as the threat of Western secularism. Many of the newer immigrants, well-educated and dedicated to the preservation of the traditional Islamic order, are concerned about what they see to be laxity of the faith and capitulation to unhealthy influences of an alien, though host, culture. Repelled by what they perceive as antireligious and immoral forces and practices in North American society, they are redoubling their efforts to provide a solid structure in which Islamic values are inculcated in the family and in the mosque. Many are having serious problems with teenage boys and girls who resent these strictures, particularly girls, who may not be allowed to date. Often these young people refuse to participate in any of the activities of the mosque, returning only when they marry, and start families of their own.

PROBLEMS OF IMMIGRANT MUSLIMS

Strains on the Muslim family in America are great. In Islamic society the family unit is the crucial area of interaction, and the welfare of the group is valued above that of any individual member.

North American society places such stress on freedom and individuality that the family is often forced to play a very secondary role. Muslim children relate first to their parents and siblings, secondarily to friends outside the family circle. In many parts of the Islamic world, social life for Muslims not only has been dictated by the family but also has been conducted within it, so that members socialize together and call on friends as a unit. This behavior is extremely difficult to maintain in the American culture, in which social contacts are generally with peers rather than family, and are designed to foster individual relationships rather than familial ties. One of the significant problems faced by many Muslim families is the American custom of dating, especially when it involves a Muslim dating a non-Muslim and the possibility of an interfaith marriage. Qur'anic law, while allowing Muslim men the option of marrying Jewish or Christian women, forbids marriage between Muslim women and non-Muslim men. Contemporary social realities make strict adherence to this law all but impossible for Muslim women if marriage is desired, a situation creating conflict for both woman and family.

Other problems face Muslim communities attempting to maintain the standards of the faith in an environment distinctly different from other parts of the Islamic world. It is difficult for business people in the United States to observe the required five daily prayers when no provision in time or facility is made in the work place. Observing the Ramadan fast is difficult enough when there is the support of the community bound by the same regulations; it becomes doubly hard when one is in a non-Muslim environment for most of the day. The long day of fasting is particularly rigorous when Ramadan, a lunar month rotating around the solar calendar, falls in the summer with its extremely long days.

Especially in times of recession and a tight economy, some Muslims have voiced questions about the necessity of paying both federal and state income taxes and the traditional Islamic zakat (charity tax), a double burden not anticipated under Muslim law. Social programs and provision for the needy, for which zakat is intended, are already covered by government welfare, yet the conscientious Muslim feels obligated to pay the tax. Even more complex to solve is the problem of the Qur'anic ban on usury in a national economy in which borrowing and paying interest are almost inescapable in any business venture, as well as in such projects as financing a house or building a mosque. A number of technical devices have been proposed in the attempt to avoid flagrant contradictions of this tenet of Qur'anic law.

Preserving an Islamic way of life is a continuing struggle in an environment in which the pressures are often strong in the opposite direction. Muslim personal status laws pertaining to marriage, divorce, and inheritance are often in tension with prevailing secular codes. The traditional role of the man as head of the household and provider for the women in the family is challenged by much in the surrounding society. Conservative dress for women and girls is increasingly being adopted as a self-conscious mark of Islamic identity, a kind of silent protest against sexual permissiveness, which is seen as dangerous and undermining Islamic values.

For those Muslims who observe strict dietary regulations, American processed food products can offer difficulties. Bread products sometimes contain lard, a problem because of the Islamic prohibition on eating pork. A prominent American cheese company was discovered a few years ago to be using pig enzymes in its cheese processing; the Muslim community responded by boycotting the company's products. Muslim law prohibits eating the meat of animals that have not been properly slaughtered. Since Muslim butcher shops are rare, many Muslims have had to look for kosher Jewish meat markets or to deal with the guilt of eating meat technically unlawful for them. *Halal* (correctly slaughtered) meat is becoming available in large metropolitan areas where there are concentrations of Muslims.

As was suggested earlier, in addition to the difficulties encountered in the tensions between acculturation and preservation of tradition, immigrant Muslims also face problems within their own communities. Many of the mosques and Islamic centers in America are extremely heterogeneous, with populations representing a variety of cultures and national groupings—as many as 65 different nationalities have been reported in one mosque. Difficulties in this context are inevitable. The way rites are performed in one country may differ from the way they are performed in another country; national and political allegiances may, on occasion, supersede the bond of Islamic identity; the confrontation of conservative and progressive may take place within the Islamic group as well as between that group and the surrounding culture.

In addition to these difficulties, the presence of a sizable community of indigenous American converts to Islam has made the situation increasingly complex for persons from abroad seeking to establish and maintain their identity as Muslims in a new land. Their responses have been varied as things have evolved in the African-American community. Let us turn, then, to what we are calling indigenous Islam in America, in particular the founding, development, and schisms of the movement that popularly has been called the Black Muslims, or the Nation of Islam in America.

ISLAM IN THE AFRICAN-AMERICAN COMMUNITY

The earliest stirrings of a kind of Islamic consciousness in the African-American community came in 1913, when an uneducated North Carolina black, born Timothy Drew, took the name Noble Drew Ali and founded the Moorish-American Science Temple in Newark, New Jersey. Like the Black Muslim movement under Elijah Muhammad, which was soon to follow, Noble Drew Ali took as his starting point the desperate situation of people of African descent in American society, and the hope that identification with a movement in which the potential for contribution is recognized could foster a transforming pride in the community. His was an eclectic amalgamation of Eastern philosophies in which Drew Ali was part of a spiritual heritage including such figures as Buddha, Confucius, Zoroaster, Jesus, and Muhammad. It was, however, based on the premise that as Christianity is the religion of Europeans, Islam is the natural religion for Asians, in which group he included Americans of African heritage. The Moorish-American movement made its way to such major northern cities as Chicago, Pittsburgh, and Detroit, as well as to a number of cities in the South. Muslim in trapping more than in content, it incorporated some of the teachings of the Qur'an with a liberal sprinkling of a fundamentalist Christianity and what was to become black nationalism. Noble Drew Ali died in 1929, following a serious schism among his followers; some vestiges of his movement remain today, but in general it has been eclipsed by the Nation of Islam, inaugurated by Elijah Muhammad.

Born in 1897 in Georgia, Elijah Poole, a small, poorly educated man, was to become one of the most significant African-American leaders of the twentieth century. Through his Muslim organization, many of the doctrines of which are at variance with those of orthodox Islam, he was to challenge his community to follow a way of life that called for self-respect, economic independence, and ethical integrity. It was, and continues to be, a movement of social consciousness and economic revolt, based on a complex set of theological underpinnings and borrowing almost randomly from orthodox Muslim law and religious structure.

Elijah Muhammad apparently learned about Islam from a figure whose identity remains obscure. Known variously as Wallace Fard, Wali Farrad, and W.F. Muhammad, he claimed to have been born in Mecca, the son of an Arab father and a European mother. This identity has been seriously challenged, but in any case he seems to have been influenced by a number of different, and often marginally Islamic, views. He appeared in Detroit, where he was heard by and had a strong influence on the young Elijah Poole. First held to be the long-expected Mahdi (Guided One) of Islamic tradition, Fard apparently later encouraged his recognition as God in human person.

Fard reportedly taught Elijah that African-Americans are all Muslims by heritage, although over the centuries they have lost touch with their past, with God, and with a sense of self-identity. Thus, the movement was originally called the Lost-Found Nation of Islam (to which "in the wilderness of North America" was sometimes added), and Elijah was commissioned as the messenger of Allah to bring the "black nation" back to a realization of its true nature. After some three years of instruction, Fard disappeared, leaving the new messenger with the responsibility of carrying out his difficult mission.

THE NATION OF ISLAM

The elaborate doctrines of the Nation of Islam form a complex underpinning to the movement of renewal led by Elijah Muhammad. While borrowing some of the teachings of normative Islam, it provides for a racially-based doctrine designed to help the "original black man" understand his identity in relation to his "satanic" white oppressors. Its eschatology does not deal with a far future event, but relates specifically to the destruction of white power structures and the establishment of the true black community. Elijah operated out of the ghettos and urban slums, preaching to those who suffered most from white oppression. It was a formidable task, not simplified by the fact of being ridiculed and rejected by the Christian church, even congregations of African heritage, by local immigrant Muslim groups, and by leaders of the African-American community.

Elijah did succeed in establishing a strong movement, the Nation of Islam, which gave hundreds of thousands of Americans a challenge and a means of rising out of their demeaning circumstances. Temples and mosques began appearing in major urban areas. Its message often spread through the prisons, where many considered Islam to be a greater rehabilitating force than movements for civil rights or government welfare programs. By the 1960s Elijah's most famous disciple, the dynamic and influential Malcolm X, had risen to prominence. From a dream entertained only by the outcasts of society, the Nation of Islam had changed to a full-blown movement to which professional and well-educated Americans of African heritage, as well as the economically disadvantaged, were attracted.

Malcolm was suspended from the Nation in 1963. In 1964 he journeyed to Mecca for the pilgrimage. Introduced to an Islamic world quite different from that of Elijah Muhammad, he began to preach a doctrine much less racially based than that of the "messenger of Allah." While he recognized the continuing oppression of blacks by whites, he no longer held the doctrine that the white race was created evil. His experience with Muslims overseas and their gestures of brotherhood while on the pilgrimage in Mecca convinced him that whites are neither categorically nor intrinsically bad. Malcolm split finally with the Nation after discovering that Elijah Muhammad was implicated in sexual scandal he considered unfitting for a messenger of God.

THE NATION AFTER ELIJAH

After Elijah's death in 1975, his son Warith Deen Muhammad assumed the leadership. Warith Deen lost no time in redefining many of the doctrines of his father, especially those concerned with the denigration of the white race. Continuing much of the later thinking of Malcolm, with whom for years he had shared ideas, he changed the emphasis from a black nationalist Islam to one clearly a part of the international body of orthodox Muslims. Warith Deen has always been a student of Arabic, Qur'an, and Islamic law, both in America and abroad. Assuming the title of *mujaddid,* a classical Arabic term for a restorer of the faith, Warith Deen continues to strive for the recognition and growth of a significant orthodox Muslim community in the United States.

Under Warith Deen, the black nationalist aspect of the Nation of Islam has been replaced by a strong appeal for Muslims to be good and responsible citizens of the United States. Muslim schools fly the American flag, and morning prayers are preceded by the pledge of allegiance. Members are encouraged to serve in the United States military rather than to evade the draft. The militant Fruit of Islam guard has been disbanded. What were formerly called ministers in the Nation are now recognized as imams; temples are now mosques or are called by the Arabic term masjid. *Muhammad Speaks,* the official newspaper of the Nation under Elijah, was renamed *Bilalian News* after the first black convert to Islam, Bilal ibn Rabah. The name was later changed to *American Muslim Journal.*

Along with these various changes in nomenclature, Warith Deen instigated the change in the name of the group from the Nation of Islam to the World Community of Islam in the West in 1976 and, in 1980, to the American Muslim Mission. Connections with Islamic orthodoxy have been strengthened, and only a few years ago, at the American Academy of Religion in New Orleans, Warith Deen was publicly recognized as a brother in Islam by leaders of the immigrant Muslim community. In the lecture that he delivered to the Academy on that occasion, entitled "Evolution of the Nation of Islam," he explained why the doctrines preached by Fard and Elijah Muhammad were necessary for the African-American community at that stage of its development, but made it clear that they were, in fact, often far from the true doctrine of Islam that he, Warith Deen, is now preaching:

> I believe that if Dr. Fard had been dealing with a higher level of knowledge of education in the Community or among people that he preached to, he would have approached it quite differently and would have come to us with a more sensible and rational, a more human doctrine. But definitely, he did not come to us with Al-Islam. He came to us with the label of Al-Islam. . . .

Warith Deen's efforts to bring his organization into the orthodox fold have been rewarded by increased recognition of his

status on the international level. He has been given the right to cer-
tify who from the United States is entitled to make the pilgrimage
to Mecca. In 1978 he was named by a number of Gulf states, including Saudi Arabia, as the consultant and trustee for the distribution
of funds for all Islamic missionary activities in the United States.

ALTERNATIVES TO THE LEADERSHIP
OF WARITH DEEN MUHAMMAD

This does not mean, however, that all of Elijah Muhammad's
followers are satisfied with the leadership of Warith Deen. While
exact numbers are difficult to obtain, it seems clear that a significant portion of the old Nation of Islam has chosen not to follow him
in his endeavors to liberalize Islam. One individual in particular has
led the movement to remain faithful to the teachings of Elijah and
to maintain the name Nation of Islam. He is Minister Louis Farrakhan, who has been likened to Malcolm X before his split from
the Nation. Farrakhan, who took Malcolm's place as the major
spokesman for the Nation, decried Malcolm's post-pilgrimage
changes and has been equally disenchanted with the moves toward
orthodoxy advocated by Warith Deen. Still persuaded that the continuing adverse circumstances of blacks, not only in America but
around the world, are due to oppression by the white man, Farrakhan has maintained Elijah's analysis of the metaphysical identification of white with evil, and the need to press with even greater
vigor for the creation of a separate state for African-Americans.

The Fruit of Islam, which Warith Deen disbanded, has been
revived by Farrakhan with both a male and a female branch. As it
did earlier, the Fruit symbolizes for many youths a way of rising
above their demeaning circumstances. While the American Muslim
Mission now seems to appeal primarily to the middle classes, the
Nation, under Farrakhan, has remained almost exclusively a lower-
class movement, appealing, as Elijah did decades ago, to ghetto residents who find in it a way to self-discipline and self-dignity in the
face of white racism.

If the two groups under Farrakhan and Warith Deen are to be
seen as rivals, it is difficult to predict how a resolution of their differences might be reached or whether one group may come to truly
eclipse the other. Imam Warith Deen has been warmly recognized

by Jimmy Carter, whose presidential campaign he endorsed, as well as by President Ronald Reagan. He is an increasingly evident participant in Jewish-Christian-Muslim trialogue sessions, and has appeared on radio and television talk shows. The American Muslim Mission, which has branches throughout the United States and in such places as the West Indies, is dedicated precisely to what the name implies—the propagation of Islam in America. With a broad base of international support, it seems destined to remain a strong force in the foreseeable future. It is also the case that Minister Louis Farrakhan speaks to the needs of a very significant segment of the African-American population, and that as long as discrimination and racism continue to remain a blight on the face of American society, he will have a ready and enthusiastic audience for his message of black nationalism.

Another Muslim organization, founded by a former national secretary of the Nation of Islam, is the Hanafi movement of Hamaas Abdul Khaalis, with whom such sports luminaries as Kareem Abdul Jabbar are connected. Khaalis seceded from the Nation in the early 1960s. Continuing tensions have led to several very unpleasant incidents, capturing the attention of the press as well as some foreign Muslim governments—another indication that Islam in America, in its various manifestations, is increasingly recognized by the international Muslim community as a noteworthy phenomenon.

This international recognition of indigenous American Islam is a source of both pleasure and concern to many immigrant Muslims, a mixed reaction that has characterized the response of the immigrant community since the beginning of the Nation in the 1930s. At first they were pleased to know that people in America found Islam attractive, but soon became alarmed at some of the doctrines propagated in the name of Islam. In particular they were appalled at the completely un-Islamic notion of God appearing in the person of W.D. Fard and of Elijah Muhammad being considered a messenger of God. Almost as unacceptable was the mythology of the white race as an evil creation, which denies the egalitarian substructure of Islam as articulated in the Qur'an.

With the assumption of leadership by Warith Deen Muhammad, and the subsequent ideological changes, came an elation among immigrants that the true teachings of Islam had been restored to the Muslim movement in the United States. They were ready to join forces with their American brothers in calling this society to the way of God. This excitement, however, has abated somewhat in the face of practical realities. It seems increasingly clear that the indigenous community is primarily interested in the economic advancement of its constituency, while the immigrants are concerned with fostering the proper image of Islam in the United States, as well as influencing U.S. foreign policy vis-à-vis Muslim countries. Such recognition as Warith Deen has received from Muslims abroad, including sizable donations to his movement, apparently has been a source of some annoyance among established groups of immigrant Muslims in this country.

FOREIGN MUSLIM STUDENTS

An addition to the various categories of immigrant and indigenous Muslims, though in a sense a subset of the former, is the increasing numbers of Muslim students who come to study in the United States. Many return to their home countries and a few stay; but at least for their term of study, many of these young men and women choose to be affiliated with campus Muslim groups and with established local mosques and Muslim communities. Before the 1970s most Muslim students were enrolled in undergraduate programs. Since 1970 there has been a sharp rise in the number of graduates, especially from the Arab world. This is due to such factors as the 1973 Arab-Israeli war, dramatically changed economic circumstances in Islamic oil nations, and the establishment of several universities in the Gulf. The revolution in Iran resulted in the arrival in the United States of some 250,000 Iranians opposed to the Khomeini regime, among them many who were students at both the undergraduate and graduate levels in various American universities.

Of the several Islamic organizations that have arisen in the United States, particularly in the last several decades, the Muslim Student Association (MSA) is one of the most active. After several earlier attempts it was finally begun in 1963 on the campus of the University of Illinois, founded for the purpose of uniting young Muslim students and stressing the commonality of the Islamic experience as it engages all aspects of life. Since the mid-1970s the goals of the organization have been broadened to include emphasis on the mission outreach of Islam and the importance of recruiting, as well as providing sustenance for members, disseminating knowledge about Islam, and establishing new Islamic institutions. Several professional groups have been organized by MSA alumni, including the Islamic Medical Association, the Association of Muslim Scientists and Engineers, and the Association of Muslim Social Scientists.

An umbrella organization subsuming the MSA is the Islamic Society of North America (ISNA). The main concern of MSA is the growing number of Muslim students in the United States and the necessity of preparing them to work for the establishment of Islamic governments and societies in their home countries. ISNA is also dedicated to the propagation of Islam in America, concentrating on such projects as the organization and establishment of mosques operated by and for Muslim alumni who have settled in university towns across America.

OTHER ISLAMIC ORGANIZATIONS

Since early in the twentieth century, there have been a variety of other Islamic organizations attempting to provide a structure to the growing number of mosques and communities in America. In 1954 the Federation of Islamic Associations (FIA) was founded, its constituency mainly second- and third-generation Muslims of Arab background. It is less militant in its efforts at propagating the faith than the MSA, and generally more social in orientation. Its publication, *The Muslim Star,* provides such services as a directory of Muslims in the United States, as well as readings on assorted Islamic topics. One of its major projects has been the continuing attempt to counter anti-Islamic and anti-Arab propaganda in the American press and media. The FIA is American-originated and American-based.

Another organization in the United States is actually a branch of a recently formed international structure based in Mecca, the Muslim World League. It is strongly dedicated to *da'wah,* propagation of the faith, and has a special interest in areas of the world in which Islam is a minority religion. The League has offices in New York City, and its efforts are concentrated on fostering a united Muslim community in the United States in which indigenous and immigrant Muslims can live in harmony and cooperation. Likening the two groups to the two major constituencies of the early Muslim community under the leadership of the Prophet Muhammad, former League director Ahmad Sakr said in a speech to the First Islamic Conference of North America in 1977:

> As you know, the Muslims of North America are composed of indigenous and immigrant Muslims who are working together and shall continue to work together. . . . They, in a way, represent the Muhajireen and the Ansar of today, working hand-in-hand, for the love of Allah. . . .

The Muslim World League is active in providing imams, primarily of Arab background, to American mosques. The Council of Masajid (Mosques), based in New York and operated by the League, is designed to promote cooperation among mosques in the United States, as well as between American and foreign mosques. It is based in Mecca and, while encouraging local mosques in the United States to be self-sufficient economically, does provide assistance when necessary in the building, furnishing, and maintenance of American mosques. Since 1974 the League has been granted nongovernmental representative status to the United Nations.

In 1972 the Islamic Party in North America was begun in Washington, D.C., for the purpose of teaching about and fostering the ideals of Islam. Primarily an indigenous Muslim organization, it provides a variety of community services for its members.

Muslim communities are located across the United States, with particular concentrations in some of the major cities. One of the densest areas of Arab Muslim population is Dearborn, Michigan, with some 80,000 immigrants. There are about 250,000 immigrant and indigenous Muslims in the Chicago area, even more in New York and on the East Coast, and over 250,000 in California, with a high concentration of Pakistanis and Iranians. Increasing numbers of Muslims from the Middle East are attracted by the climate of the Southwest, particularly Texas.

There are over 450 Islamic groupings of one sort or another in the United States, including mosques, associations, centers, and other organizational units. Immigrant Muslims have some 70 mosques, officially called mosques because they have an identifiable structure, and the American Muslim Mission has over 100 masajid.

The immigrant and indigenous communities in the United States, whatever their particular orientation, daily face the realities of being Muslim within a non-Islamic society. Of necessity chief among their concerns must be the transmission of Muslim values to the next generation. This has led to a concerted effort to provide an Islamic education to their young people. In several cities, including Chicago and Seattle, immigrant Muslims are attempting to establish separate Islamic schools in which proper instruction, behavior, and dress can be maintained. The American Muslim Mission is concentrating on reviving a former project of the Nation of Islam: to have a Muslim school associated with every mosque. Two Muslim colleges are now being established, the American Muslim Mission School in North Carolina, for teacher preparation, and the American Islamic College, being set up by immigrant Muslims in Chicago.

It is clear that Islam is a vital force in the United States and that a variety of factors, from social conditions to intensified efforts at propagation of the faith, will continue to ensure its establishment on the American scene. That difficulties will persist and new issues will arise seems certain, but it is equally certain that in the United States Islam is, and will be, a vital force that cannot be ignored. As Muhammad Abdel Rauf, former director of the Islamic Center of Washington, D.C., reflected in his talk to the First Islamic Conference of North America:

> . . . despite all these serious problems, Islam is spreading like a mighty torrent, sweeping through the doors of colleges and universities and even penetrating the thick walls of prisons. The sun rises every day on a number of new Muslims—not only the offspring of Muslim parents, but on those with a non-Muslim background who have chosen voluntarily to embrace Islam. The future looks promising for Islam. . . .

Present Tendencies, Future Trends

Seyyed Hossein Nasr

The events of the past few years in the Middle East—in fact, throughout the Islamic world—have created a flood of works on Islam and its future, some by people who but a few years before rejected the possibility of Islam's being a major force to be reckoned with in the future. This veritable new industry, often based on passing political currents or on hastily drawn conclusions from incomplete data, has already made many predictions for the Islamic world ranging from melodrama to science fiction, with a few more balanced judgments in between. My aim in this chapter is certainly not to add one more scenario to existing ones, especially since, according to a belief strongly held by all Muslims, the future lies in God's hand, and only He is aware of its content, as the Qur'an repeats in many of its verses. My goal, rather, is to delve below the surface, to bring out the nature of some of the more profound issues, ideas, and forces at work within contemporary Islamic religious thought as well as the Islamic world, and to cast an eye upon how these elements seem to be interacting with each other and with the world about them, and how they are likely to do so in the near future—all the while remaining fully aware of the unreliability of all projections based on present tendencies.

In carrying out this discussion it is important to distinguish between Islam and the Islamic world. There are currents of thought, movement, affirmations, and rejections within the world of Islamic religious thought. And there are, needless to say, very complex forces and movements at play in that part of the world called Islamic. The two are by no means identical, nor should they be confused with each other for the purpose of any scholarly analysis. Nor should they be totally separated. That part of the globe called the Islamic world is Islamic in the most profound sense: over the centuries the laws, culture, and social structure—in fact, the whole world view of the people inhabiting it—have been molded by Islam. Moreover, after over a century of retreat, and sometimes capitulation, before the West, many people of the world called Islamic are seeking again to turn in various ways and modes to Islam. So there is without doubt a "revival" of one kind or another associated with Islam in many Muslim lands, although the form and even the content of this "revival" are far from being the same everywhere. Nor are all the movements that use the name, symbols, and language of Islam of an authentically Islamic character.

There are, then, Islam and the Islamic world to consider. And there is the link between the two in the light of the pertinence of Islam, however it is understood and interpreted by different parties, to that world. The future trends of the two—Islam seen as a religion and the Islamic world—will most likely not be the same; but they cannot be totally unrelated. To study the various current schools of thought and perspectives within Islam and in the circles of Muslim thinkers will, therefore, certainly cast some light upon what is likely to happen in the Islamic world; yet one must remember that, without doubt, forces and events from outside the Islamic world are likely to have the most profound effect upon that world without being in any way related to the internal religious and theological forces of Islam. Speculation about this second type of protrusion in the future into the Islamic world and the role of these external forces in changing the destinies of the Islamic peoples, as we have seen in several Islamic countries during the past few years, cannot be the concern of this chapter. My task, rather, will be to study the trends associated with Islamic thought as it may influence and affect the future of the Islamic world. The influence of a particular form of Islamic thought on this or that segment of Islamic society is one thing; invasions by foreign troops or less overt manipulation and interference, quite another. Of necessity it is only with the former category that I can be concerned.

CONTEMPORARY FORCES AND ELEMENTS

Within the Islamic religious universe one can discern a large number of forces and forms of activity that, for the sake of this discussion, can be classified into four categories (although within each category there is a wide spectrum of diversity). These general categories may be called modernism, messianism, "fundamentalism," and traditional Islam. Despite their divergence and often inner opposition, they are likely to continue at least into the immediate future.

Modernism

Modernism, the most nebulous of these terms, continues to undergo a change of content from one decade to another. The Muslim modernists of the late nineteenth century or even of the 1940s were not defending the same theses as those of today because of the transient nature of modernism itself. But they are all called modernists because they place value and some degree of trust in the post-medieval development in the West that is called modernism, and also because they have tried, and continue to try, to interpret Islam or some aspects of it according to the ideas, values, and norms drawn from the modern outlook with its own wide range of diversity.

The modernist schools range from those that wish to reinterpret Islam in the light of the humanistic and rationalistic trends of Western thought, and ally themselves with the prevailing paradigm of liberalism in the West, to others that are drawn to the Marxist world view and have become much more numerous since World War II. The Islamic modernists range from serious scholars and thinkers like Fazlur Rahman and Muhammad Arkoun, who have been influenced by Western liberal thought, to journalist popularizers; from those attracted to French existentialism and personalism, such as Muhammad Lahbabi, to others who have been deeply influenced by Marxist thought, such as Ali Shari'ati and Abdallah Laroui. This class of modernists has usually been deeply concerned at the same time with the social aspect of Islam and often a kind of "Third World philosophy" that has been a hallmark of French intellectual circles since World War II, circles within which most of this type of Muslim "reformist" thinker have been nurtured.

Altogether, the impact of the Islamic modernists of the older generations, such as Muhammad Abduh on the one hand and Sir Ahmad Khan on the other, has decreased in most Muslim countries. Often feeling a sense of inferiority vis-à-vis the West and anxious to emulate everything Western, many of the earlier "reformers" were a strong force as long as the Western model seemed viable and world-dominating. With the gradual weakening of the prevailing Western paradigm in the West itself, combined with the tragedies of the Islamic world that are associated in the eyes of the populace with the West, there has been a decrease in the impact of the "liberal," Western-oriented Muslim thinker. This trend is likely to continue as long as the forces at play, especially in the Arab-Israeli issue, continue to be what they are.

The second type of modernist, who substitutes Marx for Locke and some form of socialism for Western capitalism, and who tries to appear as a hero of the Third World and the "downtrodden masses," may be a latecomer to the Islamic world; but his influence is far from being on the wane. On the contrary, there is every reason to think that it is on the rise in many parts of the Islamic world, being abetted materially and financially by certain sources both within and outside the Islamic world. Its force will diminish only if the traditional Muslim thinkers confront the tenets of this kind of crypto-Marxism head-on, as has happened once or twice. For example, Allamah S.M. Tabataba'i, in his *Principles of the Philosophy of Realism,* squarely faced it rather than circumventing it and refusing to consider its implications (as has usually been the case of so many contemporary Muslim figures).

Messianism

Messianism has always been present in Islam and has manifested itself whenever the Islamic community has felt an imminent danger to its world of value and meaning. The European invasion of the Islamic world in the nineteenth century stimulated a wave of messianism from West Africa to the Sudan, from Persia to India. This wave took very different forms in different areas, producing the Mahdi in the Sudan as well as the Bab in Persia. But the basis of the phenomenon was everywhere nearly the same: the appearance of a charismatic figure claiming to be the Mahdi or his representative, in direct contact with God and His agents in the universe, and representing a direct divine intervention in history with eschatological overtones. The last few years have been witness to the revival of this type of religious phenomenon. The early part of the upheavals in Iran in 1978 definitely had a messianic dimension; the same is true of the capturing of the Grand Mosque in Mecca in 1979—where, strangely enough, messianic tendencies were mixed with a brand of Wahhabism—and the recent mahdiist movement in northern Nigeria.

There is every reason to expect such forms of messianism to continue. As a billion people become ever more frustrated in failing to achieve the goals which they believe they are legitimately entitled to realize, one reaction will certainly be some kind of politicosocial eruption and upheaval. Another possible reaction, however, is a messianism that promises victory with divine help, but on the basis of the destruction of the existing order. Messianism must possess a "revolutionary" character. That is why traditional Muslims believe that only the Mahdi, who will come before the end of history, will be able to carry out a veritable religious revolution, which would mean nothing less than the establishment of the divine order on earth, all other revolutions being forms of subversion and further destruction of what remains of the religious tradition. To the extent that the world becomes a more dangerous place in which to live, and especially as the Muslim peoples see themselves confronted by alien forces that threaten their very existence, the wave of messianism is bound to increase in accordance with some of the sayings of the Prophet about the signs of the latter days.

"Fundamentalism"

As far as "fundamentalism" is concerned, use of the term by journalists and even scholars to refer to a wide variety of phenomena in the Islamic world and currents in Islamic thought is most unfortunate and misleading because the term is drawn from the Christian context, where it has quite a different connotation. "Fundamentalism" in Christian religious circles, especially in the United States refers to conservative forms of Protestantism, usually anti-modernist, with a rather narrow and literal interpretation of the Bible and a strong emphasis upon traditional Christian ethics. These characteristics have little to do with much that is classified under the name of "fundamentalism" in Islam, although some of the excessively exoteric but traditional currents of Islamic thought also called "fundamentalist" do share a few common features with "fundamentalism" as generally understood in English. The differences, however, are much greater than the similarities, especially in the more violently anti-Western and "revolutionary" currents that, despite their outward anti-Western attitude, also refer to themselves as "fundamentalist," having to invent this word for this particular context, since such a term has not traditionally existed in various Islamic languages.

The use of the term "fundamentalism" and the classification of a widely diverse set of phenomena and tendencies under such a name are misleading features of many of the current studies on Islam, and help to hide the more profound realities involved, including the essential fact that much of what is called "fundamentalist Islam" is anti-traditional and opposed to both the spirit and the letter of the Islamic tradition, as understood and practiced since the descent of the Qur'anic revelation.

Under the category of "fundamentalist" are included both organizations that hope to Islamize society fully through the application of the shari'a—but in a peaceful manner, such as the Jamaat-i-Islami of Maulana Mawdudi—and those that speak of "revolution," using the ideologies and even the techniques of modern European revolutionary movements but with an Islamic color. They include movements based on the idea of the rule of the ulama (as in Iran) and those that try to eliminate the influence of the ulama and, for all practical purposes, their existence (as in Libya). They embrace organizations as different as the Muhammadiyyah movement in Indonesia and the Muslim Brotherhood, and governments as diametrically opposed as those of Saudi Arabia and Iran.

To gain a deeper understanding of the forces that are bound to determine trends in the near future, it is important to distinguish clearly between much of what is called "fundamentalist Islam" by Western scholarship and traditional Islam. What various movements called "fundamentalist" have in common is a cultural and religious frustration before the onslaught of Western culture and the desire to reassert themselves in the name of Islam. But their common ground stops at this point because, in trying to achieve their ends, some have had recourse to revolutionary jargon drawn from the West, while others have reverted to a puritanical and rationalistic interpretation of Islam that would do away with the whole Islamic intellectual and spiritual tradition in the name of a primordial purity no longer attainable. This latter group, although limited in its understanding and appreciation of the Islamic tradition, at least accepts a part of that tradition—the shari'a, the part of "fundamentalism" closest to traditional Islam—while the former is anti-traditional in its nature and methods, despite all appearances. Moreover, in many of these "fundamentalist" movements, leftist ideology has simply replaced that of the classical, liberal schools of the West emulated by an earlier generation of Westernized Muslims, such as Ameer Ali and Zia Gokalp. Hatred, a sense of revenge, constant agitation, and blind fury may have also come to characterize many of these movements instead of the peace, tranquility, harmony, and objectivity that have usually characterized authentic manifestations of Islam and are reflected in both the Qur'an and the personality of the Prophet, and are even to be seen in movements of *tajdid* (renewal) throughout Islamic history.

In trying to render back to Islam its power on the stage of history, many of these movements have disfigured the nature of Islam. Rather than being a genuine revival of Islam, a revival that is trying to take place in many quarters, they are in reality another form of modernism—but much more dangerous than the earlier forms because they make use of the language and certain popular symbols of the Islamic religion, while adopting some of the most negative and spiritually devastating aspects of the modern West, including Marxism. Furthermore, in the name of religious fervor they close the door to all intellectual efforts and logical deliberations about the problems and dangers that confront the Islamic world.

If the hopes and aspirations of the Islamic world continue to be shattered by the force of current events, there is no doubt that the revolutionary "fundamentalist" movements will continue to manifest themselves and to spread, since many of these movements are supported and aggrandized, usually indirectly, by both the Communist world and certain forces in the West, each providing support for its own reasons. Yet, once an ideology of this kind is tried, it cannot survive for long unless it is able to achieve the goals that it has promised. Islam is still strong enough in the Islamic world for Muslims to be able to judge, in the long run, the Islamicity of the movements and ideologies that use the name of Islam. Most likely, with the passage of time the rigor of this test by the religious conscience of the community will be felt more strongly by all movements, forces, and governments that speak of "Islamic ideology." Whatever the political implications of this sifting and testing of such forces by the Islamic population might be, there seems to be little doubt that on the level of religious thought or of Islam itself considered as a religion, there is bound to be a greater discernment within Islamic society concerning movements that are dubbed "fundamentalist," especially those that try to use Islam as ideology.

ISLAM AND IDEOLOGY

A clear distinction must be made here between the Islamic religion and the ideology with which some of the modern movements within the Islamic world wish to identify Islam. An ideology is not religion, philosophy, or science, although this peculiar child of nineteenth-century European thought has been considered by some in the twentieth century as a substitute for religion and philosophy that is imbued with a kind of scientific infallibility. In the name of ideologies, which have become identified with particular states and regimes, human beings have fought and died and dedicated the fruit of their whole lives. In the modern world ideologies have claimed the totality of the life and thought of those who have fallen under their spell, but they have done so not in the name of a transcendent truth open to various earthly interpretations, but in the name of a particular worldly embodiment of the idea in question. They have substituted a this-worldly orientation for the ultimately otherworldly and spiritual one of religion, and the concern of traditional religion with establishing God's kingdom on earth has been replaced by concern with making the life of this world an end in itself. Ideology is a child of modern European thought, and nothing is quite so devastating as the confusion between it and religion as traditionally understood. This confusion is even more devastating, from the religious point of view, than the simple substitution of ideology for religion, as happened in the ideological states of the earlier decades of the twentieth century.

The Islamic religion also claims totality and is concerned with the whole of life, including the affairs of this world, which it emphasizes more than Christianity does. But its end remains the other world, to which the present world is a means. It does not limit the interpretation of Islam in such a way as to benefit the interests of a single state over other Muslims. It is not a humanly delimitable and definable "idea" that would form the heart of an ideology, as understood in the West, but a path based on the Divine Will and leading to the Divine that makes everything, including the welfare of a particular state and even the earthly well-being of a human collectivity, subservient to man's final end, which is to live the life of faith and to die as a person of faith.

In those areas and among those groups where the Islamic religion has been reduced to Islamic ideology, often with the intention of preventing anything other than Islam from becoming the source of inspiration for human thought and action, there is a clear lack of spiritual beauty, of intellectual depth, and of the traditional Islamic virtues, which have their root in the Qur'an and the very soul of the Prophet. No matter how much lip service is given to Islam's refusal to separate the sacred and the secular, the ideologization of Islam can only lead to the secularization of its norms and symbols, and a reduction of its transcendent truths to a particular opportune interpretation chosen by a certain group to protect its interests and further its goals. Moreover, those who speak of Islam as ideology are forced, especially on the plane of action, to adopt some of the most anti-religious elements of modern Western civilization and to cover them with an Islamic color in order to hide their actual anti-Islamic nature.

Once Islam is interpreted not as an all-embracing religion (*al-din*) but as an ideology that serves a particular movement or regime as its prop, the failure of that movement or regime reflects upon Islam itself. In this case either people lose their faith or they begin to scrutinize the actual nature of the forces that have presented themselves as Islamic. Both of these tendencies are bound to occur to the extent that the "fundamentalist" movements are able to wield actual power and to affect the everyday lives of human beings.

TRADITIONAL ISLAM

Finally, there is traditional Islam, which is often mistaken for "fundamentalism" as currently used. Despite waves of modernism, puritanical reactions, messianism, and violent and revolutionary or theologically limiting forms of "fundamentalism," traditional

Islam continues to survive. Most Muslims still live in a world in which the equilibrium promulgated by the shari'a and the serenity of Islamic spirituality are found to some extent, despite the experiences of European colonialism, a certain degree of decadence within the Islamic world (which became noticeable in the eighteenth century and increased during the nineteenth century), and the constant political turmoil and economic problems that many Muslim countries face. Most of the interpreters of the shari'a are still traditional ulama. The Sufi orders, far from being dead, still possess an inner vitality and one can find a few great spiritual masters within them. And the traditional intellectual and theological sciences are by no means dead.

Moreover, during the past few decades a new class of traditional scholars and thinkers, such as A.K. Brohi of Pakistan, Y. Ibish of Lebanon, Ben Abboud of Morocco, Naguib al-Attas of Malaysia, and Abd al-Halim Mahmud of Egypt, has appeared in the Islamic world. They are traditional in their adherence to and defense of the whole and integral Islamic tradition, but they also know the Western world in depth and are able to provide intellectual answers from the Islamic point of view to the problems posed by the modern world, rather than having recourse to either blind faith or simple sloganeering and rhetoric. This new class of traditional scholars and thinkers plays, and will continue to play, to an ever greater degree, a central role in the defense and propagation of traditional Islam. It will also provide, as it does already, the intellectual vision and critical knowledge of the modern world which is lacking, for the most part, among what one might call the "old" traditional groups and classes within Islamic society.

Traditional Islam is bound to survive, especially since the very structure of the Islamic tradition, with its emphasis upon the direct link between man and God and the lack of a central religious authority, contains the maximum protection for survival in a world like that of today. Moreover, the newly created class of traditional Muslim scholars and thinkers, who are also fully cognizant of the nature of the modern world, its schools of thought, philosophies, and sciences, is bound to increase—and in fact is doing so now. This trend is likely to spread, to the extent that attempts made by different groups within the "fundamentalist" camp to Islamize both society and knowledge and education, without the aid of the full import of the Islamic intellectual tradition, fail to deliver the expected results. The decay in the quality of traditional life is also likely to continue, but traditional Islam is bound to survive in its various dimensions and aspects, and will ultimately be the judge and criterion of exactly how Islamic all those revivals and resurgent movements that claim an Islamic character are.

THE ISLAMIZATION OF EDUCATION AND THE SCIENCES

For several centuries the predominant form of theology in the Sunni part of the Islamic world has been Ash'arite, based on an all-encompassing voluntarism and resulting in a theological position in which knowledge is made subservient to faith. Moreover, the rise of such movements as Wahhabism and the Salafiyyah has helped to strengthen this tendency. Even in the Shi'i world, where the prevalent theology has been more conducive to the intellectual aspects of the Islamic tradition and the exoteric element has predominated since the end of the Safavid period, there has been a certain degree of eclipse of what is traditionally called the "intellectual sciences." Therefore, by and large, and despite the survival of centers of activity of the intellectual sciences in certain areas, especially in Persia and the Indian subcontinent, when those Islamic thinkers affected by this fideism confronted the West, they did so mostly from a perspective that was helpless before the specifically intellectual and rational challenges of the modern world and had to take recourse to either an opposition based on fanaticism or refuge in faith alone.

The result was inevitably catastrophic, for the main challenge of the modern West to Islam is not primarily military, as it was with the Mongols, although the military dimension certainly has been present even after the apparent end of the colonial period. Nor is it primarily religious, as it was in the encounter of Islam with Hinduism. The challenge, rather, mainly concerns the domain of the intellect and requires a response suitable to its nature. Until recently the response of the Islamic world was not like that of the early Islamic centuries which faced the Greco-Alexandrian sciences and learning. Rather, the response in official religious circles has, for the most part, echoed the prevalent fideism and voluntarism that has dominated the religious centers of learning, the small number of new traditional scholars being an exception.

During the past few years a larger number of Islamic thinkers have begun to confront this problem more fully and to try to come to terms with both the social and the intellectual and cultural challenges of the West. Numerous educational authorities throughout the Islamic world, such as Muhammad Naseef of Saudi Arabia, S.A. Ashraf and Sajjad Husayn of Bangladesh, Hisham Nashshabi of Lebanon, and Khurshid Ahmad of Pakistan, have come to realize the importance of the re-Islamization of the educational system and the integration of the modern sciences into the Islamic world view. Many educational conferences dealing with these problems have been held and are planned for the future. There is little doubt that this trend will continue to grow in coming years. Attempts will most likely continue to be made to create a single educational system in various Islamic countries, rather than the two contending ones (the traditional Islamic and the modern) that dominate the scene in most Islamic lands. Likewise, efforts will continue to be made to try to "Islamize" disciplines ranging from the humanities to the social and even the natural sciences.

The main question is whether, while making use of only one dimension of the Islamic tradition, the shari'a, and neglecting the other dimensions and the whole intellectual and spiritual tradition of Islam, it is possible to carry out such an enterprise. Is it possible to integrate the sciences of nature into the Islamic perspective by limiting oneself to the Islamic sciences of law and the literal meaning of the verses of the Qur'an or replacing an intellectual response by piety, no matter how sincere and precious that piety might be?

At the present time there are two forces at play in this endeavor to Islamize education and the sciences. One is closely allied to certain segments of that spectrum called "fundamentalism," and sees the success of this process as being the result and consequence of the reestablishment of the shari'a in society. This group follows more or less the voluntarist-fideist theological position prevalent in the religious schools at the beginning of the modern period, to which it adds the rejection of the integral intellectual and spiritual tradition of Islam and a puritanical-rationalistic tendency going back to the "reform" movements of the nineteenth century, such as the Salafiyyah.

The second group, which is traditional rather than "fundamentalist," seeks to achieve the same goal of Islamization, but through recourse to the complete Islamic intellectual tradition, combined with a critique in depth of the modern world based on traditional principles. While agreeing with the first group on the importance of the implementation of the shari'a, it believes that the intellectual challenges posed by the modern world can be answered only by understanding the nature of these challenges in depth and by applying the intellectual principles of the Islamic tradition to counter these challenges, whether they be philosophical, ideological, or scientific. Furthermore, this latter group believes that the challenge of modernism cannot be answered until the Islamic intellectual and spiritual tradition is resuscitated and revived in its fullness and totality. It maintains that only the spiritual, inward, intellectual, and esoteric aspects of religion are able to provide answers for certain types of questions created by modernism, and solutions for certain problems brought about by the destruction of the homogeneous religious world of Islam as a result of nineteenth-century colonial penetration into that world.

Both of these groups and their ideas and goals are bound to continue in the near future. Moreover, the degree of success that each school will have will influence the course of Islamic theology and religious thought. Of course the secularizing forces, opposed to the educational aim of both groups, are also alive and active in many lands, and are bound to influence events in this domain to an appreciable degree, at least in some of the major Islamic countries. Their influence on Islamic thought through educational channels, however, is bound to be less than that of the first two groups mentioned above. Where the secularists in educational theory and practice wield their greatest influence is through the existing dual system of education. The obvious results of such a system lie in producing members of a society who hold opposing views on crucial issues and cannot agree on the basis for social order.

In the realm of education, even those who wish to Islamize the educational system may unwittingly help in the further secularization of the system by wishing to do away with or change radically the well-established "modern" educational institutions, such as the universities of Aligarh, Tehran, Cairo, and Istanbul. Muslims who have studied in them have sought to create some kind of bridge between the traditional and modern schools, and have even tried to mold the classical Islamic scientific vocabularies of such languages as Arabic and Persian so as to make them suitable vehicles for the expression of contemporary scientific disciplines. In years to come there may well be rivalry between those who wish to Islamize the existing educational institutions and those who would do away with them altogether and create "new" Islamic institutions in their place. The limited success of present-day Islamic universities in Islamizing nonreligious subjects, in the narrow meaning of the term "religious," reveals both the enormity of the task involved and the crucial importance that the process of the Islamization of education and the sciences, now taking place throughout much of the Islamic world, will have for the future of both Islamic thought and the Islamic world.

THE QUEST FOR ISLAMIC UNITY

The increase of self-awareness of the Islamic world as a single entity is an important trend that is bound to continue, since both the traditionalists and the "fundamentalists" cherish the ideal of its unity, although they envisage its realization in very different ways. Likewise, messianism has always had as an intrinsic part of its perspective and program the unification of the Islamic world. According to tradition, it is the Mahdi who will reunite the Islamic world at the end of time. The rise of greater awareness of the Islamic ethos and reactions to the onslaught of the West have made the unity of the Islamic world a motto for political and religious forces of nearly every color and persuasion—save, of course, the secularists and ethnic nationalists. There has also been manipulation of this strong Islamic sentiment by some of the "fundamentalist" forces and even by established regimes for immediate political ends—without any result but the further weakening of the Islamic world.

The desire to achieve this unity also manifests itself in a strong inclination in theological circles to have closer cooperation and better understanding between Sunnism and Shi'ism. This tendency, despite limited success, is several decades old and is bound to continue. It was highlighted by the declaration a generation ago by Shaykh al-Shaltut, then rector of al-Azhar University, that Twelve-Imam Shi'i (Ja'fari) law would be taught as one of the orthodox schools of law in that venerable Sunni institution. Intra-Islamic dialogue between Sunni and Shi'i thinkers will most likely increase on both the legal and the theological/philosophical levels.

Parallel with these religious developments, political use of Sunni-Shi'i differences not only continues but is aggravated, to the extent that Islam is used as a political instrument by one group or regime against another. These differences provide an ideal means to divide and conquer by external forces that reap their own benefits from the weakening of the Islamic world or the creation of chaos and disorder, not to speak of open warfare, therein. The disturbances and even wars of the past few years related to Sunni-Shi'i differences are unlikely to disappear in the presence of the political forces that are particularly active in the central areas of the Islamic world, such as Iraq and Iran. Yet the tendency among Islamic thinkers and the traditional ulama in both camps to benefit from dialogues with each other and from rapprochements on many theological and even legal matters is likely to increase.

Against this strong desire for "unification" and the identity of the Islamic peoples as a single people (umma) as mentioned in the Qur'an stands not only secular nationalism, which grew out of the French Revolution, but also a traditional patriotism, or what might be called "Islamic nationalism." Since the late nineteenth century the forces called Arab nationalism, Turkish nationalism, Iranian nationalism, and the like have been most powerful in the Middle East region of the Islamic world. Today, there are revolutionary Pan-Islamic movements, such as that dominant in Iran, that oppose all such forces in the name of the political unity of the Islamic world. These two contending forces are bound to struggle against each other in the years ahead. It is difficult to imagine that human efforts to unite the Islamic world will succeed in achieving what, according to Prophetic tradition, is to be accomplished only by the Mahdi—although greater cooperation, communication, and exchange are likely to take place among various Islamic nations and peoples in fields ranging from the economic and political to the cultural. Nor are the forces of nationalism likely to die out. In fact, there are now tendencies fanning the fire of even more local nationalisms, such as the Kurdish and the Baluchi, which, if successful, would not only *not* lead to a single Islamic world but would cause the creation of helpless small states at the mercy of outside forces that could then manipulate them more easily than they do now.

There is, however, a third type of force to consider in addition to ethnic and secular state nationalisms: traditional "Islamic nationalism" or patriotism in the sense of the famous hadith "The love of one's nation comes from faith." Long before the French Revolution, the Arabs knew that they were not Persians or Turks and vice versa, although an Arab could travel from Tangier and settle in Delhi without any difficulty, or a Persian could migrate to Istanbul or Hyderabad and make it his second home. Many analysts confuse this traditional awareness of an Egyptian being an Egyptian or a Persian being a Persian with the more recent forms of secular nationalism. Between the extremes of the utopian ideal of a single Islamic state covering the whole Islamic world and small warring states that continue to weaken internally as a result of constant enmity and rivalry, one can envisage the possibility of the rise, once again, of a trend toward a kind of Islamic political thought that combines the ideal of unity of the Islamic world based on culture, the Divine Law, and the intellectual life with separate political units that embrace the major peoples and cultural zones of the Islamic world, such as the Arabic, the Persian, the Turkish, and the Malay. It is very difficult to predict trends in a politically unstable world. But certainly this combining of a sense of religion with love of homeland (patriotism in a more traditional sense) is far from being extinguished among peoples already scorched by the fires of fanaticism and extremism forced upon them in the name of Islam and for the sake of an elusive and as yet nonexistent international order.

THE VITALITY OF ISLAM

There is little doubt that what has been called the "defiance of Islam" toward the modern world will continue, but it is likely to take new forms in addition to already existing ones. While political upheavals using the name of Islam are bound to continue in a world in which the forces within the Islamic world are not in a state of complete freedom to act as they will, and where external powers have access to the manipulation of such forces, other reactions of a more intellectual and deliberated nature, not based simply upon sentiments and fanaticism, are also likely to occur. As current revivalist forces use Western radio and television to attack the West, from buildings emulating Western architecture in cities laid out on Western lines, other forces in Islamic society that are still firmly enough rooted in the Islamic tradition to be able to distinguish between what is genuinely Islamic and what is only apparently so, are likely to come forward to examine the science and technology, the philosophies, the social theories, and even the ideas of urban development that the Islamic world has been blindly emulating while attacking the civilization of which they are the products.

There is likely to be a greater battle with modernism than before in the arts, architecture, literature, science, and philosophy. The recent interest in the revival of Islamic architecture and city planning, as well as arts and crafts, is a sign of this important tendency, which complements the revival of the principles of the intellectual and spiritual tradition of Islam. The battle is likely to be a bitter one, carried out with intellectual tools in fields ranging from historiography, the social sciences, language and literature, the arts and sciences, to the study of other religions. These intellectual battles will, moreover, affect the religious thought of Islam and the mentality of Muslims, and therefore will influence the course of events in the Islamic world.

As waves of mahdiism and "fundamentalism" fail to solve the problems of the Islamic world, and as the various types of modernism display their bankruptcy in a world in which the civilization that gave birth to modernism, is itself facing the greatest crises, the central reality in the Islamic world will most likely become the battle not between traditional Islam and the openly declared secularism and modernism, as was the case until recently, but between traditional Islam and various anti-traditional and leftist ideologies parading as Islam. It is one of the characteristics of the life of the late twentieth century, also seen fully in Christianity, that the forces opposed to religion no longer function only outside the citadel of religion but try to destroy it by penetrating that citadel and appearing to be part of that religion. There is a great difference between the time when Jamal al-Din Astrabadi, known as Afghani, wrote his *Refutation of the Materialists,* attacking the modern West as being materialistic and agnostic, or the scholars of al-Azhar attacked communism as being godless, and the recent exchange between traditional Muslims and those who espouse all the causes of the Communist world but also call themselves Islamic. The main battle of the future in the Islamic world will most likely be between these two forces, and the central problem will be the subversion of Islam by forces that claim to speak in the name of Islam.

Also in years to come the debates between those who would interpret Islam as religion in its traditional sense and those who speak of it as ideology are bound to continue, as are the discussions between those who seek to revive ethics by reforming Islamic society from within and those for whom reform can come only by violent changes of the norms and structures of society from without. Those who will seek to blend Islam with every aspect of society will stand against those who are not necessarily irreligious—often quite the contrary—but believe that to preserve the purity of their religion, its name should not be used in the politicoeconomic arena, where the very nature of the forces involved can sully the sacred name of Islam. One will continue to see a strong opposition between those who have a triumphalistic and often sentimental view of Islam, according to which everything of value is Islamic, and even the West is successful because of its heritage of Islamic science, and those who do not wish to identify Islam with the West and its triumphs but see Islam as an ally of other traditional religions, including Christianity and Judaism, against the modern world, which opposes not only Islam but all religion.

Finally, there will continue to be contention between those who wish to revive the Islamic tradition in its wholeness and those who contribute to the destruction of the possibility of this revival either by a misuse of the name of Islam for ideas of a completely different nature or as a result of a sense of inferiority toward the modern world that is often veiled by an emotional triumphalism. In all these cases there will be the desire, at least outwardly, to revive Islamic society and the ethical norms that govern it. This element will remain the common denominator, linking all the above variations that will most likely continue.

As the Qur'an states, the future is in God's hands and His alone. The tendencies mentioned above all exist and can be projected into trends in the near future, but only in a provisional way, for, from the Islamic point of view, there is no determinism in history. A single unforeseen event or the appearance of a single figure could change the texture of forces and tendencies that comprise the Islamic world. What can be said with certainty is that despite becoming weakened, the Islamic tradition is still very much alive in both its outer and its inner dimensions, and at this point in its history it has to react to a multiplicity of forces from without and within—some of which are openly opposed to it and others of which bear its name but are in reality of quite another nature. In any case the vitality of the Islamic tradition will continue to the end of days, as promised by the Prophet. As to which of the trends will gain the upper hand, what plans the outside world hides behind veils of secrecy in manipulating these trends and tendencies, and how these forces will affect the Islamic world itself, it is not possible to foretell. In this domain more than all others, one can best conclude with the traditional Islamic dictum: God knows best.

Glossary

Abbasid the second Muslim empire (750-1258); its capital was Baghdad

abd servant

Ali the Prophet's cousin and son-in-law

amir commander

ansar helpers; the native population of Medina who supported Muhammad

baraka a unique power transmitted by holy men or women that produces spiritual favors and miracles

caliph successor; those who succeeded Muhammad as leader of the Muslim community in the temporal sense

capitulations legal and economic privileges bestowed on Western countries by the Ottoman Empire

Dar al-Harb abode of war; non-Islamic territory

Dar al-Islam abode of peace; Islamic territory

da'wah missionary outreach

dhikr remembrance; ritual involving the rhythmic repetition, in a group setting, of one or more formulas containing the name of God

dirlik/timar revenue grant of the Ottoman Empire

Fatima the Prophet's daughter, the wife of Ali

fatwa   legal opinion given by a mufti

fuqaha   legal experts, jurisprudents

ghazis   fighters in the holy war

hadith   a report of what the Prophet said, did, or allowed

hajj   the pilgrimage to Mecca

halal   food, action, or deeds permissible for Muslims

hanifs   pre-Islamic monotheists of the Arabian peninsula

hijra   emigration: the Prophet's departure from Mecca to Medina in 622

Id al-Adha/Id al-Kabir   Festival of Sacrifice, celebrated during the pilgrimage

Id al-Fitr/Id al-Saghir   Festival of Breaking the Fast, at the end of Ramadan

ihram   sacred state of purity

ijma   consensus among the community of believers, a source of law

imam   prayer leader; in Shi'ism the head of the theocratic state

Islam   submission, surrender to God's law

Isma'ilis   Sevener Shi'is

isnad   chain of transmitters who handed down reports of the Prophet (hadith)

jagir   revenue grant of the Mughal Empire

jihad   holy war, striving to realize God's will on earth

jizya   personal tax paid by non-Muslim subjects to Muslim governments

Ka'ba   Sacred Cube located in Mecca, in whose wall is embedded the sacred Black Stone

Khadija   the Prophet's first wife

khanqahs/zawiyas   Sufi centers

khans   commercial hostels and warehouses

khasse/khalisa   imperial revenue sources

Laylat al-Qadr   Night of Power, which occurs on the twenty-seventh day of Ramadan and commemorates the beginning of God's revelation to Muhammad

madrasa   Islamic educational institution, school

Mahdi   the Guided One, who will appear in the last days to establish God's rule on earth

mamluks   professional soldiers who were military slaves and formed a ruling oligarchy

marabouts   saints

masjid/mosque   place of prayer

mihrab   niche in the mosque wall indicating the direction of prayer/Mecca

minaret   the tower of a mosque from which the call to prayer is uttered

muezzin   the individual who performs the call to prayer

mufti   specialist in Islamic law who issues fatwas

muhajirun   emigrants; those who came to Medina with the Prophet

Muhammad   the last (Seal) of the Prophets, the one to whom the Qur'an was revealed

muhtasib   market inspector; the official charged with ensuring public health, safety, welfare, and morality

mujaddid   renewer of the faith

Muslim   one who submits to God's law

Mu'tazilites   those in Abbasid times who insisted on man's absolute moral accountability

padishah   emperor

qadi   judge

qanun   administrative regulations, as opposed to the shari'a or holy law

qiyas   analogical reasoning; a source of Islamic law

qizilbash   red heads; refers to the red caps worn as a symbol of the Safavids

Qur'an   the word of God as revealed to the Prophet Muhammad; also spelled Koran

qutb   pole; the axis of spiritual power on earth who mediates between God and creation

rak'a   a multistage movement that combines bows, prostrations, and the recitation of prayer

Ramadan   the lunar month of fasting from dawn to sunset

rasul   messenger; one who brings a message of God

salat   daily ritual prayer

sama'   audition; a musical recital of religious poetry, usually accompanied by Qur'anic recitations and involving ritual dance

shahada   the profession of faith: There is no God but God and Muhammad is the messenger of God

shari'a   path; Islamic law

shaykh/pir   Sufi master

Shi'is   partisans or supporters of Ali who believed him to be Muhammad's rightful successor; those believing the Islamic community should be led by an Imam

shirk   idolatry, associating someone or something with God

shura   consultation

Sufism   mysticism

sunna   model of behavior demonstrated by the Prophet; a source of Islamic law

Sunni   dominant faction in Islam; it believes in a communal rather than a hereditary determination of spiritual authority

sura   chapter of the Qur'an

tafsir   the exoteric meaning of the Qur'an

tajdid   renewal of the faith

taqlid   doctrine of obedience to established authority

tariqah   a Sufi brotherhood

ta'wil   the esoteric, interpretive meaning of the Qur'an

tiyul   revenue grant of the Safavid Empire

ulama   knowers of religious sciences; whose who study, preserve, and interpret Islamic law; Muslim clerics

Umayyad   first Muslim dynasty (661-750); the capital was Damascus

umma   community of believers

umrah   the lesser pilgrimage

vizier   an administrative official

waqf   religious endowments used for constructing mosques and law schools, assisting the ulama and the poor, and other philanthropic activities

zakat   alms tax

Selected Bibliography

The items listed below reflect suggestions made by this volume's contributors as well as selections made by its editor and research assistant. In some cases they also function as sources for specific material quoted in a particular chapter. The entries have been limited to English-language publications; most are currently in print and available from American publishers.

GENERAL REFERENCE WORKS

Ede, David, et al., eds. *Guide to Islam.* Boston: G.K. Hall and Co., 1983.

*Gauhar, Altaf, ed. *The Challenge of Islam.* London: Islamic Council of Europe, 1978.

*Geertz, Clifford. *Islam Observed: Religious Development in Morocco and Indonesia.* Chicago: University of Chicago Press, 1971.

*Gellner, Ernest. *Muslim Society.* New York: Cambridge University Press, 1981.

Gibb, H.A.R., and J.H. Kramers. *Shorter Encyclopedia of Islam.* Ithaca, N.Y.: Cornell University Press, 1965.

*Gilsenan, Michael. *Recognizing Islam: Religion and Society in the Modern Arab World.* New York: Pantheon, 1983.

*Hodgson, Marshall G. *The Venture of Islam.* Chicago: University of Chicago Press, 1977.

---

*Available in paperback.

*Holt, P.M., Ann K.S. Lambton, and Bernard Lewis, eds. *The Cambridge History of Islam.* New York: Cambridge University Press, 1977-78.

Pearson, James Douglas, ed. *Index Islamicus.* London: Mansell, 1958 (published quarterly).

Robinson, Francis. *Atlas of the Islamic World Since 1500.* New York: Facts on File, 1982.

*Smith, Wilfred Cantwell. *Islam in Modern History.* Princeton: Princeton University Press, 1957.

PERIODICALS

Arabia, the Islamic World Review
Aramco World Magazine
Arts, the Islamic World
International Journal of Middle East Studies
Middle East Journal
Muslim World

CHAPTER 1: FAITH AND PRACTICE

*Ahmad, Kurshid, ed. *Islam: Its Meaning and Message.* London: Islamic Council of Europe, 1976.

Awn, Peter J. *Satan's Tragedy and Redemption: Iblis in Sufi Psychology.* Leiden: E.J. Brill, 1983.

*Goldziher, Ignaz. *Introduction to Islamic Theology and Law.* Princeton: Princeton University Press, 1981.

McCarthy, Richard J. *Freedom and Fulfillment.* Boston: Twayne, 1980.

*Schimmel, Annemarie. *Mystical Dimensions of Islam.* Chapel Hill: University of North Carolina Press, 1975.

*al-Tabataba'i, Muhammad H. *Shi'ite Islam.* 2nd ed. Albany: State University of New York Press, 1979.

von Grunebaum, Gustave E. *Muhammadan Festivals.* Totowa, N.J.: Rowman and Littlefield, 1976.

Watt, W. Montgomery. *The Formative Period of Islamic Thought.* New York: Columbia University Press, 1973.

CHAPTER 2: THE MESSAGE AND THE MESSENGER

*Andrae, Tor. *Mohammed: The Man and His Faith.* New York: Harper and Row, 1977.

*Arberry, Arthur J. *The Koran Interpreted.* New York: Macmillan, 1964.

Gatje, Helmut. *The Qur'an and Its Exegesis: Selected Texts with Classical and Modern Muslim Interpretations.* Berkeley: University of California Press, 1977.

*Rahman, Fazlur. *Major Themes of the Qur'an.* Chicago: Bibliotheca Islamica, 1980.

*Rodinson, Maxime. *Muhammad.* New York: Pantheon, 1980.

*Watt, W. Montgomery. *Muhammad: Prophet and Statesman.* New York: Oxford University Press, 1974.

CHAPTER 3: THE FOUNDATIONS OF STATE AND SOCIETY

*Gibb, Hamilton A.R. *Mohammedanism: An Historical Survey.* 2nd ed. New York: Oxford University Press, 1953.

*Hitti, Philip K. *A History of the Arabs.* 10th ed. New York: St. Martin's Press, 1970.

Lambton, Ann K.S. *State and Government in Medieval Islam.* New York: Oxford University Press, 1981.

Mottahedeh, Roy P. *Loyalty and Leadership in an Early Islamic Society.* Princeton: Princeton University Press, 1980.

Rahman, Fazlur. *Islam.* 2nd ed. Chicago: University of Chicago Press, 1979.

*Schacht, Joseph, and C.E. Bosworth, eds. *The Legacy of Islam.* 2nd ed. New York: Oxford University Press, 1979.

*Watt, W. Montgomery. *Islamic Political Thought.* New York: Columbia University Press, 1980.

CHAPTER 4: THE EARLY MUSLIM EMPIRES

Donner, Fred M. *The Early Islamic Conquests.* Princeton: Princeton University Press, 1981.

*Grabar, Oleg. *The Formation of Islamic Art.* New Haven: Yale University Press, 1973.

Lasser, Jacob. *The Shaping of Abbasid Rule.* Princeton: Princeton University Press, 1980.

*Lewis, Bernard, ed. *Islam, from the Prophet Muhammad to the Capture of Constantinople.* New York: Harper and Row, 1973.

*Peters, Francis E. *Allah's Commonwealth.* New York: Simon and Schuster, 1974.

von Grunebaum, Gustave E. *Classical Islam.* Winchester, Mass.: Allen and Unwin, 1970.

*Watt, W. Montgomery. *The Majesty That Was Islam.* London: Sidgwick and Jackson, 1974.

CHAPTER 5: ISLAMIC UNIVERSALISM IN THE LATER MIDDLE AGES

Boyle, J.A., ed. *The Cambridge History of Iran.* Vol. V: *The Saljuq and Mongol Periods.* New York: Cambridge University Press, 1968.

Cahen, Claude. *Pre-Ottoman Turkey.* New York: Taplinger, 1968.

Gibb, Hamilton A.R., ed. *The Travels of Ibn Battuta, 1325-1354.* New York: Cambridge University Press, 1971.

Grousset, Rene. *The Empire of the Steppes: A History of Central Asia.* New Brunswick, N.J.: Rutgers University Press, 1970.

Lapidus, Ira M. *Muslim Cities in the Later Middle Ages.* Cambridge, Mass.: Harvard University Press, 1967.

Saunders, J.J. *The History of the Mongol Conquests.* Boston: Routledge and Kegan Paul, 1971.

*Trimingham, J. Spencer. *The Sufi Orders in Islam.* New York: Oxford University Press, 1973.

CHAPTER 6: THE LATER MUSLIM EMPIRES

Ahmad, Aziz. *Studies in Islamic Culture in the Indian Environment.* New York: Oxford University Press, 1964.

Blunt, Wilfrid, and Wim Swamm. *Isfahan: Pearl of Persia.* London: Elek Books, 1966.

Gascoigne, Bamber. *The Great Moguls.* London: Jonathan Cape, 1971.

Ikram, S.M. *Muslim Civilization in India.* New York: Columbia University Press, 1964.

Inalcik, Halil. *The Ottoman Empire: The Classical Age, 1300-1600.* New York: Weidenfeld and Nicolson, 1973.

*Itzkowitz, Norman. *Ottoman Empire and Islamic Tradition.* Chicago: University of Chicago Press, 1980.

Saunders, John J., ed. *The Muslim World on the Eve of Europe's Expansion.* Englewood Cliffs, N.J.: Prentice-Hall, 1966.

Savory, Roger M. *Iran Under the Safavids.* New York: Cambridge University Press, 1980.

CHAPTER 7: THE COLONIAL PERIOD

*Anderson, M.S. *The Eastern Question, 1774-1923: A Study in International Relations.* New York: St. Martin's Press, 1966.

Daniel, Norman. *Islam, Europe, and Empire.* Edinburgh: Edinburgh University Press, 1966.

*Goldschmidt, Arthur, Jr. *A Concise History of the Middle East.* 2nd ed. Boulder, Colo.: Westview Press, 1983.

*Keddie, Nikki R. *Roots of Revolution: An Interpretive History of Modern Iran.* New Haven: Yale University Press, 1981.

Kiernan, V.G. *From Conquest to Collapse: European Empires from 1815 to 1960.* New York: Pantheon, 1982.

*Lewis, Bernard. *The Emergence of Modern Turkey.* 2nd ed. New York: Oxford University Press, 1968.

* _____. *The Middle East and the West.* New York: Harper and Row, 1968.

Mansfield, Peter. *The British in Egypt.* New York: Holt, Rinehart and Winston, 1971.

Polk, William R., and Richard L. Chambers, eds. *Beginnings of Modernization in the Middle East: The Nineteenth Century.* Chicago: University of Chicago Press, 1968.

CHAPTER 8: MUSLIM RESPONSES TO COLONIALISM

Ahmad, Aziz. *Islamic Modernism in India and Pakistan, 1857-1964.* New York: Oxford University Press, 1967.

Evans-Pritchard, E.E. *The Sanusi of Cyrenaica.* New York: Oxford University Press, 1949.

*Keddie, Nikki R., ed. *Scholars, Saints, and Sufis: Muslim Religious Institutions Since 1500.* Berkeley: University of California Press, 1972.

Lewis, Bernard. *The Muslim Discovery of Europe.* New York: W.W. Norton, 1982.

Martin, B.G. *Muslim Brotherhoods in Nineteenth Century Africa.* New York: Cambridge University Press, 1977.

*Voll, John Obert. *Islam: Continuity and Change in the Modern World.* Boulder, Colo.: Westview Press, 1982.

CHAPTER 9: MUSLIM NATION-STATES

Abu Jaber, Kamel S. *The Arab Ba'th Socialist Party.* Syracuse, N.Y.: Syracuse University Press, 1966.

*Ajami, Fouad. *The Arab Predicament.* New York: Cambridge University Press, 1982.

*Hourani, Albert. *Arabic Thought in the Liberal Age 1798-1939.* New York: Cambridge University Press, 1983.

*Hudson, Michael C. *Arab Politics: The Search for Legitimacy.* New Haven: Yale University Press, 1977.

*Karpat, Kemal H., ed. *Political and Social Thought in the Contemporary Middle East.* New York: Praeger, 1982.

*Kerr, Malcolm H. *The Arab Cold War.* 3rd ed. New York: Oxford University Press, 1971.

Mitchell, Richard. *The Society of Muslim Brothers.* New York: Oxford University Press, 1969.

Safran, Nadav. *Egypt in Search of Political Community.* Cambridge, Mass.: Harvard University Press, 1961.

*Waterbury, John. *The Egypt of Nasser and Sadat.* Princeton: Princeton University Press, 1983.

CHAPTER 10: MUSLIM SOCIETIES TODAY

Ayoob, Mohammed, ed. *The Politics of Islamic Reassertion.* New York: St. Martin's Press, 1981.

*Azzam, Salem, ed. *Islam and Contemporary Society.* London: Islamic Council of Europe, 1982.

*Curtis, Michael, ed. *Religion and Politics in the Middle East.* Boulder, Colo.: Westview Press, 1982.

Dessouki, Ali E. Hillal, ed. *Islamic Resurgence in the Arab World.* New York: Praeger, 1982.

*Enayat, Hamid. *Modern Islamic Political Thought.* Austin: University of Texas Press, 1982.

*Esposito, John L., ed. *Islam and Development.* Syracuse, N.Y.: Syracuse University Press, 1980.

* _____. *Islam and Politics.* Syracuse, N.Y.: Syracuse University Press, 1984.

*Piscatori, James P., ed. *Islam in the Political Process.* New York: Cambridge University Press, 1983.

*Pullapilly, Cyriac K., ed. *Islam in the Contemporary World.* Notre Dame, Ind.: Cross Roads Press, 1980.

CHAPTER 11: ISLAMIC LAW

Anderson, James Norman. *Islamic Law in the Modern World.* Westport, Conn.: Greenwood Press, 1976.

*Coulson, Noel. *A History of Islamic Law.* New York: Columbia University Press, 1979.

* _____. *Conflicts and Tensions in Islamic Jurisprudence.* Chicago: University of Chicago Press, 1969.

Liebesny, Herbert. *The Law of the Near and Middle East.* Albany: State University of New York Press, 1975.

Schacht, Joseph. *An Introduction to Islamic Law.* New York: Oxford University Press, 1964.

CHAPTER 12: THE CHANGING ARAB MUSLIM FAMILY

Allman, James, ed. *Women's Status and Fertility in the Muslim World.* New York: Praeger, 1978.

*Esposito, John L. *Women in Muslim Family Law.* Syracuse, N.Y.: Syracuse University Press, 1982.

*Fernea, Elizabeth, and Basima Bezirgan, eds. *Middle Eastern Muslim Women Speak*. Austin: University of Texas Press, 1977.

*Keddie, Nikki, and Lois Beck, eds. *Women in the Muslim World*. Cambridge, Mass.: Harvard University Press, 1978.

*Kerr, Malcolm H., and El Sayed Yassin, eds. *Rich and Poor Nations in the Middle East*. Boulder, Colo.: Westview Press, 1982.

Minai, Naila. *Women in Islam*. New York: Putnam Publishing Group, 1981.

*Nashat, Guity, ed. *Women and Revolution in Iran*. Boulder, Colo.: Westview Press, 1983.

Smith, Jane, ed. *Women in Contemporary Muslim Societies*. Lewisburg, Pa.: Bucknell University Press, 1980.

CHAPTER 13: MUSLIMS IN THE UNITED STATES

*Abraham, Sameer, and Nabeel Abraham. *Arabs in the New World*. Detroit: Wayne State University Press, 1983.

Haddad, Yvonne Y. *The Muslim Experience in the United States*. New York: Oxford University Press, forthcoming.

*Lincoln, C. Eric. *The Black Muslims in America*. Boston: Beacon Press, 1961.

*Muhammad, Warith Deen. *As the Light Shineth from the East*. Chicago: WDM Publishing Co., 1980.

Thernstrom, Stephan, et al., eds. *Harvard Encyclopedia of American Ethnic Groups*. Cambridge, Mass.: Harvard University Press, 1980.

*Waugh, Earle H., Baha Abu Laban, and Regula Qureshi, eds. *The Muslim Community in North America*. Edmonton: University of Alberta Press, 1983.

CHAPTER 14: PRESENT TENDENCIES, FUTURE TRENDS

*Esposito, John L., ed. *Voices of Resurgent Islam.* New York: Oxford University Press, 1983.

*Haddad, Yvonne Y. *Contemporary Islam and the Challenge of History.* Albany: State University of New York Press, 1982.

Nasr, Seyyed Hossein. *Islam and the Plight of the Modern Man.* New York: Longman, 1976.

Rahman, Fazlur. *Islam and Modernity.* Chicago: University of Chicago Press, 1982.

*Schuon, Frithjof. *Understanding Islam.* Winchester, Mass.: Allen and Unwin, 1976.

OUTREACH CENTERS

Near Eastern Center
University of Arizona
Tucson, Arizona 85721

Center for Middle Eastern Studies
University of California-Berkeley
Berkeley, California 94720

von Grunebaum Center for Near Eastern Studies
UCLA
Los Angeles, California 90024

Duncan Black Macdonald Center for the Study of Islam and Christian-Muslim Relations
Hartford Seminary
Hartford, Connecticut 06105

Center for Contemporary Arab Studies
Georgetown University
Washington, D.C. 20057

American Institute for Islamic Affairs at The American University
4900 Massachusetts Avenue, NW
Washington, D.C. 20016

Middle East Institute
1761 N Street, NW
Washington, D.C. 20036

The Center for Middle Eastern Studies
University of Chicago
Chicago, Illinois 60637

Center for Middle East Studies
Harvard University
Cambridge, Massachusetts 02138

Outreach Program for North African and Near Eastern Studies
University of Michigan
Ann Arbor, Michigan 48109

Southwest Asia and North African Program
State University of New York
Binghamton, New York 13901

Joint Center for Near Eastern Studies
New York University and Princeton University
New York University
New York, New York 10003

Middle East Center
University of Pennsylvania
Philadelphia, Pennsylvania 19104

Center for Middle Eastern Studies
University of Texas
Austin, Texas 78712

Middle East Center
University of Utah
Salt Lake City, Utah 84112

Southeast Regional Middle East
  and Islamic Studies Specialists
c/o Jerome Weiner
Old Dominion University
Norfolk, Virginia 23508

Near East Resource Center
University of Washington
Seattle, Washington 98105

TEACHING AIDS
The Islamic Teaching Materials Project was designed to provide materials for the study of Islamic civilization at the college and advanced secondary levels, to be used by both generalists and specialists. Among the project's components are the following:

1. *Islamic Ritual Practices*—180 slides and a 115-page manual covering formal rituals, pilgrimage, life-cycle rites, Shi'i observances, and religious symbols ($100)

   Available from: Paul Vieth Center
   Yale Divinity School
   New Haven, Connecticut 06511

2. *The World of Islam, Images and Echoes*—a volume reviewing 250 selected 16-mm films and 200 sound recordings about the Muslim world. ($9.50)

   Available from: American Council of Learned Societies
   228 East 45 Street
   New York, New York 10017

3. *Islam Fiche*—in microfiche, excerpts from Islamic primary source materials from pre-Islamic to contemporary times, translated into English.

   Available from: Inter Documentation Company
   Hogewoerd 151-153
   2311HK Leiden
   The Netherlands

Other components of the project scheduled for completion are 600 slides on Islamic art and architecture, 376 slides on lands and peoples of Islam, an atlas and teacher's guide. Project Director: Herbert L. Bodman, University of North Carolina, Chapel Hill, North Carolina 27514.

An article for teachers, "Teaching Contemporary Islam," by John L. Esposito, appears in the April 1983 *Bulletin* of The Council

on the Study of Religion, 300 West Chestnut Street, Ephrata,
Pennsylvania 17522.

ISLAMIC CENTERS IN THE UNITED STATES

International Islamic Community
Room #3351A
United Nations Secretariat
New York, New York 10017

Muslim Students Association of U.S. and Canada
Headquarters
P.O. Box 38
Plainfield, Indiana 46168

Muslim World League
P.O. Box 4174
Grand Central Station
New York, New York 10017

DISTRIBUTORS OF ISLAMIC MATERIALS AND THIRD
WORLD LITERATURE IN TRANSLATION

Kazi Publications
1647 North Wells Street
Chicago, Illinois 60614

Mizan Press
P.O. Box 4065
Berkeley, California 94704

New Era Publications
P.O. Box 8139
Ann Arbor, Michigan 48107

Three Continents Press
1340 Connecticut Avenue, Suite 224
Washington, D.C. 20036

Index

Abu Bakr: and conquest, wars of, 66; as follower of Muhammad, 34; as leader of Muslims, 63-64; and Qur'an, 48-49
Abbas, 129-130
Abbasids: in Baghdad, 79-80; and Hanbalis, 71; overthrow of, 69, 78; rule of, 64-65
Abduh, Muhammad, 167
ablutions, 7-8, 13
Abraha, 29
Abu Sufyan, Umayyad, 38-39
Ad, 46
Adam and Eve, 4, 43
Afghani, 167-169, 291
al-Afghani, Jamal al-Din, 167-169, 291
Afghanistan, 142
Aflaq, Michel, 189
Africa, 97
Aga Khan IV, 17, 233, 246
Ahmad, Jalal Al-e, 218
Ahmad, Muhammad, 163-164
Akbar, 125-126
Alawis, 190
Algeria, 148
Ali, 16, 58-59
Alids, 60
Ali, Muhammad, 140, 176-178
almsgiving, 9
American Islamic College, 274
American Muslim Journal, 268
American Muslim Mission, 268, 274
American Muslim Mission School, 274
amirs, 65, 90
Anglo-Iraqi Treaty of 1930, 183
al-Aqsa, 77
al-Ash'ari, 5-6
Arab bedouin, 30-31
Arabi, Sufi ibn, 54

Arabia, pre-Islamic: Arab bedouin in, 30-31; Jewish community in, 29; Quraysh tribein, 30; "religious" problem in, 30; women in, 31
Arab League, 184
Arabs, 181-184, 191
Arab Socialist Resurrection Party, 189
Arafat, mount of, 12
Ardabil, 123
Aristotle, 50
Ascension, 24-25
Asharite, 285
Asia, 97
al-Ashraf, Ka'b ibn, 38
associationism, 5
Astrabadi, Jamal al-Din, 291
Ataturk. *See* Kemal Ataturk
Attar, 20
Aus, 37
Austria, 139
Avrangzib, 135

Babur, 125
Badr, 38
Baghdad, 19, 79-80
Baghdad Pact of 1955, 186
Balfour Declaration, 149
al-Banna, Hassan, 180, 185, 214-215
Banu Hashim, 34-35
Banu Nadir, 37, 40
Banu Qainuga, 37, 40
Banu Qurayza, 37, 40
Banu Taghlib, 29
baraka, 23, 25
Baring, Evelyn, 150
Ba'th Party, 189
Ba'thist socialism, 189-191
Bazargan, Mehdi, 218, 222

World War I, 144; motives of for colonization, 147; and Syria, division of, 182; in Tunisia, 141; in West Africa, colonization of, 140
Franks, 86-87
Free Officers, 185, 213-214
Fruit of Islam, 268-269
fundamentalism, 279-282, 286

Genghis Khan, 101-102, 108, 116
ghazis, 99
Golden Horde, 116
Grand Mosque, seizure of, 204-205
Great Britain: and agreement with France, 142; in India, colonization of, 140-141, 148-149; in Libya, colonization of, 144; motives of for colonization, 139, 145-146
Green Book, The, 207-209
Gulf Cooperation Council, 205-206

hadith, 4, 57-59, 230
Hafiz, 20
hagiography, 19
hajj, 9, 11-13
halal, 264
al-Hallaj, Husayn ibn Mansur, 20
al-Hamid, Abd II, 168-169
Hanbalism, 71-72, 233
Hanifism, 233
hanifs, 29
ul-Haq, Zia, 209, 211-212, 240
Hasan, 59, 62, 121
Hassan II, 26
Hawrani, Akram, 189
Haykal, Muhammad Husayn, 180
hijra, 36
Hinduism, 1
Holland: in Borneo, colonization of, 144; and discrimination of Muslims, 147; motives of for colonization, 139, 146
Holy House of God, 8
holy war, 13, 86-87
Hulagu, 101-102
Hugronje, Snouck C., 147, 150
Husayn: and Arab identity, separate, 182; and Arab revolt, 143;

and imamate, 62; martyrdom of, 16, 25; relationship of to Ali, 59
Hypocrites, 39-40

Iblis, 20
Ibn 'Arabi, 21-22
Ibn Battuta, Abu Abdallah Muhammad: in China, 107; in Kipchak, 103; as legal scholar, 104; and Sufism, 106-107; travels of, 95-97, 104
Id al-Adha, 10, 12
Id al-Fitr, 10
Id al-Kabir, 10
Id as-Saghir, 10 '
Idris I., 25
Idris II, 25-26
ihram, 13
ijma, *see* consensus
Ikhwan, 202
Ilkhans, 102-103, 116
Ilms, 58
imam, 8, 261
Imam, Shi'ism, 8, 16-17
imam-hatep, 201
Inan, Abu, 104
India: British colonization of, 140, 169-170; French colonization of, 140; Islam in, 99; and Muslim conquerors, 125
inheritance, 46-47, 248-249
Iran: Islamic law in, 222-223; as Muslim society, modern, 217-223; and treaty with Britain, 143
Iraq, 75-76
Islam: in Africa, 97; in African-American Community, 265-266; in Asia, 97; calendar of, 9-10, 36; city network of, 104-109; and colonialism (*see* colonialism); community of (*see* Islamic community); debate of in formative period, 5; diversity of, cultural, 13-14; division of, in sixteenth century, 117; divisions of, sectarian, 66; dualism in, social, 26-27; and education, 285-288; in Egypt, 213-217; and Europe, 83-84; expansion of, 109-111; festivals of, 10,

About the Editor and Contributors

MARJORIE KELLY is a consultant to the Foreign Policy Association and previously served as director of community programs for FPA's national Great Decisions program. She holds a B.A. in political science from the University of Illinois-Urbana, where she graduated Phi Beta Kappa, an M.A. in Islamic studies from the University of California-Los Angeles, and an M.A. in anthropology from the State University of New York-Binghamton. She has traveled, studied, and worked in seven Middle Eastern countries.

PETER J. AWN is assistant professor of Islamic religion and history of religions at Columbia University.

FAZLUR RAHMAN is professor in the Department of Near Eastern Languages and Civilizations at the University of Chicago.

ROY P. MOTTAHEDEH is professor of Islamic history at Princeton University.

FRANCIS E. PETERS is professor of Near Eastern languages and literatures at New York University.

ROSS E. DUNN is professor of history at San Diego State University.

I. METIN KUNT has taught at Bosporus University in Istanbul.

ARTHUR GOLDSCHMIDT, JR., is associate professor of history at Pennsylvania State University.

JOHN O. VOLL is professor of history at the University of New Hampshire.

JOHN L. ESPOSITO is professor of religious studies at the College of the Holy Cross.

ANN ELIZABETH MAYER is associate professor in the Department of Legal Studies and Public Management at the University of Pennsylvania.

AFAF LUTFI AL-SAYYID MARSOT is professor of history at the University of California-Los Angeles.

YVONNE YAZBECK HADDAD is associate professor of Islamic studies at Hartford Seminary Foundation.

SEYYED HOSSEIN NASR is university professor of Islamic studies at George Washington University.